# Contents

## Dedication

*This book is dedicated to those who made it possible:*

*The Villemaire Family, especially*
*Norman, Christopher, and Valerie Villemaire, and Robert Oberg*

*and*

*The Sisters of St. Joseph of Springfield, MA*
*especially Mary Patricia Carr, SSJ*

# Preface

*Grammar and Writing Skills for the Health Professional,* 2nd edition, was written to provide health care professionals with the necessary tools they need to learn and apply good writing skills to common writing situations found in various medical settings. These may include a range of activities, from writing medical letters and taking meeting minutes to documenting patient information and writing grant proposals.

The success of the first edition of this book affirmed that effective writing skills are essential for good communication across all medical professions. Health care continues to diversify at a rapid pace and is one of the largest industries in the country today. Both the constant evolution of health services and the frequency of litigation increase the need for meticulous written documentation. Recent concerns about maintaining and protecting patient privacy and the confidentiality of health information have led to the implementation of the Health Insurance Portability and Accountability Act (HIPAA). The rules and standards of this mandatory legislation make it more important than ever that health professionals be clear in their written communications, whether that communication is part of a medical report, patient history, or a medical letter.

The goal of this revised text is to place grammar and writing skills in the context of common health care writing situations in order to facilitate learning these important skills. To this end, this second edition consists of two major revisions. The chapter titled "Guidelines for Effective Writing" was moved to the front of the book in order to immediately emphasize the writing process and to provide the foundation in writing skills necessary to complete the writing assignments that follow in each chapter. The second revision was to reorganize the contents of each chapter so that users can begin to apply writing and grammar skills to examples of "real world" medical communications as they learn.

## ORGANIZATION OF TEXT

This book is divided into 11 chapters. The first chapter introduces the five steps of the Writing Process. The subsequent chapters cover grammar rules regarding parts of speech and sentence structure. For practical application, each of these chapters is paired with a Practical Writing

Component, such as the Medical Letter, Medical Records, Charting and Documentation, and Promotional Writing.

## NEW TO THIS EDITION:

- Computerized Test Bank consisting of over 500 questions for more in-depth skills evaluation

- Comprehensive Reviews at end of each chapter that help synthesize skills learned

- Answers to Practice Exercises in the back of the book that allow users to check progress

- Extra Practice tests in Instructor's Manual

## CONTENT ALSO INCLUDES:

- Medical spelling and abbreviation translation exercises

- Practice exercises and Skills Review in each chapter

- Appendices on Spelling Rules, Capitalization Rules, Number Use, Clichés, Titles and Salutations, Instructor's Symbols for Correction, Medical Abbreviations and Symbols, Use of a Thesaurus, Use of the English Dictionary, Use of the Medical Dictionary.

# CHAPTER 1

# Guidelines for Effective Writing Skills

**OBJECTIVES** *Upon completion of this chapter, the learner should be able to:*

❖ implement the five stages of the writing process

❖ apply the criteria of a good writing style

❖ understand the advantages and disadvantages of writing on the computer

❖ spell various medical terms

❖ translate various medical abbreviations and symbols

The most important word in the preceding subtitle is the word *process*. A process is a series of steps from beginning to end for achieving a desired result. Writing becomes easier when broken down into manageable steps. A process is not a one-step operation that magically produces a finished product on the first attempt. Many people wrongfully assume that once something is written, it is acceptable and the task is over. For both beginners and experienced writers, the implementation of all steps in the writing process is crucial to successful documentation. Dr. Seuss, a prestigious writer of children's literature, pondered hours and days on which preposition (to, of, for, by) conveyed the best meaning and rhythm.

In this chapter, we have included a Writing Process Worksheet to facilitate the integration of this key process. The expectation is that learners will use this worksheet as they practice applying effective writing skills to medical reports, documents, and office correspondence.

## The Writing Process

The writing process includes five steps: prewriting, writing, rewriting, finalizing, and proofreading. These steps remain the same for any type of writing: a single sentence, narrative, speech, proposal, instruction, summary, description, paragraph, short story, novel, report, memo, or medical documentation. To demonstrate the steps of the writing process, we use a short paragraph on legal issues in health care as an example.

## STEP ONE: PREWRITING

The prewriting stage is the planning stage during which an outline of everything the author wants to write about the topic is prepared. At this initial step, the writer thinks about the reading audience and begins to focus more clearly on the subject. Details are jotted down in any order. If necessary, the author researches and limits the amount and length of writing. Correct spelling is not necessary at this stage. See Figure 1-1 for a sample of the prewriting process.

| | |
|---|---|
| TOPIC | Legal Issues Affecting Health Care |
| SPECIFICS | Negligence |
| | Asault and batery |
| | Invasion of pivacy |
| NOTES | Research definitions |
| | Place issues in alphabetical order |
| | Have a good opening and closing sentence |
| | Keep the language simple |
| | Limit paragraph to five or six sentences |

**FIGURE 1-1**  *Prewriting Sample*

## STEP TWO: WRITING

In the second step of the writing process, a pencil is placed on paper or fingers on the keyboard. The task is to start writing and keep it flowing. Forget about spelling, grammar, or punctuation at this point. Do not try to make things perfect. Just write. Let anything happen. Present facts or ideas about the topic. See Figure 1-2 for a sample of step two.

The Patients bill of Rights require that patients be treated with respect Some violations against patients right are asault, negligence, invasion of privacy, verble abuse. Asault is verble or physical treats that cause harm, injury or fear. Failure to give proper care to patients is called negligense. Discussing information about patients publically without there soncent is unlawful. Failure to obey these areas make one lible or legally responsible.

**FIGURE 1-2**  *Writing Sample*

## STEP THREE: REWRITING

Read the first draft. Does it say what it is meant to say? Is the message clear and complete? Are facts or events in the right order? Does the writing follow the plan established in the prewriting stage? Concentrate on *each* word. Now correct grammar, spelling, and punctuation. (When using a computer, never depend solely on it to check spelling and grammar.) Change what needs to be changed. If necessary, consult others for feedback. Notice any satisfaction or discomfort that comes with reading the words. If there is discomfort, more work is needed. Review Figure 1-3 for the rewriting phase.

**FIGURE 1-3** *Rewriting Sample*

Note that special proofreaders' marks are used during the rewriting step. The most commonly used proofreaders' marks appear in Figure 1-4.

| Symbol | Meaning | Symbol | Meaning |
|--------|---------|--------|---------|
| ds | double-space | — | insert underscore |
| ss | single-space | bold | boldface print |
| ital | use italic print | ⋀ | insert a comma |
| ⊙ | insert a period | ⋁ | insert an apostrophe |
| ¶ | new paragraph | # ⋀ | insert space |
| ◡ | delete a space; close up | ⋏ | insert a letter |
| sp | spell out | w/f | wrong font |
| ∪ | transpose | ⋿ ⋾ | insert quotation marks |
| ⋀ | insert a word | stet | let it stand |
| ≡ or caps | capitalize | ; | insert semicolon |
| ℓ | delete | : | insert colon |
| / or lc | lowercase letter | ? | insert question mark |
| = | insert a hyphen | | |

**FIGURE 1-4** *Proofreaders' Marks*

## STEP 4: FINALIZING

Once you are satisfied with the corrections, rewrite or type the final version. Figure 1-5 shows the result of finalizing your work.

The Patient's Bill of Rights requires that patients be treated with respect and dignity. Some violations against patient's rights are assault and battery, negligence, invasion of privacy, and verbal abuse. Assault and battery are verbal or physical treats that cause injury or fear. Failure to give proper care to patients is called negligence. Discussing information about patients without their consent is an invasion of privacy. Failure to obey these laws can have serious consequences.

**FIGURE 1-5**  *Finalizing Sample*

## STEP FIVE: PROOFREADING

The purpose of proofreading is to check and correct the final printed product. The proofreading stage is not the time to make major changes. It is the time to check for typing errors or slips of the pen. Mistakes reflect a negative image to the reader about the management of the medical office. Patients may assume or conclude that poor office performance means poor patient care. In the final copy of the sample paragraph resulting from step four (Figure 1-5) find the two errors that still remain.

In summary, it should be evident that good writing does not just happen. A writer must follow a systematic approach that calls for planning, organizing, writing, evaluating, and revising. Just as you learn to read by reading, you learn to write by writing. Writing improves with practice, and practice is the key to successful writing. When writing, it would be beneficial to use the five steps of the writing process. The Writing Process Worksheet that follows can be used for all writing assignments throughout this book.

## Practice 1-1

*Using the five steps of the writing process, write a paragraph of approximately six to eight sentences on the topic of effective writing.*

# Writing Style

The dictionary defines the word *style* as a manner in which something is said, done, expressed, or performed. Style reveals how a writer thinks and feels about the people and situations that are the subjects of the writing. The two basic rules that apply to all types of writing are:

1. The writing style should be appropriate for the situation.

2. The writing style should be consistent throughout the writing.

Following are some of the criteria of a good writing style:

❖ *Purpose.* Initially, writers should know their audience and the purpose for which a particular writing task is being done. Is it to persuade, inform, entertain, or explain? Whatever the purpose, the writing must be clear, original, and focused on the message to be conveyed. What does the writer want the reader to understand? If the writer is not clear about the message, the reader will not be either. Writing is done for someone to read and should immediately engage the reader's interest.

In a medical office setting, the purpose for writing is to document, transcribe, and organize patients' medical data in order to form a quality environment for good medical care.

---

*No matter how technical a subject, all writing is done for human beings by human beings.*

Jacqueline Berke

---

❖ *Appropriate Wording.* Writing style is developed from a series of choices that makes the writer's style unique. One of those choices involves the words that are used. Words are combined to convey an intended meaning or attitude. A message with the same meaning can be written in many different ways for different situations:

His heart is fluttering.

His heart flutters whenever he sees you.

His heart is in tachycardia.

The patient has tachycardia.

The rate of heart palpitations has reached a serious level.

This medicine does things to my heart.

The patient has an increased heart rate.

My heart is all worked up over this health problem.

The style of writing for a newspaper is quite different from that of a novel, textbook, romance, research paper, biography, poem, narrative, short story, business letter, autobiography, or medical report. The writing style of the medical profession is unique. In medical documentation, writing is brief and detailed. For example:

Acetaminophen 2 tabs. q. 4 h.

Acetaminophen 1000 mg. q. 4 h. p.r.n.

To be skilled in the style of medical documentation, knowledge of medical terms and abbreviations is of utmost importance. Use words that are precise and concise so the reader can easily understand what is said.

---

*Doctors bury their mistakes. Lawyers hang them. Journalists put their mistakes on the front page.*

Anonymous

---

# Writing Process Worksheet

1. PREWRITING – write down facts, organize ideas

   _____     _____
   _____     _____
   _____     _____
   _____     _____
   _____     _____

2. WRITING – write without concern for grammar or punctuation

   _____
   _____
   _____
   _____
   _____
   _____
   _____

3. REWRITING – correct grammar, make changes using proofreaders' marks

   _____
   _____
   _____
   _____
   _____
   _____
   _____
   _____

4. FINALIZING – type or write final copy

   _____
   _____
   _____
   _____
   _____

5. PROOFREAD – read the final copy aloud for a final check

   _____
   _____
   _____
   _____

❖ *Explicitness.* Good writing avoids generalization and is as specific as possible.

| General | Give the patient aspirin for pain. |
|---|---|
| Specific | Pt. gets ASA 500 mg. q. 4 h. p.r.n. for pain. |

| General | Patient says he has pain in the back. |
|---|---|
| Specific | Pt. states he has low back pain in the lumbar region. |

| General | The patient suffered from pain. |
|---|---|
| Specific | The patient suffered from a migraine headache. |

| General | The physician began the treatment. |
|---|---|
| Specific | The physician reluctantly began the treatment. |

| General | The patient is not to eat before the exam. Upper GI series is to be done. |
|---|---|
| Specific | Pt. is n.p.o. after 2 a.m. UGI series in the a.m. |

| General | The patient is coughing after surgery. |
|---|---|
| Specific | Pt. is coughing/deep breathing q. 15 min. while awake. |

---

*Trim sentences, like trim bodies, usually require far more effort than flabby ones.*

Clair Kehrwald Cook

---

❖ *Conciseness.* A complete message stated in as few words as possible and without unnecessary words is another feature of good writing style.

| Wordy | The pt. was violent, abusive, and was hitting the nurse. |
|---|---|
| Clearer | Patient showed violent behavior. |

| Wordy | Place the reports in the file. After the reports are in the file, put them in alphabetical order. |
|---|---|
| Clearer | File the reports alphabetically. |

| Wordy | The reason I was late was due to the fact that my alarm clock didn't ring. |
|---|---|
| Clearer | I was late because I forgot to set the alarm. |

---

*The beautiful part of writing is that you don't have to get it right the first time, unlike, say, a brain surgeon.*

Robert Cormier

---

❖ *Correct Grammar.* The use of good grammar is usually equated with writing well. Although the two are interconnected, one does not necessarily guarantee the other. While it may be useful to learn isolated skills at times, grammatical concepts must be learned by integrating them into the context of writing. Writers must transfer what they learn from studying grammar to their own writing.

❖ *Smoothness.* The use of transitional words to unite one sentence or paragraph with another helps to eliminate bumps or rough spots. Each sentence or paragraph should lead clearly and logically to the next, providing a smooth flow of ideas.

The x-rays were negative. *Therefore,* additional testing is unnecessary.

The patient didn't follow directions when using the medication. *Consequently,* her blood pressure reading was invalid.

❖ *Inclusive Language.* All types of medical writing should contain gender-free language. At one point in history, nursing was considered only a woman's career and most physicians were men:

The doctor and his patients . . .        The nurse and her patients . . .

The use of the word *his* often implies both men and women.

The hospital employee must sign *his* name.

Some feel that one way to overcome non-inclusive language is to use both *his* and *her* together.

The hospital employee signed *his/her* name.

Many professionals feel that the *his/her* combination is awkward. Two ways to avoid its use are (1) by changing nouns to their plural form and using the pronoun *their,* and (2) by rewriting the sentence to avoid using a pronoun.

Hospital employees must sign *their* benefit plans.

All hospital employees must sign benefit plans.

Use of gender-free language in written (and spoken) language fosters equality in the workplace. Note how gender-specific terms have changed over the years:

| | |
|---|---|
| mankind | humankind |
| chairman | chairperson |
| housewife | homemaker |
| my girl/boy | my assistant |
| policeman | police officer |
| salesman | salesperson |
| stewardess | flight attendant |

Developing a good writing style requires commitment to the writing process. Writing is hard work and needs constant editing and revising. No matter how experienced a writer, there is always room for improvement. The health-care professional must be committed to the writing process in order to give the task the proper attention it needs and the practice it requires. Practice is the key to becoming a good writer. Practice is what makes good writing better. All writings possess the challenge to improve. Good writing is achieved by working and reworking ideas again and again.

Finally, learning to write well goes beyond good grammar skills, proofreading, revising, and organizing. Developing writing skills also comes from reading the works of good writers.

# Practice 1-2

*Rewrite to simplify these sentences:*

1. I can't tell you, Doctor, how I really, really appreciate what you did for me. _____

2. Working in the operating room, the nurse did not see the doctor. _____

3. Cathy was Dr. Villmare's medical assistant. She worked two years for him. _____

4. Read the medical report literally, word for word. _____

5. It is the hospital's intention to issue bonuses based on a worker's performance. _____

# Computer Writing

A computer is a writer's best friend, if the writer has keyboard, writing, and computer skills. If the learner is competent in two of these skills, the other skill can be learned. Otherwise, using the computer to improve writing may be counterproductive.

The advantages to using a computer far outweigh the disadvantages for many reasons:

❖ The computer is faster than longhand writing.

❖ The writer can focus more freely on ideas.

❖ The writer can endure longer periods of writing time and cover a topic more thoroughly.

❖ Revisions are easier to make.

❖ Small and large sections can be added, moved, or deleted.

❖ Pages have uniform margins and formats.

❖ Nice touches can be added to work: type styles, italics, bold print, illustrations, tables and charts, and colors.

❖ Spell check and grammar check help spot errors quickly.

❖ Printouts are clean and easier to read.

Among the disadvantages are:

❖ The writer has to continually stop and read what was written.

❖ Some errors, such as missing words, commas, and periods, are hard to see on the screen.

❖ For some writers, revising, rereading, and evaluating from the screen is more difficult than from a paper.

# Medical Spelling

*Become familiar with the spelling of the following words:*

| | |
|---|---|
| absorbent | necessary |
| accessible | occurrence |
| accommodation | opportunity |
| analysis | palliative |
| analyze | perseverance |
| beneficial | precede |
| canceled | prescription |
| conscious | procedure |
| comparative | quantity |
| convalescent | recurrence |
| deficiency | referral |
| diarrhea | reiterated |
| eligible | rheumatism |
| flatulence | severity |
| hemorrhage | successful |
| hygiene | sufficient |
| inadvertently | susceptible |
| infectious | suture |
| intermittent | tachycardia |
| irritated | technique |
| irrigated | umbilicus |
| judgment | xiphoid |

# Guidelines for Effective Writing Summary

| **The Writing Process:** | a series of steps for achieving effective writing. |
|---|---|
| 1. Prewriting | Outline the topics to include in the writing. |
| 2. Writing | Write and keep it flowing, without regard to correct spelling, grammar, or punctuation. |
| 3. Rewriting | Correct errors and determine if the message is clear. |
| 4. Finalizing | Write or type the final copy. |
| 5. Proofreading | Check the final version for remaining errors. |

Characteristics of Good Writing

| | |
|---|---|
| Purpose | Understand why a message is written. |
| Appropriate wording | Use the style that fits the message. |
| Explicitness | Avoid generalizations and be specific. |
| Conciseness | State the message once and in as few words as possible. |
| Correct grammar | Transfer grammar skills to writing. |
| Smoothness | Use transitional words to unite sentences. |
| Inclusive language | Use gender-free language. |

# Skills Review

*Answer true or false to the following statements:*

1. A writer with good grammar skills will automatically write well. _____

2. Reading the works of famous authors can help improve one's writing. _____

3. Ordinarily, the works of good experienced writers don't need much revision. _____

4. The purpose of a topic sentence is to tie ideas together. _____

5. For an experienced writer, skipping a stage of the writing process is allowed. _____

6. Writing for health-care personnel consists mainly of transcribing medical manuscripts. _____

7. Correct spelling and grammar are necessary through all phases of the writing process. _____

8. If one word conveys a clear message, use it. _____

9. A broad vocabulary makes reading more interesting. _____

10. The informal writing style for medical personnel should exclude abbreviations. _____

*Circle the letter of the best-constructed sentence in each group:*

1. A. Because patients pay the bill, invoices are their responsibility.
   B. Invoices are the patients' responsibility.
   C. Medical assistants send invoices to patients.

2. A. When the patient was young, the patient had frequent urinary tract infections as a child.
   B. The patient had urinary tract infections as a child.
   C. The patient had frequent urinary tract infections as a child.

3. A. Most likely, the syndrome is viral hepatitis.
   B. I thought the syndrome presented viral hepatitis.
   C. The syndrome is thought by me to be most likely viral hepatitis.

4. A. I am thrilled that you referred this pleasant, beautiful patient to me.
   B. Thank you for referring this patient for neurological evaluation.
   C. Thank you for the reference.

5. A. Avoidance of the infection is the best approach.
   B. Avoidance of the infection includes polio vaccination.
   C. Avoidance includes vaccination of anyone with the disease.

## Practice 1-3

Use the Writing Process Worksheet to complete.

Explain why you want to be a medical professional.

*Circle the correctly spelled word in each line:*

| | | | |
|---|---|---|---|
| 1. perservirance | perseverance | preseverance | preseverence |
| 2. paliative | palliative | paleative | palleative |
| 3. necsesary | nessessary | necessary | necissary |
| 4. prescription | perscripition | perscription | prescishun |
| 5. rhumatism | ruematism | rhuematism | rheumatism |
| 6. acomodation | accomodation | accommodation | acommodation |
| 7. benificial | beneficial | benefecial | beneficle |
| 8. ocurrence | occurence | occurrance | occurrence |
| 9. intermittent | interrmittant | intermittant | intermitant |
| 10. diarhea | diarea | diarrhhea | diarrhea |

*Translate medical symbols using a medical dictionary or appendix.*

1. / _____

2. → _____

3. c̄ _____

4. s̄ _____

5. > _____

6. < _____

7. ∴ _____

8. Δ _____

9. ® _____

10. Ⓛ _____

# Comprehensive Review

*Use the Writing Process Worksheet to summarize this paragraph in your own words.*

Hand washing is one important step that helps limit the spread of germs. Before and after contact with each patient, wet your hands and wrists. Work soap into lather, getting between fingers and under nails. Lower hands with fingernails downward and rinse well. Dry your hands carefully with a paper towel. Turn off the water tap with a paper towel to avoid any germs on the faucet. Apply lotion if desired.

# Writing Process Worksheet

1. PREWRITING – write down facts, organize ideas

_____     _____
_____     _____
_____     _____
_____     _____
_____     _____

2. WRITING – write without concern for grammar or punctuation

_____
_____
_____
_____
_____
_____
_____
_____

3. REWRITING – correct grammar, make changes using proofreaders' marks

_____
_____
_____
_____
_____
_____
_____
_____

4. FINALIZING – type or write final copy

_____
_____
_____
_____
_____
_____
_____

5. PROOFREAD – read the final copy aloud for a final check

_____
_____

# *Writing Process Worksheet*

1. PREWRITING – write down facts, organize ideas

_____     _____
_____     _____
_____     _____
_____     _____

2. WRITING – write without concern for grammar or punctuation

_____
_____
_____
_____
_____
_____
_____

3. REWRITING – correct grammar, make changes using proofreaders' marks

_____
_____
_____
_____
_____
_____
_____
_____

4. FINALIZING – type or write final copy

_____
_____
_____
_____
_____
_____
_____

5. PROOFREAD – read the final copy aloud for a final check

_____
_____

# CHAPTER 2

# Nouns

PRACTICAL WRITING COMPONENT:
MEDICAL LETTER AND ENVELOPE

OBJECTIVES *Upon completion of this chapter, the learner should be able to:*

❖ identify basic types of nouns

❖ identify nouns by gender, number, and function

❖ explain the difference between apposition and direct address

❖ spell various medical terms

❖ translate various medical abbreviations

❖ form the plurals of regular nouns and medical nouns

❖ prepare block and modified block letters with accompanying envelope

❖ identify medical nouns

Grammar is a set of rules about words and how they are used in sentences for the purpose of conveying a message. A sentence is a group of words that expresses a complete thought. Words improperly arranged in a sentence cannot be understood, as illustrated in this example:

Classes conference in Carr room Doctor supervisor the arranged.

Rearranged according to the rules of grammar, the words form a logical sentence:

The supervisor, Doctor Carr, arranged classes in the conference room.

The individual words that make up a sentence are called *parts of speech* (see Figure 2-1). They direct the manner in which words are used in sentences. The parts of speech are:

Noun          names a person, place, thing, or idea

Pronoun       substitutes for a noun

Verb          shows action, being, or linking

Adjective     describes a noun or pronoun

Adverb        describes a verb, adjective, or other adverb

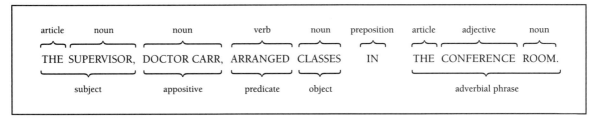

**FIGURE 2-1** *Sentence Structure*

Preposition    shows relationship to a noun or pronoun

Conjunction    connects words or groups of words

Article    points out or limits

# Types of Nouns

Knowledge of the different types of nouns and how they are used in sentences is essential for accurate medical documentation. Nouns are used more frequently than any other part of speech. Sentences abound with them. Note the number of nouns (in italic) in this sentence:

The *supervisor, Doctor Carr,* arranged *classes* in the conference *room.*

The English language has more nouns than any other part of speech. A noun is a word used to name a person, place, object (thing, activity), or quality (idea). The types of nouns covered in this chapter are proper, common, collective, concrete, and abstract.

## PROPER AND COMMON NOUNS

Proper and common nouns are easy to understand. A proper noun names a particular person, place, object, or quality. To help remember the definition, think of the words *proper* and *particular* that both begin with the letter *P.* Words like *Main Street, Dr. Villes, Massachusetts, Memorial Hospital, American Association of Medical Assistants (A.A.M.A.), Red Cross,* and *University Hospital* are proper nouns. Proper nouns begin with a capital letter.

Common nouns do not name any specific or particular person, place, object, or quality. They are general words such as *book, vegetable, hospital, patient, artery, muscle, temperature, admission, bacteria, examination, physician, specimen,* and *bone.* Common nouns do not begin with a capital letter.

## Examples

The *physician* [common] worked with the medical *assistant* [common] in the *office* [common].

*Dr. Valerie Brown* [proper] worked with *Lorry* [proper] in the *Mayo Clinic* [proper].

The *patient* [common] went to the *hospital* [common].

*Chris Villes* [proper] went to *Mercy Hospital* [proper].

*January* [proper] is the *month* [common] to review medical *forms* [common].

In the medical field, proper nouns often begin with eponyms. Eponyms are surnames of people used as descriptive adjectives for diseases, instruments, syndromes, procedures, drugs, parts of the human body, and other medical nouns. Words such as *Bell's palsy, Babinski's reflex, Foley catheter,* and *Buck's extension* are eponymic terms. The eponym is capitalized, but not the noun following it. It is important to check the spelling of eponyms in a medical dictionary.

The names of specific departments in a hospital or clinic are capitalized proper nouns. The reference to a general department is not a proper noun and so is not capitalized.

The brand or trade name of a drug is a capitalized proper noun, but the generic or common name of the drug is not; for example, aspirin or Bayer aspirin, and meperidine or Demerol. When in doubt about capitalizing, consult the *PDR (Physicians' Desk Reference)*.

## Examples

| Proper | Common |
|---|---|
| *Taber's Cyclopedic Medical Dictionary* | chickenpox |
| German measles | flu |
| Medical Records Department | operating room |
| Amoxicillin | penicillin |
| Tylenol | acetaminophen |
| Meckel's diverticulum | diverticulitis |
| Marshall-Marchetti operation | laparotomy |

# Practice 2-1

*Identify the italicized words as proper or common nouns:*

1. The largest *artery* in the body is the *aorta.* _____

2. *Scientists* were watching changes in the *DNA.* _____

3. Pulmonary *veins* are the only *veins* in the *body* that carry oxygenated *blood.*

   _____

4. *Croup* is the narrowing of the air passage in the *larynx.* _____

5. *Cholesterol* is a lipid found in saturated *fats.* _____

## COLLECTIVE NOUNS

Collective nouns represent a group of persons, animals, or things. One of the meanings of the word collective is a number of people working together. Examples of collective nouns are:

| | | | | |
|---|---|---|---|---|
| audience | committee | faculty | nation | school |
| board | company | family | navy | society |
| choir | crew | group | panel | staff |
| club | crowd | jury | public | union |

## *Examples*

The *staff* of physicians works as a *team*.

The *family* consented to the operation.

## Practice 2-2

*Identify the collective nouns in the following sentences.*

1. The patient was on the faculty at the medical school. _____

2. A group of muscles helps the movement of the mouth. _____

3. Chris joined the faculty after graduation. _____

4. The family is the basic structure of society. _____

5. The hospital welcomed the inclusion of a union. _____

## CONCRETE NOUNS

Concrete nouns are easy to identify because they name things that are touchable, visible, and audible; that is, they are perceived by the senses.

## *Examples*

*Bones* and *muscles* work together.

*Muscles* are attached to *bones* by *tendons*.

*Massachusetts General Hospital* is in *Boston*.

The *New England Journal of Medicine* is an excellent *journal*.

## ABSTRACT NOUNS

Abstract nouns are more difficult to identify because they name a feeling, quality, or idea. Think of abstract nouns as untouchables. Abstract nouns often have *-ness, -dom, -th, -ance, -cy,* and *-ism* for endings. Examples of abstract nouns are:

| | | | | |
|---|---|---|---|---|
| acceptance | courage | foolishness | intelligence | security |
| accuracy | danger | freedom | love | strength |
| case | emotion | function | memory | theories |
| concept | energy | grief | method | truth |
| condition | evidence | honesty | personality | type |

## Examples

The *concept* portrayed the *personality* and *honesty* of the individual.

The *strength* of this *concept* lies in the facts about the musculoskeletal system.

*Patience* is an admirable *quality* in any medical assistant.

*Wordiness* is inexcusable in written communication.

## Practice 2-3

*State whether the italicized words are collective or abstract:*

1. The Patient's Bill of Rights provides greater *satisfaction* and *care* for the patient.

   _____

2. The medical *staff* is meeting at 10 A.M. _____

3. After class, the *group* celebrated its hard work. _____

4. Members of the A.M.A. worked as a *team.* _____

5. The *evidence* is questionable. _____

# Characteristics and Functions of Nouns

Nouns have three characteristics: gender, number, and case.

## GENDER

Gender categorizes nouns as masculine, feminine, neuter, or indefinite. Masculine gender words include *men, uncle, boy, rooster, bull,* and *stallion. Mother, girl, woman, queen, hen*, and *daughter* are nouns that belong in the feminine category. Words such as *tree, bicycle, pencil, phone, car, bed, ligament, room, tendons, thermometer, stethoscope,* and *medication* have no male or female references and are called neuter. Indefinite nouns are words that can be either masculine or feminine: *president, plumber, parent, doctor, teacher,* and *clerk.*

Why is there a gender for words in the English language? One reason is that writers may wish to vary their text by substituting a pronoun in place of a noun. Gender guides the selection of the correct pronoun. This concept is more fully developed in Chapter 3.

## Practice 2-4

*State whether the italicized nouns are masculine, feminine, neuter, or indefinite:*

1. The *doctor* won the *award* for the research. _____

2. Many *men* agree that *women* deserve equal pay. _____

3. The *winner* of the *prize* was elated. _____

4. A *tourniquet* was used on the man's *limb.* _____

5. When visiting the *hospital*, we saw the *nurses* with *signs* at the picket *line.*

   _____

## NUMBER

Number is the form of a noun that indicates whether it is singular (one person or thing) or plural (more than one).

### Forming Plurals in General

A few basic rules help to form the plurals of nouns (Figure 2-2). However, like many rules, there are some exceptions. When in doubt about the spelling of any word, always consult a dictionary. If there are two acceptable spellings of plural words given, the first is preferred.

### Forming the Plurals of Medical Terms

Many medical terms are derived from Greek and Latin words. Forming the plurals of medical terms is somewhat different from forming the plurals of regular nouns (Figure 2-3). Reviewing the following rules may be helpful when charting, correcting, typing, or corresponding.

1. Most singular nouns are made plural just by adding *s*: *patient, patients; bone, bones; tendon, tendons; symptom, symptoms; friend, friends; nurse, nurses; writing; writings.*

2. To form the plurals of nouns ending in *s, x, ch, sh,* and *z,* add *es; dress, dresses; church, churches; tax, taxes; wish, wishes; quiz, quizzes; process, processes; larynx, larynxes.*

3. Singular nouns ending in *y* preceded by a vowel form their plurals by adding *s*: *attorney, attorneys; boy, boys; x-ray, x-rays; key, keys.*

4. Nouns ending in *y* preceded by a consonant form the plural by changing *y* to *i* and adding *es*: *policy, policies; copy, copies; allergy, allergies; extremity, extremities; study, studies; dichotomy, dichotomies; deficiency, deficiencies.*

5. Singular nouns ending in *f* and *fe* form the plural in two ways. If the final *f* in the plural form is heard, add *s: belief, beliefs; safe, safes; staff, staffs.* If the final *f* in the plural has a *v* sound, change the *f* to *v* and add *es: life, lives; half, halves; wife, wives; leaf, leaves.*

6. Singular nouns ending in *o* preceded by a vowel form their plurals by adding *s: studio, studios; duo, duos; portfolio, portfolios.* Singular nouns ending in *o* preceded by a consonant form the plural by adding *s* or *es: echo, echoes; hero, heroes; two, twos; potato, potatoes.* Usage varies, so consult a dictionary when in doubt. Note that there are two acceptable plurals of *zero* (*zeros, zeroes*) and *no* (*nos, noes*).

**FIGURE 2-2** *Rules for Forming Plurals*

## Practice 2-5

*Form the plurals of the words in italics.*

1. Protect *child* from electrical shock by covering unused *outlet*. _____

2. Maslow arranges human *need* into five *category*. _____

3. The *diagnosis* were negative. _____

4. Congenital *anomaly* are physical *abnormality* at birth. _____

5. There are seven cervical *vertebra*. _____

*Identify the singular form of these nouns:*

1. nuclei            nuclae, nuclons, nucleus          _____

2. foci              focus, focis, focae              _____

3. strata           stratae, strati, stratum           _____

1. Change *x* to *c* or *g* and add *es*: *apex, apices; thorax, thoraces; meninx, meninges; appendix, appendices; phalanx, phalanges.*

2. Change *is* to *es*: *diagnosis, diagnoses; prognosis, prognoses.*

3. Change *oma* to *omata*: *stoma, stomata; sarcoma, sarcomata; carcinoma, carcinomata* (but *carcinomas* is also acceptable).

4. Change *a* to *ae*: *sequela, sequelae; vertebra, vertebrae; pleura, pleurae.*

5. Change *um* to *a*: *ovum, ova; bacterium, bacteria; diverticulum, diverticula.*

6. Change *us* to *i*: *fungus, fungi; streptococcus, streptococci; thrombus, thrombi; bronchus, bronchi.*

7. Change *on* to *a*: *ganglion, ganglia.*

8. Change *en* to *ina*: *lumen, lumina.*

**FIGURE 2-3** *Rules for Forming Plurals of Medical Terms*

4. emboli          emblae, embolum, embolus          _____

5. ova             ovae, ovum, ovi                   _____

*Identify the plural form of these nouns:*

1. septum          septae, section, septa            _____

2. fimbria         fimbrium, fimbri, fimbriae        _____

3. thorax          throaxses, thoraxae, thoraces     _____

4. bronchus        bronchae, bronchi, bronchum       _____

5. aponeurosis     aponeursum, aponeurosae, aponeuroses   _____

## FUNCTIONS OF NOUNS

Nouns can be used in different ways in a sentence (see Figure 2-4):

| | |
|---|---|
| Subject | the person, place, thing, or idea that the sentence is about |
| Predicate Noun | a word that follows a *linking* verb and that tells something about the subject |
| Direct Object | the person, place, thing, or idea that receives the action of the verb |
| Indirect Object | a word that answers "to whom?" or "to what?" about the verb |
| Possessive Noun | a word that indicates possession or ownership by its form |
| Appositive | a word or group of words following a word to identify or give information about that word |

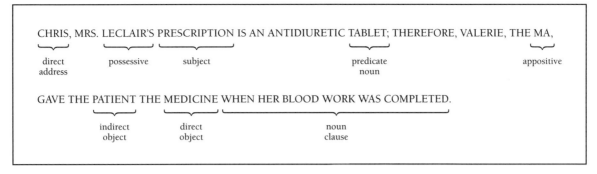

**FIGURE 2-4** *Some Uses of Nouns*

| | |
|---|---|
| Direct Address | a word or group of words naming or denoting the person or persons spoken to |
| Noun Phrase or Clause | a group of words used as a noun |

The use of a noun in a sentence is described by its case, which shows its relationship to other words in the sentence. In English there are three cases: subjective (or nominative), objective, and possessive (or genitive).

## Nominative Case: Subject

Nominative case refers to the *subject* (abbreviated S) of a sentence. The subject is always a noun or a group of words that functions as a noun. The subject of a sentence is the person, place, thing, or idea about which something is said. It is determined by asking "who?" or "what?" about the verb and can be found anywhere in the sentence.

## *Examples*

The *supervisor* scheduled six nurses. [Who scheduled? The *supervisor* scheduled.]

*Students* increased their skills with practice. [Who increased? *Students* increased.]

*Bones* of the skull protect the brain. [What protects? *Bones* protect.]

The *attitude* of our staff makes working in the O.R. enjoyable. [What makes? *Attitude* makes.]

## Practice 2-6

*Identify the subject in each sentence by placing an S above it:*

1. The instructor's approach to writing excited the students.

2. The embolus traveled to the lungs.

3. The symptoms are fever and headache.

4. The ability to proofread is a plus in the doctor's office.

5. The otologist diagnosed otitis media.

### Nominative Case: Predicate Noun

A noun can also function as a subject complement that completes the sense of a verb, or a predicate noun (PN). Sometimes it is referred to as the predicate nominative. It follows immediately after a *linking verb*: forms of "to be" (am, is, are, was, were, be, being, been), become, and seem, as well as weak intransitive verbs such as appear, feel, grow, look, smell, sound, taste. It is the same person, place, thing, or idea as the subject.

## Examples

Doctors are *specialists*. [*Specialists* is a predicate noun of the subject, *Doctors*; *are* is the linking verb.]

Valerie is a good *friend*. [*Friend* is the predicate noun of the subject, *Valerie*; *is* is the linking verb.]

Jose Ramos is a medical *assistant*. [*Assistant* is the predicate noun of the subject, *Jose Ramos*; *is* is the linking verb.]

## Practice 2-7

*Identify the predicate noun in each sentence by placing PN above it:*

1. Clothing is a nonverbal message.

2. Communication with patients is an essential skill.

3. Meninges is the term for the protective covering of the brain.

4. The patient's response to the illness was denial.

5. The elderly patient is Mrs. Leclair, the CVA in room 513.

### Objective Case

Think of the word *object* in connection with the objective case. The direct *object,* the indirect *object*, and the *object* of a preposition constitute the objective case. The direct object and indirect object complete the action of the verb and are found in the predicate.

The direct object (DO) receives the action expressed by the verb. It is found by asking "what?" or "whom?" about the verb.

## Examples

The physician dictated a *report*. [Dictated *what*? A *report*.]

Pat discussed *Mary* at the meeting. [Discussed *whom*? *Mary*.]

Can you help *John*? [Help whom? John.]

## Practice 2-8

*Identify the direct object in each sentence by placing DO above it:*

1. The neurologist prescribed medication for the condition.

2. The gastroenterologist did the colonoscopy.

3. Patients have a right to information in the medical record.

4. The doctor owns the medical record.

5. The cell contains complex structures.

The indirect object (IO) is the noun denoting *to whom, for whom, to what,* or *for what* the action of the verb is being done. It follows the verb and comes before the direct object.

## Examples

The patient wrote the *pharmacist* a check. [Wrote to *whom*? The *pharmacist*.]

The entertainer gave the *audience* a real show. [Gave *to whom*? The *audience*.]

Villes Medical Associates pays its *employees* competitive salaries. [Pays to whom? Its *employees*.]

## Practice 2-9

*Identify the indirect object in each sentence by placing IO above it.*

1. The surgeon gave the residents an opportunity to operate.

2. The patient mailed the doctor the check.

3. The scrub nurse handed the doctor a scalpel.

4. Matthew told the Medicare class his ideas.

5. The nurse fed the patient some soup.

The object of a preposition (OP) is the noun or pronoun that follows a preposition and joins it to other words in the sentence. The preposition along with its object is called a prepositional phrase. The noun that is used as the object of a preposition is never the subject of a sentence.

Some common prepositions are *to, for, on, with, off, in, during, by,* and *over.*

## Examples

The doctor wrote a letter *to* the *cardiologist.* [*Cardiologist* is the object of the preposition *to.*]

Arthroscopy is visualization *with* an *endoscope.* [*Endoscope* is the object of the preposition *with.*]

Osteomalacia *in children* is called rickets. [*Children* is the object of the preposition *in.*]

# Practice 2-10

*Identify the object of the preposition by placing OP above it:*

1. The ileum is the distal portion of the small intestines.

2. Ethics is a branch of moral science.

3. CHAMPUS is insurance for military families.

4. A statute of limitations fixes the period of time for legal action.

5. Skills in verbal communication are required of the health-care team.

## Possessive Case

Possessive case indicates possession or ownership. Possessive nouns express something that is part of a person, place, thing, or idea. For example, *patient's medication* shows that the patient is the owner of the medication. *Medication* is the noun that follows the possessive noun, *patient's.* To check the accuracy of the possessive, change the words to *the medication of the patient.*

Use an apostrophe (') to form the possessive. The six rules for forming a possessive noun are listed in Figure 2-5.

1. To form the possessive of singular nouns, add an apostrophe and the letter s ('s) to the noun. The word that has the apostrophe is the word that owns something.

   *patient's* bed [the bed of the patient]

   *doctor's* white coat [the white coat of the doctor]

2. The possessive of plural nouns ending in s is formed by adding only an apostrophe after the s (s').

   *doctors'* dressing room [the dressing room of the doctors]

   *nurses'* scrub gowns [the scrub gowns of the nurses]

3. Irregular plural nouns not ending in s need an apostrophe s ('s) to form the possessive.

   The *children's* ward is on the fourth floor.

   The *women's* lounge is down the hall.

4. If two people own an item, only the last name takes the possessive form.

   *Lorry and Doreen's* book on *Grammar and Writing Skills for the Health Professional* is on the shelf.

   If each person owns the item, both names take the possessive form.

   *Dr. Archie's* and *Dr. Villes's* stethoscopes are on the treatment table.

5. To form the possessive of singular nouns ending in s, add an apostrophe and an s ('s).

   *Mr. Jones's* daughter.

6. To form the possessive of plural nouns ending in s, add only an apostrophe (').

   The *Jones'* families.

**FIGURE 2-5**   *Rules for Forming Possessive Nouns*

# Practice 2-11

*Form the possessive of the italicized nouns:*

1. The *doctor* examination revealed no fracture. _____

2. The *parent* children showed their concern. _____

3. The *children* dentist is a pedodontist. _____

4. The dental *technician* surgical scrubs are at the office. _____

5. The *pharmacy* location is near the atrium of the hospital. _____

### Appositives and Direct Address

Nouns may also be used as appositives (APP). An appositive is a word or group of words that immediately follows and further identifies another noun. It is usually separated by commas.

## Examples

Dr. Villes, *the doctor on call*, performed the ORIF. [The phrase *the doctor on call* identifies and renames the noun, *Dr. Villes.*]

Carr Insurance, *an independent firm*, covered all medical expenses. [The phrase *an independent firm* identifies and renames *Carr Insurance.*]

The noun of direct address (DA) names the listener. The speaker tries to catch the listener's attention by using the person's name. The use of direct address makes messages more direct and personal. Because it interrupts the message, a noun of direct address is separated by commas.

## Examples

This equipment, *Miss Archie*, belongs in the treatment room. [The speaker is requesting *Miss Archie* to listen.]

What do you think, *Christopher*?

*Sara*, please see me after class.

After class, *Sara*, please see me.

Note that commas separate both appositives and nouns of direct address.

## Practice 2-12

*Indicate whether the italicized noun or phrase is appositive or direct address by placing APP or DA above it:*

1. Tell me, *Doctor*, what is the normal course of treatment for this condition?

2. Do you think, *Dr. Paul*, that the biopsy is necessary?

3. My husband, *Bob*, developed atrial fibrillation.

4. Schedule an appointment, *Pat*, in six months.

5. The assistant, *Lorry*, set the room up for the next patient.

## Nouns Functioning as Phrases or Clauses

A group of two or more words may also function as a noun, either as a noun phrase or a noun clause. Phrases and clauses are nouns when they are used as a subject, direct object, indirect object, or predicate noun.

A noun phrase lacks a subject or a predicate.

*To cure disease* is the goal of medical research.

The phrase *To cure disease* has no subject or predicate. The group of words functions as a noun because it is used as the subject of the entire sentence.

In the following sentence, the phrase is a noun used as a predicate noun after the linking verb *is:*

The goal of medical research is *to cure disease.*

A noun clause does contain a subject and a predicate. It can also function as a noun.

The patient didn't understand *why two tests were scheduled.*

The clause *why two tests were scheduled* contains a subject (*two tests*) and a predicate (*were scheduled*). The clause in this sentence is a noun that functions as a direct object.

## Practice 2-13

*Fill in the blanks below with the correct word from the following group:*

| | | | | |
|---|---|---|---|---|
| direct object | appositive | possessive | predicate noun | gender |
| collective noun | subject noun | abstract noun | proper noun | number |

1. Tells what the sentence is about: _____

2. Names an idea: _____

3. Refers to a group: _____

4. Identifies masculine, feminine, neuter: _____

5. Determines singular or plural: _____

6. Follows a linking verb: _____

7. Receives the verb's action: _____

8. Shows ownership: _____

9. Renames a noun: _____

10. Names a particular person, place, or thing: _____

*Identify how the italicized nouns are used in the sentences:*

1. *Reports* are dictated by the *physician*.: _____

2. The *doctor* gave the *nurse* explicit *directions*.: _____

3. *Nurse*, please administer the *medication* now.: _____

4. Listen, *Doctor Lee*, the heart is normal.: _____

5. *Susan* is the best *nurse* on the *floor*.: _____

# Nouns Summary

| Noun | Names a person, place, thing, or quality. |
|---|---|
| Common | Names a *class* of persons, places, objects, or qualities: politician, state, author, couple, drug, disease, clinic, company, physician, specimen, virus, therapy, artery, temperature, x-ray. |
| Proper | Names a *particular* person, place, object, or quality: Republican, Massachusetts, Emily Dickinson, Jack and Jill, Darvon, Hodgkin, Mayo Clinic, Microsoft, Joan Mullins, M.D., Museum of Fine Arts, Basketball Hall of Fame, American Medical Association (AMA), American Association of Medical Assistants (AAMA). Proper nouns are capitalized. |
| Collective | Names a group of persons, animals, or things: government, association, board, public, society, organization, audience, police, nation, flock. |
| Abstract | Names a quality or idea not perceived by the senses: honesty, goodness, joy, integrity, honor, worth, value, thought, courage, freedom, fear. |
| Concrete | Names things that are touchable, visible, and audible: pharmacist, therapist, instrument, forceps, alcohol, ointment, medication, hospital. |
| **Gender** | **Categorizes nouns as masculine, feminine, neuter, or indefinite.** |
| Masculine | Represents noun words like male, bull, rooster, Mr. |
| Feminine | Represents noun words like women, princess, girl. |
| Neuter | Represents noun words that are neither male nor female: plant, river, desk. |
| Indefinite | Represents nouns that can be either masculine or feminine: clerk, doctor. |
| **Number** | **Categorizes nouns as singular or plural.** |
| Forming plurals | Add the letter *s* to most nouns: patient, patients; pen, pens; symptom, symptoms; quota, quotas; bone, bones; nurse, nurses. |
| Nouns ending in *s, x, ch, sh, z* | Add *es*: pass, passes; box, boxes; wish, wishes; index, indexes; quiz, quizzes; phalanx, phalanxes; larynx, larynxes. |
| Nouns ending in *y* preceded by a *vowel* | Add *s* only: boy, boys; key, keys; attorney, attorneys; delay, delays; donkey, donkeys; Saturday, Saturdays. |

| | |
|---|---|
| Nouns ending in *y* preceded by a *consonant* | Change the *y* to *i* and add *es*: city, cities; allergy, allergies; dictionary, dictionaries; extremity, extremities; dichotomy, dichotomies; deficiency, deficiencies. |
| Nouns ending in *o* preceded by a *vowel* | Add the letter *s*: studio, studios; shampoo, shampoos; ratio, ratios; stereo, stereos; portfolio, portfolios. |
| Nouns ending in *o* preceded by a *consonant* | Add *s* or *es*: ego, egos; memo, memos; potato, potatoes; hero, heroes; zero, zeros; auto, autos; typo, typos. |
| Nouns ending in *f* or *fe* | Add the letter *s* if the plural form has an *f* sound: belief, beliefs; proof, proofs; safe, safes; staff, staffs. If the plural form has the *v* sound, change the *f* to *v* and add *es*: life, lives; wife, wives; calf, calves; loaf, loaves. |
| Plurals of Medical Nouns | Make the following changes: |

*x* to *c* or *g* and add *es*: apex, apices; appendix, appendices; thorax, thoraces; phalanx, phalanges.

*is* to *es*: diagnosis, diagnoses; prognosis, prognoses.

*oma* to *omata*: stoma, stomata; sarcoma, sarcomata.

*a* to *ae*: sequela, sequelae; vertebra, vertebrae.

*um* to *a*: ovum, ova; bacterium, bacteria.

*us* to *i*: fungus, fungi; streptococcus, streptococci.

*on* to *a*: ganglion, ganglia.

*en* to *ina*: lumen, lumina.

| **Function** | **Categories of usage.** |
|---|---|
| *Nominative* | Refers to the subject of the sentence about which something is said. |
| Subject | "The patient receives excellent care." *Receives excellent care* is what is said about the subject, *patient*. |
| Predicate Noun | Means the same as the subject but comes right after a linking verb. "English is a language." *Language* is the predicate noun that comes after the linking verb, *is*. |
| *Objective* | Refers to the object of the sentence or preposition. |
| Direct Object | Directly receives the action of the verb and answers *who* or *what* about the verb. "Students read [*what?*] books." The direct object is *books*. |
| Indirect Object | Relates indirectly to the verb and answers *to/for whom* and *to/for what* about the verb. "The physician gave [*to whom?*] the patient [*what?*] a prescription." The *patient* is the indirect object. |
| Object of a Preposition | Follows a preposition and shows its relationship to the rest of the sentence. "The patient came to the office." *Office* is the object of the preposition *to*. |
| *Possessive* | Shows ownership or possession. |
| Singular | Add an apostrophe and an *s* to singular nouns: ship's name, Chris's truck, month's allotment, boss's approval. |

| | |
|---|---|
| Plural | Add only an apostrophe to plural nouns ending in s: boys' games, heroes' medal. |
| Irregular | Add an apostrophe and an s: children's toys, women's blouses. |
| *Appositive* | Follows a noun and renames it. "The disease, *an inflammation of the spinal cord and brain*, involves the meninges." Note the separation by commas. |
| *Direct Address* | Speaks directly to a person and names the listener. "Listen, *Jane*, to the sounds through the stethoscope." Note the separation by commas. |
| *Noun Phrase* | Lacks a subject or predicate. "*To alleviate symptoms* is the goal of taking this medication." |
| *Noun Clause* | Contains a subject and a predicate. "*Confidentiality is necessary when health professionals care for patients*." |

# Medical Spelling

*Become familiar with the spelling of the following words:*

| | |
|---|---|
| allergy, allergies | orthodontist |
| anesthesiologist | orthopedist |
| anomaly, anomalies | osteoporosis |
| appendix, appendices | otitis |
| bacterium, bacteria | otolaryngologist |
| biopsy | otologist |
| bronchus, bronchi | ovum, ova |
| cardiologist | pathologist |
| deficiency, deficiencies | pharmacist |
| dermatologist | pharmacologist |
| diagnosis, diagnoses | physician |
| embolus, emboli | process, processes |
| endocrinologist | psychiatrist |
| extremity, extremities | psychologist |
| gastroenterologist | psychosomatic |
| gynecologist | radiologist |
| immunologist | stratum, strata |
| medication | symptoms |
| neurologist | thorax, thoraces |
| nucleus, nuclei | thrombus, thrombi |
| oncologist | urologist |
| ophthalmologist | vertebra, vertebrae |

# Medical Office Correspondence

Writing in the medical field is a highly structured form of communication. Correspondence is a process of sharing medical-related information through standardized letters, memos, reports, and electronic messages. Through these means, both the receiver and the sender have a document that holds more legality than the spoken word. This chapter outlines some of the varied communication tasks that medical professionals need to perform.

# The Medical Letter

This chapter has covered types of nouns, including common nouns, proper nouns, and medical nouns, all of which are essential parts of a medical letter, especially in the heading, subject line, and inside address. These parts are key because they indicate who the letter is from, what is being communicated, and to whom it is being communicated. These key sections of a medical letter can provide information about clients, medical records, and other medical concerns at a glance. Since medical letters may pass important and private information from doctor to client, between doctors, or between facilities and insurance companies, it is important that the appearance of the medical letter reflect competence by utilizing correct formatting and organization to facilitate communication.

## LETTER COMPONENTS

A letter has six basic parts: the heading, inside address, salutation, body, closing, and signature.

## Heading

The heading includes the letterhead and the date line. The letterhead is usually commercially printed with a logo, physician's name or medical group, and address. Some may include a telephone number or medical specialty. When using letterhead paper, only the date needs to be typed, including the month, day, and year with no abbreviations. The date is placed *three lines* below the letterhead, flush with the left margin. Figure 2-6 shows a sample heading.

VMC

*VILLES MEDICAL CENTER*
*One Morey Place*
*Anywhere, MA 01102*
*(555) 555-4727 Phone*
*(555) 555-4000 Fax*

July 15, 20XX

**FIGURE 2-6** *Heading*

## Inside Address

The inside address gives the name and address of the person or facility to which the letter is going. It is the mailing address. It is placed *four lines* below the date line, flush with the left margin (Figure 2-7).

**V**
**M**
**C**   *VILLES MEDICAL CENTER*
*One Morey Place*
*Anywhere, MA 01102*
*(555) 555-4727 Phone*
*(555) 555-4000 Fax*

July 15, 20XX

Dr. Valerie Christopher
Carr and Oberg Associates
25 Brewster Street
Anywhere, MA 01518

**FIGURE 2-7**   *Inside Address*

If the title of the person is included in the inside address, it goes after the name on the same line. If the title is too long, place it on the second line.

## Examples

Dr. Valerie Christopher, President
Carr and Oberg Associates
25 Brewster Street
Anywhere, MA 01518

Mary Louise Norman, M.D.
Chairperson, Board of Directors
25 Brewster Street
Anywhere, MA 01518

## Salutation

The salutation is the greeting of the letter. It is placed *two lines* below the inside address, flush with the left margin. A colon (:) follows the salutation (Figure 2-8). All words in the salutation begin with capital letters, except articles and prepositions.

## Examples

| | |
|---|---|
| Firm or Group | Dear Customer Service Representative, Colleagues, Friends, Members of the Search Committee, Gentlemen, Ladies, Editors, Physicians, Students |
| Special Unknown Person | Dear Personnel Director, Sir, Madame, Clerk of Deeds, Nurse Supervisor |

**VILLES MEDICAL CENTER**
*One Morey Place*
*Anywhere, MA 01102*
*(555) 555-4727 Phone*
*(555) 555-4000 Fax*

July 15, 20XX

Dr. Valerie Christopher
Carr and Oberg Associates
25 Brewster Street
Anywhere, MA 01518

Dear Dr. Christopher:

**FIGURE 2-8**  *Salutation*

| | |
|---|---|
| Special Known Persons | Dear Dr. Norman, Nurse Rose, Mr. Oberg, Mary, Miss Leclaire |

## Body

The body of the letter contains the message. The first line of the body is placed *two lines* below the salutation, flush with the left margin (Figure 2-9). The body may have more than one paragraph with double spacing between each paragraph.

Sometimes in medical correspondence, a subject line is used to call attention to what's important in the letter. The subject line is typed two lines before the salutation, flush with the left margin in the block style (Figure 2-10). The subject line or RE: in most cases is a patient's name or medical topic and is considered part of the body of a letter.

## Closing and Signature

The closing is the leave-taking part of the letter. It is typed on the *second line* below the last line of the body. Only the first word in the closing is capitalized. A comma is placed after the last word.

## Examples

| | | |
|---|---|---|
| Yours truly, | Sincerely, | Thank you, |
| Very truly yours, | Sincerely yours, | With best wishes, |
| With best regards, | Cordially, | Respectfully yours, |

---

**V**
**M**    *VILLES MEDICAL CENTER*
**C**    *One Morey Place*
*Anywhere, MA 01102*
*(555) 555-4727 Phone*
*(555) 555-4000 Fax*

July 15, 20XX


Dr. Valerie Christopher
Carr and Oberg Associates
25 Brewster Street
Anywhere, MA 01518


Dear Dr. Christopher:


Thank you for referring your patient, Mr. Burt Weaver, to Villes Medical Center. Mr.Weaver's psychological status on his initial evaluation necessitated an emergency evaluation. I diagnosed the patient as having an adjustment disorder and major depression. He was placed on antidepressant medication for three months.


During this time, Mr. Weaver also participated in six group sessions and ten individual psychotherapy sessions before reaching his maximum rehabilitation. At the time of his discharge, Mr. Weaver was made aware that he could return to Villes Medical Center at any time, if warranted.


If you have any further questions, please call my office at (555) 555-4727.

---

**FIGURE 2-9**    *Body*


The signature is handwritten in ink right after and *directly below* the closing. In addition, the writer's name is typed *four lines* directly below the closing (Figure 2-11). The typed name may also include the writer's position.

## Other Notations

If the author of the letter did not type it, the typist's initials are typed on the second line below the typewritten signature, flush with the left margin. If there are enclosures with the letter, an "Enc." is typed directly below the typist's initials. If copies of a letter are given to other people, "C:" and the name of the person to whom the copy is sent should be typed on a new line following "Enc.," or the typist's initials if there is no "Enc."

**VILLES MEDICAL CENTER**
*One Morey Place*
*Anywhere, MA 01102*
*(555) 555-4727 Phone*
*(555) 555-4000 Fax*

July 15, 20XX

Dr. Valerie Christopher
Carr and Oberg Associates
25 Brewster Street
Anywhere, MA 01518

Mr. Burt Weaver

Dear Dr. Christopher:

Thank you for referring. . . .

**FIGURE 2-10** *Use of Subject Line*

## Example

Yours truly,

Dr. Mary Louis Norman

LNV
Enc.
C: Mary Pat Leonard, M.D.

If the office's name and address do not appear at the top of the stationery, type this information under the writer's typed name (or title) following the signature.

## Example

Dr. Mary Louis Norman
Villes Medical Center
One Morey Place

VMC | **VILLES MEDICAL CENTER**
One Morey Place
Anywhere, MA 01102
(555) 555-4727 Phone
(555) 555-4000 Fax

July 15, 20XX

Dr. Valerie Christopher
Carr and Oberg Associates
25 Brewster Street
Anywhere, MA 01518

Dear Dr. Christopher:

Thank you for referring your patient, Mr. Burt Weaver, to Villes Medical Center. Mr. Weaver's psychological status on his initial evaluation necessitated an emergency evaluation. I diagnosed the patient as having an adjustment disorder and major depression. He was placed on antidepressant medication for three months.

During this time, Mr. Weaver also participated in six group sessions and ten individual psychotherapy sessions before reaching his maximum rehabilitation. At the time of his discharge, Mr. Weaver was made aware that he could return to Villes Medical Center at any time, if warranted.

If you have any further questions, please call my office at (555) 555-4727.

Yours truly,

Dr. Mary Louis Norman

**FIGURE 2-11**  *Closing and Signature*

Anywhere, MA 01102
(555) 555-4727
(555) 555-4000 Fax

If a letter runs longer than one page, the heading on the second page should contain the name of the writer, the page number, and the date. It should begin flush with the left margin.

## Examples

(1)  Mary Louis Norman, M.D.          -2-          July 15, 20XX

(2)  Mary Louis Norman, M.D.
     Page 2
     July 15, 20XX

(3)  Mary Louis Norman, M.D.
     Page 2
     July 15, 20XX
     Subject: Mr. Burt Weaver

## FORMATS AND PRESENTATION OF LETTERS

The two most common styles of formal letters are the block style and the modified block style. The difference between the two is that the block style has no indentations and the modified block does. The modified block style has the date, closing, and signature indented to the middle of the page. The example letter used in this chapter to explain the basic letter parts uses the block style (Figure 2-12). A modified block example of the same letter is also included (Figure 2-13).

Most medical offices and clinics use official letterhead paper. The standard size is 8/1/2/-by-11-inch or 5/1/2/-by-8/1/2/-inch paper for shorter notes. Whether using letterhead stationery or plain stationery, the margins must be equal on the top, bottom, and left and right sides, usually one inch. Margins can be compared to the matting on a picture. Margins are the frame of the letter. Letters are typed single spaced unless the message is extremely short, in which case double spacing is acceptable.

To be most effective, the letter should be as short as possible. A single page is preferable.

## *Practice 2-14*

*Match the terms with their definitions:*

1. body _____          A.  leave-taking of the letter

2. written signature _____          B.  typed name of sender

3. heading _____          C.  the greeting

4. closing _____          D.  parts of the letter are indented

5. inside address _____          E.  everything in letter begins at the left margin

6. letterhead stationery _____          F.  company's name and address printed on stationery

7. typed signature _____          G.  message of the letter

## V M C  VILLES MEDICAL CENTER
*One Morey Place*
*Anywhere, MA 01102*
*(555) 555-4727 Phone*
*(555) 555-4000 Fax*

July 15, 20XX

Dr. Valerie Christopher
Carr and Oberg Associates
25 Brewster Street
Anywhere, MA 01518

Dear Dr. Christopher:

Thank you for referring your patient, Mr. Burt Weaver, to Villes Medical Center. Mr. Weaver's psychological status on his initial evaluation necessitated an emergency evaluation. I diagnosed the patient as having an adjustment disorder and major depression. He was placed on antidepressant medication for three months.

During this time, Mr. Weaver also participated in six group sessions and ten individual psychotherapy sessions before reaching his maximum rehabilitation. At the time of his discharge, Mr. Weaver was made aware that he could return to Villes Medical Center at any time, if warranted.

If you have any further questions, please call my office at (555) 555-4727.

Yours truly,

Dr. Mary Louis Norman

LNV

**FIGURE 2-12**  *Block Style Letter*

**V**
**M**   *VILLES MEDICAL CENTER*
**C**   *One Morey Place*
       *Anywhere, MA 01102*
       *(555) 555-4727 Phone*
       *(555) 555-4000 Fax*

July 15, 20XX

Dr. Valerie Christopher
Carr and Oberg Associates
25 Brewster Street
Anywhere, MA 01518

Dear Dr. Christopher:

Thank you for referring your patient, Mr. Burt Weaver, to Villes Medical Center. Mr. Weaver's psychological status on his initial evaluation necessitated an emergency evaluation. I diagnosed the patient as having an adjustment disorder and major depression. He was placed on antidepressant medication for three months.

During this time, Mr. Weaver also participated in six group sessions and ten individual psychotherapy sessions before reaching his maximum rehabilitation. At the time of his discharge, Mr. Weaver was made aware that he could return to Villes Medical Center at any time, if warranted.

If you have any further questions, please call my office at (555) 555-4727.

Yours truly,

Dr. Mary Louis Norman

LNV

**FIGURE 2-13**   *Modified Block Letter*

8. block style letter _____     H. person and address to whom the letter is written

9. salutation _____     I. address of person writing the letter

10. modified block letter _____     J. written in ink after the closing

## FOLDING THE LETTER

The manner in which the letter is folded depends on the size of the envelope used. The following folds apply to an 8½-by-11-inch letter.

### *Business Envelope (9½ by 4³⁄₁₆ inches)*

Step One      Bring the bottom third of the paper up and fold.

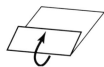

Step Two      Fold the top third downward to within about ⅜ inch of fold made in step one.

Step Three    Insert the folded edge of the letter into the envelope.

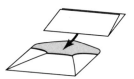

### *Use the Envelope to Get the Folds Right*

Step One      Slip the top edge of the letter all the way up under the flap.

Step Two      Fold the bottom part of the letter so that the bottom edge of the letter and the envelope align.

Step Three    Pull the letter out from under the flap of the envelope and fold the top over to within ⅜ inch of the bottom fold.

### *Smaller Envelopes*

Step One      Fold from the bottom to a quarter of an inch from the top.

Step Two      Fold over the right-hand third of the letter.

Step Three      The left side is folded over the first fold.

Step Four      Insert the letter with the fold at the bottom of the envelope.

## Envelopes with Windows

Step One      Bring the bottom third of the letter up and fold.

Step Two      Fold the top part *back* to the fold made in step one.

Step Three      Insert the letter toward the *front* of the envelope so that the mailing address shows through the window.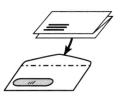

# Practice 2-15

*Number these folds in the correct order.*

A.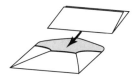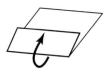

B.

C.

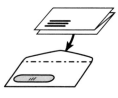

## ADDRESSING THE ENVELOPE

For envelopes with a preprinted return address, only the recipient's address is typed. This address should correspond to the inside address on the letter. Begin the address in the middle of the envelope, slightly to the right. Use proper titles, including the first name or initial of the person to whom the letter is sent. Directly below that line is the street address. The third line contains the city, state, and zip code. If the envelope has no return address, it must be typed in the upper left corner. The envelope should be typed in all captial letters with no punctuation to comply with post office guidelines. Information for the post office, such as "certified mail," is usually written under the stamp. Information for the addressee, such as "personal or private," is written under the return address. See Figure 2-14 for a properly typed envelope.

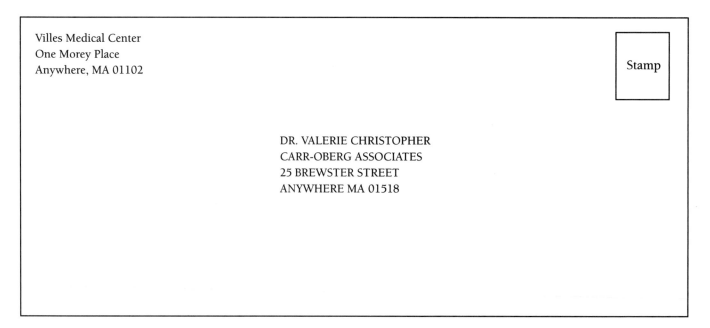

**FIGURE 2-14** *Addressing an Envelope*

# *Medical Office Correspondence Summary*

## MEDICAL LETTER FORMAT

Heading

**V**
**M**
**C**

*VILLES MEDICAL CENTER*
*One Morey Place*
*Anywhere, MA 01102*
*(555) 555-4727 Phone*
*(555) 555-4000 Fax*

(3 spaces)

| | |
|---|---|
| June 5, 20XX | Date |

(4 spaces)

| | |
|---|---|
| Mary LeClair | Name and address |
| Anystreet | of the person |
| Anywhere, MA 00000 | receiving the mail |

(2 spaces)

| | |
|---|---|
| Dear Mrs. LeClair, | Salutation |

(2 spaces)

The purpose of this letter. . . . . . . . . . .
. . . . . . . . . . . . . . . . . . . . . . . . . . . . . .
. . . . . . . . . . . . . . . . . . . . . . . . . . . . .
. . . . . . . . . . . . . . . end of letter.        Body—Message of the letter

(2 spaces)

| | |
|---|---|
| Sincerely, | Closing—Leaving-taking |

(4 spaces)

Written signature

| | |
|---|---|
| Valerie Christopher, M.D. | Typed signature—author of |
| | the letter |

(2 spaces)

| | |
|---|---|
| VC: Inv | Typist's Initials |

(2 spaces)

| | |
|---|---|
| C: Dr. Michael Paul | C—Others receiving copy |

(2 spaces)

| | |
|---|---|
| Enc. Consultation report | Enc.—Enclosures |
| | (notations follow in this order) |

# Skills Review

*Write the noun usage for the italicized word in each sentence: S for subject, DO for direct object, IO for indirect object, OP for object of preposition, APP for appositive, PN for predicate noun, and DA for direct address.*

1. The left *knee* was limited in motion due to intrinsic pathology.

2. Hillside Medical Associates pays its *employees* competitive *salaries*.

3. Most *physicians* read several *journals* each week.

4. The *AMA* will hold its *election* next month.

5. *Visualization* of the *joint* is done with an *endoscope*.

6. The medical *assistant* transcribed the *report* for the *doctor*.

7. *Nurse*, would you please check my *temperature*?

8. *Muscles* can perform a variety of *actions*.

9. *Cramps* are painful *contractions* of *muscles*.

10. The *calcaneus* is the heel *bone*.

*Rewrite these sentences correcting capitals, spellings, possessives, and plurals where necessary.*

1. Dr. smith is on call for orthopedic consultation.

   _____

2. Bones cannot move without the help of muscles'.

   _____

3. the admitting diagnosis is acute intertrochanteric fracture of the Right Hip.

   _____

4. Copys of the report were mailed to the patients physician.

   _____

5. Thousands of patients spread bacterium to other workers.

   _____

*If the noun in italic print is singular, make it plural. If the noun is plural, make it singular.*

1. The patient had multiple *diagnosis*. _____

2. The bacterium responsible for the disease is the *gonococci*. _____

3. The outer layer of skin has cells that are arranged in *stratum*. _____

4. In a colostomy, the proximal *stomata* drains the feces. _____

5. Many *villus* in the small intestines absorb nutrients. _____

6. Diverticulosis is saclike swellings present in the wall of the colon called *diverticulum*. _____

7. The blocking of a coronary artery by *thrombi* could lead to an M.I. _____

*Change proper nouns in italics to common nouns and common nouns in italics to proper nouns.*

1. The *patient* expects and appreciates courtesy. _____

2. Due to an accident, *James* has a greenstick fracture of the right ulna. _____

3. The *doctor* praised the *medical assistant* for her efficiency. _____

4. The *AMA* is a prestigious group. _____

5. Most doctors send their patients to the *Mayo Clinic*. _____

6. The *hospital* hired a new *specialist*. _____

*Identify the medical nouns in the following sentences:*

1. Health information coding is transferring the description of disease, injuries, and procedures into letters and numbers (alphanumeric).

2. Congenital anomaly is a birth defect.

3. The symptoms are similar to a myocardial infarction.

4. Otitis media is common in young patients.

5. The dermatologist wants a biopsy sent to the pathologist.

*Indicate whether these statements are true or false.*

1. The modified block style letter has no indentation.

2. "Yours truly" is a common salutation in a medical letter.

3. "C" in a letter means a copy was sent to an additional person/s.

4. The number of folds for an 8½-inch by 1-inch paper is three.

5. "Re:" and "Subject" have the same meaning.

*Use the Writing Process Worksheet to write a letter and address an envelope to your primary-care physician asking for a referral to an ophthalmologist. When completed, underline the nouns in the letter.*

# Writing Process Worksheet

1. PREWRITING – write down facts, organize ideas

_____     _____
_____     _____
_____     _____
_____     _____
_____     _____

2. WRITING – write without concern for grammar or punctuation

_____
_____
_____
_____
_____
_____
_____

3. REWRITING – correct grammar, make changes using proofreaders' marks

_____
_____
_____
_____
_____
_____
_____

4. FINALIZING – type or write final copy

_____
_____
_____
_____
_____
_____
_____

5. PROOFREAD – read the final copy aloud for a final check

_____
_____
_____

*Circle the correct plural form of these words. If necessary, check a medical dictionary.*

|   |   |   |
|---|---|---|
| 1. | antenna | antennas, antenni, antennae |
| 2. | extremity | extremities, extremites, extremmities |
| 3. | metamorphosis | metamorphos, metamorphos, metamorphoses |
| 4. | bacterium | bacteria, bacteri, bacteriac |
| 5. | symptom | symptam, symptim, symptoms |
| 6. | anomaly | anomilies, anomalys, anomalies |
| 7. | diaphysis | diaphysises, diaphyses, diaphysiss |
| 8. | vertebra | vertebrum, vertebrae, vertebri |
| 9. | process | processes, processos, processs |
| 10. | phalanx | phalanxes, phalanges, phalanxs |
| 11. | diagnosis | diagnoss, diagnosiss, diagnosing, diagnoses |
| 12. | ganglion | ganglionss, ganglia, gangli |

*Translate medical abbreviations using a medical dictionary or appendix.*

1. a.c.        _____
2. AIDS        _____
3. alt. noc.        _____
4. AROM        _____
5. AS        _____
6. amb        _____
7. B/S        _____
8. ASA        _____
9. BE        _____
10. A&P        _____

# Comprehensive Review

*Match these words with the corresponding numbers found in the letter.*

a. appositive
b. salutation
c. direct object
d. object of a preposition

e. proper noun
f. subject
g. closing

h. predicate noun
i. inside address
j. common noun

1. \_\_\_\_\_
2. \_\_\_\_\_
3. \_\_\_\_\_

4. _____
5. _____
6. _____
7. _____
8. _____
9. _____
10. _____

---

# LINCOLN MEDICAL OFFICE
## 1 VASSER STREET
## BOSTON, MA 05440

June 14, 20XX

Dr. William Ward
5609 Main Street ②
Boston, MA 05402  } ①

Dear Dr. Ward: ③

Thank you for referring your *patient*, ④ *Ms. Emily Parker*, ⑤ to this office. My diagnosis of this woman was major *depression*. ⑥ I prescribed *an antidepressant* ⑦ for a period of three months. *Ms. Parker* ⑧ will return in September for a follow-up *appointment*. ⑨

Call me if you have any questions.

Sincerely, ⑩

*Dr. Peter Morin*

Dr. Peter Morin

# CHAPTER 3

# *Pronouns*

PRACTICAL WRITING COMPONENT:
MEMO AND ELECTRONIC MAIL

## OBJECTIVES

*Upon completion of this chapter, the learner should be able to:*

❖ identify basic types of pronouns

❖ identify personal pronouns by gender, number, and function

❖ use pronouns that agree with their antecedents in number, gender, and person

❖ spell various medical terms

❖ translate various medical abbreviations

❖ Compose an office memorandum and e-mail using the proper format.

Once upon a time there was a medical office unit with four medical assistants named *Everybody, Somebody, Anybody*, and *Nobody*. There was an important job to be done, and *Everybody* was sure that *Somebody* would do it. *Anybody* could have done it, but *Nobody* did it. *Somebody* got angry with this because it was *Everybody*'s job. *Everybody* thought *Anybody* could do it, but *Nobody* realized that *Everybody* wouldn't do it. It ended up that *Everybody* blamed *Somebody* when *Nobody* did what *Anybody* could have done. (Author unknown)

Welcome to the world of pronouns. A pronoun is a word that replaces or substitutes for a noun; for example,

*Leah* borrowed *books* from the library. *She* returned *them* yesterday.

Note that the pronouns *she* and *them* take the place of the nouns *Leah* and *books*.

Because of the close relationship between nouns and pronouns, there are a lot of similarities in how both are used in sentences. Therefore, anyone with a good understanding of nouns will have no difficulty with pronouns.

# *Types of Pronouns*

The different types of pronouns are personal, reflexive, relative, indefinite, interrogative, and demonstrative. The meaning of each pronoun is contained within its name, which makes the definitions easier to understand:

❖ Personal pronouns refer to persons (and things).

❖ Reflexive pronouns throw back or reflect.

❖ Relative pronouns relate to other words.

❖ Indefinite pronouns refer to the unknown.

❖ Interrogative pronouns ask questions.

❖ Demonstrative pronouns point out or demonstrate.

## PERSONAL PRONOUNS

Personal pronouns refer to specific people and things. They are used more frequently than any other pronoun. Personal pronouns have three characteristics: gender, number, and person. They are also distinguished by case, being either nominative, objective, or possessive. Choosing which personal pronoun to use depends on how it is used in a sentence.

---

### Personal Pronouns

I, you, he, she, it, we, you, they
me, you, him, her, it, us, you, them, my, mine, your,
yours, his, her, hers, its, our, ours, your, yours, their, theirs

---

## Gender

Like nouns, pronouns are characterized by gender: masculine, feminine, neuter, and indefinite. Masculine pronouns are *he, his, him*. Feminine pronouns are *she, her, hers*. The word *it* is an example of a neuter pronoun. Indefinite pronouns represent unknown persons or things, such as *all, anything, someone*.

## *Examples*

*He* is very protective of *his* property. [masculine]

*Anyone* can be successful. [indefinite]

*It* belongs to the person who finds *it,* I believe. [neuter]

*She* was all ears after *she* learned about *her* grades. [feminine]

## Number and Person

Number shows whether a pronoun refers to one person or thing (singular) or more than one (plural). Person denotes whether one is speaking (first person), spoken to (second person), or spoken about (third person). Table 3-1 shows pronoun forms categorized by person and number.

## *Examples*

*I* am always right. [first person singular]

*We* are at the medical conference. [first person plural]

## TABLE 3-1 *Number and Person of Pronouns*

| Person | Meaning | Number | |
|--------|---------|--------|---|
| | | **Singular** | **Plural** |
| First | Speaker | I, me, my, mine | we, us, our, ours |
| Second | Individual addressed | you, your, yours | you, your, yours |
| Third | Person or thing spoken about | he, she, it, its, him, his, her, hers | they, them, their, theirs |

*My* schedule is very busy. [first person singular]

*You* should check the treatment room for antiseptics. [second person singular or plural]

*You* make *your* own way. [second person singular or plural]

*He* said the matter could be settled now. [third person singular]

*They* should have signed the medical consent form. [third person plural]

The anatomy books belong to *them*. [third person plural]

# Practice 3-1

*Use Table 3-1 to identify the italicized pronouns in the following sentences as first, second, or third person and singular or plural:*

1. The exam took a long time but *it* was simple. _____

2. As nurses, *we* need to help lessen health-care disparities. _____

3. Are they *your* new patients? _____

4. The medical history given to *us* was complete. _____

5. *They* found a kidney stone in the strainer. _____

The choice of pronouns depends on how they function in a sentence, which heads to the explanation of case.

## Nominative Case

The subject pronoun—*I, you, he, she, it, we,* and *they*—is the person or thing talked about in a sentence.

## Examples

*He* tripped on the stairs.

*They* work at the Medical Center.

*She* is the Chief Resident.

*I* felt confident I could do the job.

Although the bronchoscopy was simple, *it* took a long time to do.

# Practice 3-2

*Choose the correct pronoun from within the parentheses:*

1. Dr. Jones, (you, your) have no idea how much work is involved in preparing the patient.

2. (She, Her) answered the office telephone immediately.

3. (It, Its) doesn't make any difference what the EKG reads.

4. As a medical group, (we, us) support our diagnosis.

5. Studies indicate (it, its) takes 4–6 doses before the symptoms disappear.

Predicate pronouns are the same as subject pronouns: *I, you, he, she, it, we,* and *they.* They are found following a linking verb such as am, is, are, was, or were.

## Examples

The visitor must have been *she.*

Is *she* the owner?

Is it *I?*

It is *she* who pays the bill.

Was it *he* who called?

# Practice 3-3

*Choose the correct predicate pronoun from within the parentheses:*

1. It was (me, I) who administered cardiopulmonary resuscitation.

2. The resident who did the physical exam on the patients was (he, him).

3. Is it (she, her) who has the diagnosis of hypertension?

4. The cholecystectomy patient is (it, she).

5. Born in a foreign country, (them, they) felt fearful and uneasy in the hospital.

## Objective Case

A pronoun that receives the action of the verb either directly or indirectly is an object pronoun.

The direct object pronoun—*me, you, him, her, it, us, you,* and *them*—receives the action of the sentence.

# Examples

The patient paid *them* in cash.

Laurie helped *me* with the amniocentesis.

The indirect object pronoun, like the noun, receives the indirect action of the verb.

The indirect object pronouns are the same as the object pronouns: *me, you, him, her, it, us, you,* and *them.*

# Examples

Dr. Rodriguez gave *you* some medication.

The change in surgical procedures saved *them* time.

The AMA loaned *us* medical literature.

Evelyn sent *me* the x-ray report.

Pronouns that follow a preposition are also objective: *me, you, him, her, it, us, you,* and *them.*

# Examples

I gave the sphygmomanometer to *them.*

Jane spoke to *her* several times on the phone.

It was a good thing for *them* to do.

English is taught to *her* and *me.*

## Possessive Case

The possessive case shows ownership or possession. The possessive pronouns are *my, mine, your, yours, his, her, hers, our, ours, their,* and *theirs.*

# Examples

The patient refused to eat *his* food.

The blue lab coat is *mine.*

The urinalysis is *hers.*

Table 3-2 provides a review of the personal pronouns categorized by case.

### TABLE 3-2 *Cases of Personal Pronouns*

| Nominative Case | Objective Case | Possessive Case |
|---|---|---|
| Subject and predicate pronouns: I, you, he, she, it, we, they | Direct and indirect object or object of a preposition: me, you, him, her, it, us, you, them | Possessive pronouns: my, mine, your, yours, his, her, hers, its, our, ours, their, theirs |

# Practice 3-4

*Select the correct pronoun from within the parentheses. State how it is used in each sentence: subject, predicate, direct object, indirect object, object of a preposition, or possessive.*

1. (He, Me) had no idea about the aneurysm. _____

2. I carried a stethoscope with (me, I). _____

3. (Them, They) should get the electrocardiogram from (he, him). _____

4. (Her, Hers) bronchoscopy showed carcinoma of the lungs. _____

5. Is (she, her) doing the urinalysis? _____

## REFLEXIVE PRONOUNS

Reflexive pronouns reflect back to the person. The pronoun refers to a noun or pronoun that appears earlier in the sentence. To form them, add *self* or *selves* to the personal pronoun. Depending on how it is used in the sentence, a reflexive pronoun can be a direct object, indirect object, object of a preposition, or a predicate pronoun.

---

### Reflexive Pronouns

myself, yourself, himself, herself, itself, ourselves, themselves

---

## Examples

She buys *herself* a stethoscope. [indirect object]

He gives *himself* insulin injections every day. [indirect object]

I am *myself* only when I feel good. [predicate pronoun after the linking verb *am*]

They smiled at *themselves* when the procedure was over. [object of a preposition]

# Practice 3-5

*Provide the correct reflexive pronoun:*

1. Doreen and Val enjoyed _____.

2. Lorry volunteered the information _____.

3. Ms. Ville did the procedure _____.

4. Dr. Archie gave _____ an hour to complete the amniocentesis.

5. John canceled the appointments _____.

## RELATIVE PRONOUNS

Relative pronouns relate one part of a sentence to a word in another part of the sentence.

---

### Relative Pronouns

who, whom, whose, which, what, that

---

A relative pronoun helps to join a relative clause to the rest of the sentence. The most important relative pronouns are *who, which,* and *that.*

*Who* refers to people.

# Examples

The patient *who* needs the antiemetic is in room 430.

*Who* is the relative pronoun that refers to the patient.

The physician *who* ordered the procedure is on rounds.

*Which* refers to things. *Which* is used when the clause that it introduces is not essential to the meaning of the sentence.

# Examples

The medical record, *which* is confidential, shows the diagnosis.

The crash cart, *which* is used for emergencies, needs to be restocked.

*That* refers to people or things. *That* is used when the clause that it introduces is essential to the meaning of the sentence.

## Examples

The type *that* is needed for this wound is a figure eight bandage.

The doctor wrote the letter *that* has the information.

## Practice 3-6

*Select the correct pronoun:*

1. The patient has Dr. Villes, (who, that) is scheduled to go on vacation tomorrow.

2. Diagnostic tests, (which, who) are used for cardiopathy, should be read by a cardiologist.

3. This is the telemetry (which, that) records the heart rate.

4. Progress notes (who, that) are documented in various styles are legal documents.

5. The patient had cryotherapy (who, that) included cold compresses.

## INDEFINITE PRONOUNS

Indefinite pronouns refer to persons or things in general. Most indefinite pronouns are singular and require a singular verb.

---

### Indefinite Pronouns

all, another, any, anybody, anyone, anything, both, each, each one, either, everybody, everyone, everything, few, many, most, much, neither, nobody, none, no one, nothing, one, other, several, some, somebody, someone, something, such

---

## Examples

*Each* of the employees wants [singular verb] *her* surgical scrubs ordered through the catalog.

*Anyone* who gives [singular verb] to charity is twice blessed.

*Neither* person knows [singular verb] the correct answer.

*Every* pharmaceutical company has *its* own sales person.

*Everyone* will send *his/her* consultation to the medical team by Friday.

Some indefinite pronouns are always plural, such as *many, several, few, these,* and *those.* The indefinite pronouns *this, that, each, either,* and *neither* are always singular.

## Examples

*Many* on the medical staff expressed *their* concerns about the care given to patients.

*Several* voiced *their* anger.

*All* staff members are to report to *their* stations.

Neither nurse wants to change shifts.

The indefinite pronouns *all, some, any,* and *none* are either singular or plural depending on the number of the noun to which they refer.

## Examples

*None* of the equipment is [singular verb] modern.

*All* the students knew *their* [plural verb] abbreviations by heart.

## Practice 3-7

*Write S if the pronoun is singular and P if the pronoun is plural.*

1. Either of the girls can perform her procedure._____

2. Each of the PDRs was returned to its proper place._____

3. Many of the assistants brought their dictation equipment._____

4. Both raised their quality standards._____

5. Few of the pharmacies wanted their prices to increase._____

## INTERROGATIVE PRONOUNS

Interrogative pronouns are used simply to ask questions. They are *who, whom, whose, which,* and *what.* Note that these pronouns are also relative.

---

### Interrogative Pronouns

who, whom, whose, which, what

---

## Examples

*Who* ordered this type of medication?

*What* caused the fever?

## DEMONSTRATIVE PRONOUNS

The easiest pronouns to learn are the demonstrative pronouns: *this, that, these,* and *those.* They point out. The singular pronouns *this* and *that* point out people or things that are near in space or time. *These* and *those* are plural pronouns referring to people or things that are farther away in space or time.

---

### Demonstrative Pronouns

this, that, these, those

---

When writing, place a noun close to the demonstrative pronoun to make the sentence clearer.

## *Examples*

*This* is the first restaurant on the street. [The demonstrative pronoun *this* points out the *restaurant.*]

*These* need sterilizing.

*That* was a good decision.

*Those* are rare tumors.

# *Practice 3-8*

*Identify the pronouns as demonstrative or interrogative:*

1. This needs to be filed in the medical records._____

2. These are the suture scissors._____

3. Which is your health insurance plan?_____

4. Those are found with the retractors._____

5. Who read the EKG?_____

# *Practice 3-9*

*Identify each pronoun as personal, reflexive, relative, indefinite, interrogative, or demonstrative:*

1. The medical report was given to me to transcribe._____

2. Who would think the illness was a malignancy?_____

3. We have to sterilize the instruments ourselves._____

4. The doctor examined his patient._____

5. I didn't know the etiology of the disease._____

# Pronoun-Antecedent Agreement

The noun that a pronoun replaces is called its antecedent. All pronouns have noun antecedents. The antecedent usually appears before the noun.

*Bill* applied an *antiseptic*. He applied *it*. [*Bill* is the antecedent for the pronoun *he*, and *antiseptic* is the antecedent for the pronoun *it*.]

Pronouns may also be antecedents of other pronouns.

*He* took *his* antibiotics. [*He* is the antecedent of *his*.]

Pronouns must agree with their noun antecedents in three ways: number, gender, and person.

## Number

Use a singular pronoun to refer to a singular noun.

*Alice* wants *her* report finished today. [*Alice* and *her* are singular.]

Use plural pronouns to refer to plural nouns.

The *Smiths* are giving a party at *their* home. [*Smiths* and *their* are plural.]

When antecedents are joined by *or* or *nor*, the pronoun agrees with the antecedent nearest to the pronoun.

## Examples

Neither Jim nor the *assistants* want *their* positions taken away. [The word *assistants* is closer and plural, so the plural pronoun *their* is used.]

Either Mary or *Ellen* wants to do *her* share.

Use a plural pronoun when two antecedents are joined by the word *and*.

*Harry and I* think *we* need a raise in pay.

## Gender

Use masculine, feminine, or neuter pronouns depending on the gender of their antecedents.

## Examples

The *man* brought *his* antibiotics to work. [*Man* and *his* are masculine.]

*Mary* increased *her* skills with practice. [*Mary* and *her* are feminine.]

The *tracing* is irregular; *it* shows artifacts. [*Tracing* and *it* are neuter.]

When in doubt about the gender, two options are possible:

1. Use *his/her:* One of the students bought *his or her* book.

2. Make the noun plural and use the plural pronoun: *Students* bought *their* books.

## PERSON

Recall that the first person is the speaker, the second person is the individual addressed, and the third person is the person or thing spoken about. In the sentence "*Mary* likes *her* aerosols kept in the closet," *Mary* is the first person singular noun, so a first person singular pronoun must be used: *her*. In "The *girls* left *their* books at the library," *girls* is third person plural noun and *their* is a third person plural pronoun. Finally, consider the following sentences:

> *Bill* changed the *catheters*. *He* changed *them*.

*Bill* is third person singular, and *he* is third person singular. The antecedent *catheters* is third person plural, and its pronoun, *them*, is third person plural.

## Practice 3-10

*Identify the antecedent of the pronoun in each sentence:*

1. The doctor wrote *his* cerebrovascular article._____

2. The patient corrected *his* insulin injection._____

3. Val and I practiced *our* medical terminology._____

4. Pat wondered if *she* qualified._____

5. Medical personnel should know *their* CPR technique._____

*Select the correct pronoun from within the parentheses:*

1. Bill and (she, her) went to (her, their) class on cardiopulmonary resuscitation.

2. When a patient has a cerebrovascular accident, (they, she/he) may become hemiplegic.

---

### Commonly Confused: The Use of Its and It's

| | |
|---|---|
| It | Used only to refer to a specific noun: "When the *code alarm* rings, *it* can be heard a mile away." |
| Its | The possessive pronoun: "The *stethoscope* is missing *its* diaphragm." |
| It's | The contraction for "it is." The apostrophe is the sign that the word is used as a contraction: "*it's* a normal EKG" means "*it is* a normal EKG." |

One way to check the correct usage of "it's" is to say *it is* instead when reading the sentence. For example, in "The computer printed (it's, its) hardcopy," using *it's* would make it read: "The computer printed *it is* hardcopy." That is not correct. The possessive, *its*, shows that the computer owns the hardcopy, and that is the correct form of the pronoun to use.

3. Some people develop hypertension as (they, his/her) get older.

4. They plan to explain (their, them) reasons for diagnosing pancreatitis.

5. Can you and the committee give us (their, them) decision?

# Pronoun Summary

| Pronoun | A word that replaces or substitutes for a noun. |
|---|---|
| Personal | Refers to persons. *Singular*: I, me, my, mine, you, your, yours, he, she, it, him, her, his, hers, its. *Plural:* we, us, our, ours, you, your, yours, they, them, their, theirs. |
| Reflexive | Reflects, throws back: myself, yourself, himself, herself, itself, ourselves, themselves. |
| Relative | Relates to other words: who, whom, whose, which, what, that, whomever, whichever, whatever. |
| Indefinite | Refers to persons or things in general: all, another, any, anybody, anyone, anything, both, each, each one, either, everybody, everyone, everything, few, many, most, much, neither, nobody, none, no one, nothing, one, other, several, some, somebody, someone, something, such. |
| Interrogative | Asks questions: who, whom, whose, which, what. |
| Demonstrative | Points out, demonstrates: this, that, these, those. |

# Usage Forms

| | Subjective (subject) | Objective (object) | Possessive with Noun | Possessive without Noun | Reflexive (same person or thing as subject) |
|---|---|---|---|---|---|
| **Singular** | | | | | |
| First person | I | me | my | mine | myself |
| Second person | you | you | your | yours | yourself |
| Third person | he, she, it | him, her, it | his, her, its | his, hers, its | himself |
| | | | | | herself |
| | | | | | itself |
| **Plural** | | | | | |
| First person | we | us | our | ours | ourselves |
| Second person | you | you | your | yours | yourself |
| Third person | they | them | their | theirs | themselves |

| | |
|---|---|
| **Antecedent** | The noun that is replaced by a pronoun. Pronouns must agree with their noun antecedents in three ways: number, gender, and person. |
| Number | Singular: *Bill* took the EKGs. *He* took five. |
| | Plural: The *doctors* gave *their* off duty time to volunteer. |
| Gender | Masculine singular: *Jonathan* liked *his* care. |
| | Feminine plural: *Medical assistants* wear *their* hair at a certain length. |
| Person | 1st (speaker): *Norma* is my name. *I* am named after my father, Norman. |
| | 2nd (spoken to): *Pat*, are you sure? Do *you* mean what you say? |
| | 3rd (spoken about): *Norman and Leonard* know how to scrub. *They* understand surgical technique. |
| | Antecedents joined by *and* need a plural pronoun: *Tom and Mary* are friends. *They* study together. |
| | For antecedents joined by *or* or *nor*, the pronoun agrees with the nearest antecedent: Either the doctor or the *nurses* left *their* charts here. |

# Medical Spelling

*Become familiar with the spelling of the following words:*

| | |
|---|---|
| aerosols | fontanel |
| amniocentesis | gallbladder |
| antibiotics | glaucoma |
| aneurysm | hemiplegic |
| antiemetic | hemorrhoids |
| antiseptic | hypertension |
| auscultation | hypotension |
| bronchoscopy | insulin |
| cardiopulmonary resuscitation (CPR) | meninges |
| cataract | mesentery |
| catheter | occlusion |
| cerebrovascular | prostatitis |
| cholecystectomy | palpitations |
| cirrhosis | pancreas |
| coagulation | pancreatitis |
| conjunctiva | paraplegia |
| electrocardiogram | quadriplegia |
| esophagus | sphygmomanometer |
| etiology | stethoscope |
| fallopian tube | urinalysis |

# The Office Memorandum

The office memo is a written message sent to coworkers *in the same company or organization*. Its purpose is to expedite the flow of all types of information; ask or answer questions; describe procedures or policies; remind people of meetings or appointments; or list names, schedules, written records, pronouncements, or work activities.

Although memos are most often used for short communication, their length can vary from one sentence to many pages. Because they are intended for internal circulation, they are less formal than a business letter and do not include the inside address, salutation, or complimentary close. However, the writer must ensure that pronouns agree with their noun antecedents in number, gender, and person. The remaining portion of this chapter applies pronoun use to two common types of informal office communication—the office memo and electronic mail (e-mail).

## STRUCTURE OF A MEMO

Some organizations have special printed forms for office memos, but a plain piece of paper is sufficient. The format for the content of a memo must be very simple. Consider this structure as an example:

| | |
|---|---|
| **To:** | (the person to whom the message is written) |
| **From:** | (the name of the person writing the message) |
| **Subject:** (or **Re:**) | (the precise purpose or topic of the memo) |
| **Date:** | (month, day, and year the memo is written) |

(The message of the memo follows.)

In large facilities, another category may be added after the "From" line, namely, "Dept./Floor/Ext."

## WRITING THE MEMO

The writing style of a memo is direct, concise, and clear. The language is plain and simple, with short sentences averaging about 15 words. The memo must be written so readers understand the message. It is sent only to those for whom the message applies. It should look attractive, command attention, and entice the reader.

The most important message of the memo is stated in the first line, followed by any necessary detailed or supportive information. In addition to narrative paragraphs, facts may be listed with numbers or bullets. Make directives and requests specific. Avoid vague messages like "get back to me about this matter." Replace it with "call me Tuesday morning, July 30."

The name or initials of the writer appear after "From" in the heading of the memo, yet some people prefer to sign their name below the final line of the body. If added, the signature is always more effective when it is handwritten.

Before closing the body of the memo, state any task or positive result that the writer might expect from the reader. At the end of the message, a "C:" or "ENC:" may be added, if applicable. Memos that are double spaced should have a paragraph indention of one-half inch. Single spaced paragraphs have no paragraph indention and have a blank line between paragraphs. This is done so readers are able to tell where the paragraphs begin and end. See Figure 3-1 for an example of a properly written memo.

**V**
**M**   **VILLES MEDICAL CENTER**
**C**        *OFFICE MEMO*

**Date:**        August 1, 20XX

**To:**          Office Medical Assistants

**From:**       Rose Villes, RN, Office Manager

**Subject:**    Upgrade of Computer Systems


Computer World is giving a training workshop on the MedSoft Computer

Program that BMC plans to implement before September 15. Here are the details:

Tuesday, July 15, from 9 : 00 a.m. to 4 : 00 p.m.

Second Floor Conference Room

Read the enclosed brochure about the program before attending the

workshop.


C: Dr. Luke Christopher

Enc.

**FIGURE 3-1**   *Sample Memo*

## Practice 3-11

Using the **Writing Process Worksheet**, *Write an office memo that includes this information:*

❖ change in office hours from 8 a.m. to 5 p.m. to 9 a.m. to 4 p.m.

❖ new hours effective only during the week between Christmas and New Year's

❖ applies to all staff members

❖ the message is from Dr. Sarah to staff members

# Writing Process Worksheet

1. PREWRITING – write down facts, organize ideas

_____     _____
_____     _____
_____     _____
_____     _____
_____     _____

2. WRITING – write without concern for grammar or punctuation

_____
_____
_____
_____
_____
_____
_____

3. REWRITING – correct grammar, make changes using proofreaders' marks

_____
_____
_____
_____
_____
_____
_____

4. FINALIZING – type or write final copy

_____
_____
_____
_____
_____
_____
_____

5. PROOFREAD – read the final copy aloud for a final check

_____
_____

---

V
M   VILLES MEDICAL CENTER
C   *OFFICE MEMO*

Date:

To:

From:

Subject:

---

# Electronic Mail

Electronic mail, or e-mail, is a computer-to-computer communication system that transmits messages from one point to another anywhere in the world. This medium is popular because it is convenient, fast, and less expensive than a phone call. E-mail can also include any type of text, files, or other documents as part of the message.

### E-Mail Guidelines

1. Write only the main message.

2. Put the most important information first.

3. Make the message short, complete, and accurate.

4. Write an attention-getting opening sentence.

5. Limit the message to one screen.

6. Use correct grammar.

7. Proofread the message before sending it. Professionalism is important in e-mail.

8. Save a copy if a record is needed.

9. Eliminate unnecessary closing.

10. Just as e-mail can be sent, e-mail can also be received. Check the office e-mail two or three times a day and respond to incoming messages promptly.

Figure 3-2 gives an example of a properly prepared e-mail.

---

**To:** Lorry Villes, R.N.
**From:** Mary Louise Norman, M.D.
**Subject:** Staff Meeting, March 5, 20XX, 9 a.m.
**CC:** Louis Villes, Chairperson
**Date:** February 17, 20XX


Add three additional topics to the agenda for the March 5 meeting. The topics are **as follows:**

1. Written policies regarding safety procedures
2. Documentation procedures update
3. New computer software needs

If you have any questions, call me at ext. 229.

---

**FIGURE 3-2** *E-mail Format*

# Office Memorandum and Electronic Mail Summary

| Type of Communication | Definition | Format/Structure |
|---|---|---|
| Memo | A written message to coworkers in the same company | **To:**<br>**From:**<br>**Re:**<br>**Date:** |
| E-mail | A computer-to-computer communication system that transmits messages electronically | To:<br>From:<br>Subject:<br>CC: (optional)<br>Date: |

# Skills Review

*Circle the correct pronoun from within the parentheses:*

1. Each procedure has (its, their) own requirements.

2. Lorry and (she, her) were getting the patient ready for the cholecystectomy.

3. (Who, Whom) did the cross-reference on these files?

4. The doctor appointed (he, him) to the Quality Assurance Program.

5. Someone called with a medical office emergency. I did schedule (him, them) STAT.

6. It was (she, her) who established the matrix on the appointment schedule.

7. One of the patients developed (his, their) symptoms over two years.

8. Norm and (I, me) are leaving for the conference in the morning.

9. (Who, Whom) shall we hire to do the insurance claims?

10. The PT (coagulation test) was done by (we, us).

*Circle the indefinite pronoun and above it write S if singular or P if plural:*

1. Everyone suffering from orthopnea must sit up to breathe.

2. Not one of the orthopedic patients has traction.

3. Many of our students realize that their oral communication skills are vital to their success.

4. The tumors were not visible, but he found several when he conducted the examination.

5. None of the symptoms indicated an emergency.

*Circle the pronouns in the e-mail message. Write them below and identify the type of pronoun as personal, relative, reflexive, indefinite, interrogative, or demonstrative. Identify any noun antecedents, if applicable.*

---

### E-MAIL    July 15, 20XX

I received your e-mail message today. The mailing that you sent contained all laboratory reports Dr. John needed to plan his procedure. John thanks you, as does everyone here.

---

| PRONOUN | TYPE | NOUN ANTECEDENT |
| --- | --- | --- |
| _____ | _____ | _____ |
| _____ | _____ | _____ |
| _____ | _____ | _____ |
| _____ | _____ | _____ |
| _____ | _____ | _____ |
| _____ | _____ | _____ |
| _____ | _____ | _____ |
| _____ | _____ | _____ |

*Circle the correctly spelled word in each line:*

1. coagulation      caogulation      coaguletion      coaggulation
2. antimetic        cataract         mininges         cirhosis
3. prostetitis      prostattitis     prostatetis      prostatitis
4. esofagus         oclusion         aerosols         anteseptic
5. hemorhoids       hemmorrhoids     hemorrhaids      hemorrhoids
6. insulin          misentery        cateter          anurysm
7. urenalysis       hypotension      cholecystectamy  meningis
8. eteology         cerebrovescular  broncuscopy      etiology
9. antibiotics      arosols          antibiautics     glowcoma
10. electrokardiogram  electrocardigram  electrocardiogram  eletrocardiogram

*Translate medical abbreviations using a medical dictionary or appendix.*

1. b.i.d. _____
2. BUN _____
3. BPH _____
4. CABG _____
5. Bx _____
6. CBC _____
7. C/O _____

8. COPD _____

9. C&S _____

10. C/C _____

# Comprehensive Review

*Using the **Writing Process Worksheet**, write an office memo to Dr. William Freeze to reschedule the August 15, 20XX meeting to August 30. Use at least three pronouns with two noun antecedents. Circle the pronouns and underline the noun antecedents.*

---

**LINCOLN MEDICAL CENTER**
**OFFICE MEMO**

TO:                                                                        DATE:

FROM:

RE:

---

# Writing Process Worksheet

1. PREWRITING – write down facts, organize ideas

_____     _____
_____     _____
_____     _____
_____     _____
_____     _____

2. WRITING – write without concern for grammar or punctuation

_____
_____
_____
_____
_____
_____

3. REWRITING – correct grammar, make changes using proofreaders' marks

_____
_____
_____
_____
_____
_____
_____

4. FINALIZING – type or write final copy

_____
_____
_____
_____
_____
_____

5. PROOFREAD – read the final copy aloud for a final check

_____
_____
_____

# CHAPTER 4

# Verbs

## PRACTICAL WRITING COMPONENT: MEDICAL RECORD

**OBJECTIVES** *Upon completion of this chapter, the learner should be able to:*

- ❖ identify verb types

- ❖ define the difference between transitive and intransitive verbs

- ❖ use verbs that agree with the subject in number and person

- ❖ distinguish between active and passive voices

- ❖ form the principal parts of regular and irregular verbs

- ❖ use the simple past, present, and future tenses correctly

- ❖ explain how the mood of verbs affects the action of a sentence

- ❖ spell various medical terms

- ❖ translate various medical abbreviations

- ❖ explain the purpose of the medical record

- ❖ describe the Health Insurance Portability and Accountability Act (HIPPA) compliance tools

## Types of Verbs

Verbs are *the* essential components of sentences. They denote action or being. Verbs are a challenge to master because they have a variety of forms that perform many functions.

## Action Verbs

Action verbs are words that express activity, both physical and mental.

## Examples

Blood *circulates* through the heart, arteries, and veins.

*Ask* for an appointment.

The patient *complains* of extreme thirst.

The doctor *performed* the operation.

He *proved* his point.

The doctor *evaluates* the physical and mental condition of the patient.

### BEING VERBS

Verbs can also express a state of being. Any form of the verb *to be* that stands alone is a being verb: *am, is, are, was, were,* any form of *be* or *been.*

## Examples

I *am* the nurse in charge.

Bob *is* the patient in question.

We *were* watching for obvious symptoms.

Being verbs may be used as the only verb in a sentence or they may be combined with another verb. When a being verb is used with another verb, it can be a linking verb, a helping verb, an auxiliary verb, or a verb phrase.

## Examples

I *was* at the hospital.

I *was helping* the nurse.

Phil was doing his procedures.

The exam *was* thorough.

 *Practice 4-1*

*Identify the verb in each sentence:*

1. Antibiotics are expensive. _____

2. Cataracts are common in the elderly. _____

3.  Hands washed frequently prevent the transmission of disease. _____

4.  Palpation is one of the five Ps. _____

5.  Tetracycline is a broad-spectrum antibiotic. _____

## MAIN VERBS AND HELPING VERBS

A single verb in a sentence is called the main verb:

Janet *disclosed* the information.  The dentist *cleaned* the teeth.

Sometimes the main verb is accompanied by one or more helping verbs. The most common helping verbs are as follows:

### Common Helping Verbs

| | | |
|---|---|---|
| am | has | can (may) have |
| are | had | could (would, should) be |
| is | can | could (would, should) have |
| was | may | will (shall) have been |
| were | will (shall) be | might have |
| do | will (shall) have | might have been |
| did | has (had) been | must |
| have | can (may) be | must have been |

The combination of a helping verb and a main verb is referred to as a verb phrase. In a verb phrase, the last verb is always the main verb.

## *Examples*

The intern *had studied* all night. [*Had* is the helping verb and *studied* is the main verb.]

Operations *were delayed* for one hour. [The verb phrase is *were delayed*.]

Verbs may be separated by other words that are not part of the verb phrase.

## *Examples*

Mark *has* never *liked* working in the laboratory.

*Can* Dr. Villmarie *operate* next Thursday?

Helping verbs may also stand alone as the main verb:

May Tom leave the room? Yes, he *may*.

## LINKING VERBS

A linking verb connects a complement. A complement is a word or phrase that completes the meaning of a linking verb.

The most common linking verb is the verb *be*, which has the following forms: *am, is, are, was, were, be, being, been* (and all verb phrases ending in *be, being,* or *been*, such as *can be, is being,* and *could have been*). Other common linking verbs are listed below.

## Common Linking Verbs

| | | | |
|---|---|---|---|
| appear | grow | seem | stay |
| become | look | smell | taste |
| feel | remain | sound | |

The complement may be a predicate noun, pronoun, or adjective (describer).

# Examples

Mary *is* my *assistant*. [*Is* is the linking verb; *assistant* is the complement (predicate noun).]

John *is* the *supervisor*. [*Is* is the linking verb; *supervisor* is the complement (noun).]

The employees *were they*. [*Were* is the linking verb; *they* is the complement (pronoun).]

The ideas *are excellent*. [*Are* is the linking verb; *excellent* is the complement (adjective).]

Sometimes linking verbs may be separated by other words in the sentence.

# Examples

Cardiovascular disease, end-stage renal disease, loss of visual acuity, and limb amputations *are* some of the chronic complications.

The ideal goal of treatment *is* blood glucose normalization.

## Practice 4-2

*Identify the verb or verb phrases in each sentence:*

1. We have read the article in the journal. _____

2. A patient has the right to privacy. _____

3. Has the B.P. been stabilized? _____

4. Fluid accumulated in the lungs. _____

5. Caffeine stimulates the nervous system. _____

## TRANSITIVE AND INTRANSITIVE VERBS

A transitive verb shows action and needs a direct object to complete its meaning.

# Examples

The patient ate solid *food*. [*Food* is the *direct object*, so the verb is transitive.]

The anesthesiologist intubated the *patient*.

The surgeon sutured the *laceration*.

The surgical team changed scrub *clothes*.

Verbs that do not have a direct object are called intransitive verbs. These verbs have no object to receive the action.

# Examples

The patient ate poorly. [There is no direct object so the verb is intransitive.]

The surgeon sutured.

Cancer radiates quickly from the lymph nodes.

The students studied for three hours.

The surgical team changed.

# Practice 4-3

*Identify the verbs and indicate whether they are transitive or intransitive:*

1. The doctor introduced the scope. _____

2. The music relaxed the surgical team in the OR. _____

3. The IV punctured the skin. _____

4. The trachea bifurcates into the right and left bronchi. _____

5. The test reveals normal blood cholesterol. _____

## GERUNDS

A gerund ends in *-ing* and acts as a noun.

# Examples:

*Nursing* is her profession. Nursing is a gerund. It acts as a noun and is the subject of the sentence.

Dr. Tran likes *operating* at the Memorial. Operating acts as a noun and is the object of the verb (direct object).

## INFINITIVES

An infinitive consists of the word *to* plus a verb. The two words together usually acts as a noun.

## Examples:

*To work* in the medical professions is noble. To work acts as a noun and is the subject of the sentence.

Dr. Tran likes *to operate* at the Memorial. To operate acts as a noun and is the object of the verb (direct object).

The patient was about *to speak*. To speak is an infinitive. To speak acts as a noun and is the object of the preposition "about."

# Person of a Verb

Like pronouns, verbs also have first, second, and third person. Person helps determine whether the subject is singular or plural. For example:

|  | **Singular** |  | **Plural** |  |
|---|---|---|---|---|
| 1st person | I | I walk | we | we walk |
| 2nd person | you | you walk | you | you walk |
| 3rd person | he, she, it | he walks | they | they walk |

Notice that the third person singular form of the verb *walk* ends in *s*. The verb ends in *s*, but it is not plural. It is singular. The third person verb needs the *s* to make the verb singular. Sometimes the English language does strange things.

# Number of a Verb

Verbs, like nouns and pronouns, also have a number. Number indicates whether the verb is singular or plural. The verb must agree in number and person with the subject. If the subject is plural, the verb must be plural; if the subject is singular, the verb must be singular. The relationship between the subject and the verb forms the core of any sentence.

## Examples

The *pharmacy* is conveniently located. [*Pharmacy* is singular. The verb *is* is singular.]

A *child dreams* many things when she is young.

*Children dream* many things when they are young.

*Dr. Villmarie* and *Dr. Archie operate* together.

*Dr. Villmarie* also *operates* alone.

*Dr. Archie doesn't* care to work long hours.

*They have* too many patients.

*Lorry evaluated* the problem.

*Students work* hard on their projects.

*Janet works* harder on her anatomy than on medical terminology.

Sometimes a group of words separates the subject from the verb, but number agreement between the subject and verb must be maintained.

## Examples

The *hygienists* in the office next to the garden *examine* teeth.

*Joe*, with the extra hours, *accumulated* vacation time.

A compound subject (two or more words joined by *and*) requires a plural verb.

## Examples

The *stethoscope and reflex hammer are* tools of the physician.

*Jeff and Lorry make* good salaries.

When two subjects are combined by *either. . . or, neither. . . nor,* and *not only. . . but also,* the verb agrees with the subject closest to it.

## Examples

Neither Janet nor her *sister likes* to give injections.

Neither Janet nor her *sister like* to give injections.

Not only John but also his *mother lives* near the medical office.

Not only John but also his *parents live* near the medical office.

# Practice 4-4

*Identify the subject in each sentence and select the correct verb from within the parentheses:*

1. Shock (is, are) a serious condition. _____

2. The EMTs (resuscitate, resuscitates) patients. _____

3. The instruments (need, needs) to be calibrated regularly. _____

4. The patient's tumor (has, have) impaired many systems. _____

5. Neither the physician nor the employees (disclose, discloses) patient information.

_____

# Verb Tenses

Verbs in the English language have many tenses (see Figures 4-1 through 4-4). This chapter covers only three: past, present, and future. These are the tenses used most frequently in the allied health setting.

## PRESENT TENSE

Present tense expresses action that is happening at the *present* time, or action that happens regularly.

## Examples

You *work* in a doctor's office.

The doctor *sutures* the laceration in the ER.

The doctor *examines* the patients.

|  | Meaning | How Formed | Examples Singular | Plural | Use in Sentence |
|---|---|---|---|---|---|
| Present | Action happens now or regularly | Use main verb | I work<br>Your work<br>He she, it works | We work<br>You work<br>They work | I work 35 hours a week now. |
| Past | Action begins and ends in the past | Add *d* or *ed* to the main verb | I worked<br>You worked<br>He, she, it workd | We workd<br>You worked<br>They worked | I worked 30 hours a week last year. |
| Future | Action will occur sometime in the future | Add *will* to the main verb | I will work<br>You will work<br>He, she, it will work | We will work<br>You will work<br>They will work | I will work 40 hours a week next year. |

**FIGURE 4-1** *Forms of a Regular Verb*

## PAST TENSE

Past tense expresses action that is completed in the past. Notice that *ed* is used to form the past tense of the regular verbs in the examples.

## Examples

You *worked* in a doctor's office.

The doctor *sutured* the laceration in the ER.

The doctor *examined* the patients.

## FUTURE TENSE

The future tense expresses action that will take place any time after now. To form the future tense, the word *will* is used with the main verb. *Will* is the sign of the future tense.

## Examples

You *will work* in a doctor's office.

The doctor *will suture* the laceration in the ER.

The doctor *will examine* the patients.

## Practice 4-5

*Identify the verbs and state whether they are in the past, present, or future tense:*

1. The physician decides on the most efficient scheduling policy. _____

2. The cancer originated in the lungs. _____

3. Blood cells circulate through the body in one minute. _____

4. The surgeon resected the diseased colon. _____

5. Results of the health survey will be published. _____

# Principal Parts of Verbs

As a noun and in connection with grammar, the word *tense* means *time*. Verb tenses tell when an action or state of being occurs. Every verb has four principal parts for denoting tense: the present, past, past participle, and present participle. How verb forms change from one principal part to another categorizes them as regular or irregular verbs.

### REGULAR VERBS

The past tense of regular verbs is formed by adding the letters *d* or *ed* to the present form of the verb. A helping verb is added to the *past* form of the verb to make a *past participle*. Adding *ing* to the present tense forms the *present participle*.

## Examples

| Present | Present Participle | Past | Past Participle |
|---|---|---|---|
| introduce | introducing | introduced | has, had, have introduced |
| look | looking | looked | has, had, have looked |
| tolerate | tolerating | tolerated | has, had, have tolerated |
| diagnose | diagnosing | diagnosed | had diagnosed |
| compare | comparing | compared | have compared |

| drop | dropping | dropped | has dropped |
|------|----------|---------|-------------|
| perform | performing | performed | has performed |

Notice that some regular verbs change their spelling to form the past tense or present participle. The rules shown in Figures 4-2 and 4-3 help make the spelling easier.

---

1. Verbs ending in *e* add *d: hope, hoped.*

2. One-syllable verbs ending in a consonant preceded by one vowel double the final consonant and add *ed: stop, stopped;* preceded by two vowels add *ed: rain, rained.*

3. Two-syllable verbs ending in a consonant with the accent on the first syllable add *ed: open, opened;* with the accent on the second syllable double the final consonant and add *ed: recur, recurred.*

4. Verbs ending in two consonants add *ed: start, started.*

5. Verbs ending in *y* preceded by a vowel keep the *y* and add *ed: pray, prayed;* preceded by a consonant change *y* to *i* and *ed: try, tried.*

6. Verbs ending in *ie* add *d: lie, lied.*

---

**FIGURE 4-2**   *Rules for Forming the Past Tense of Regular Verbs*

---

1. Verbs ending in *e* drop the *e* and add *ing: hope, hoping.*

2. One-syllable verbs ending in a consonant preceded by one vowel double the final consonant and add *ing: stop, stopping;* preceded by two vowels add *ing: rain, raining.*

3. Two-syllable verbs ending in a consonant with the accent on the first syllable add *ing: open, opening;* with the accent on the second syllable double the final consonant and add *ing: recur, recurring.*

4. Verbs ending in two consonants add *ing: start, starting.*

5. Verbs ending in *y* keep the *y* and add *ing: pray, praying; try, trying.*

6. Verbs ending in *ie* chane the *ie* to *y* and add *ing: lie, lied.*

---

**FIGURE 4-3**   *Rules for Forming the Present Participle of Regular Verbs*

# Practice 4-6

*Form the present participle, past, and past participle of these regular verbs:*

1. accumulate _____ _____ _____

2. elicit _____ _____ _____

3. reveal _____ _____ _____

4. bifurcate _____ _____ _____

5. palpate _____ _____ _____

## IRREGULAR VERBS

Only regular verbs follow the rule to add *d* or *ed* to form the past. Many verbs in the English language do not follow this rule. The verbs that do not are called irregular verbs.

Some irregular verbs keep the same form in three of the four parts:

| Present | Present Participle | Past | Past Participle |
|---|---|---|---|
| burst | bursting | burst | had burst |
| cost | costing | cost | had cost |
| let | letting | let | had let |
| set | setting | set | have set |
| hit | hitting | hit | had hit |
| read | reading | read | has read |
| put | putting | put | had put |
| hurt | hurting | hurt | has hurt |

Some irregular verbs change form twice:

| Present | Present Participle | Past | Past Participle |
|---|---|---|---|
| sleep | sleeping | slept | had slept |
| say | saying | said | had said |
| buy | buying | bought | had bought |
| have | having | had | had |
| find | finding | found | had found |

Some irregular verbs change three forms:

| Present | Present Participle | Past | Past Participle |
|---|---|---|---|
| eat | eating | ate | had eaten |
| tear | tearing | tore | had torn |
| throw | throwing | threw | had thrown |
| break | breaking | broke | had broken |
| drink | drinking | drank | had drunk |
| forgive | forgiving | forgave | had forgiven |

Many errors are made using irregular verbs. Try to memorize as many principal parts of irregular verbs as possible. See Figure 4-4 for the more commonly encountered irregular verb forms.

| Simple Present | Past | Past Participle | Simple Present | Past | Past Participle |
|---|---|---|---|---|---|
| awake | awoke | awoken | know | knew | known |
| am/are | was/were | been | leave | left | left |
| beat | beat | beaten | lose | lost | lost |
| begin | began | begun | make | made | made |
| bend | bent | bent | prove | proved | proven |
| bite | bit | bitten | ring | rang | rung |
| blow | blew | blown | run | ran | run |
| bring | brought | brought | see | saw | seen |
| burst | burst | burst | send | sent | sent |
| catch | caught | caught | sew | sewed | sewn |
| choose | chose | chosen | shake | shook | shaken |
| come | came | come | show | showed | shown |
| cost | cost | cost | shut | shut | shut |
| cut | cut | cut | sing | sang | sung |
| do | did | done | sit | sat | sat |
| draw | drew | drawn | slay | slew | slain |
| drive | drove | driven | slit | slit | slit |
| fall | fell | fallen | speak | spoke | spoken |
| feed | fed | fed | spread | spread | spread |
| fight | fought | fought | spring | sprang | sprung |
| flee | fled | fled | steal | stole | stolen |
| fly | flew | flown | strive | strove | striven |
| find | found | found | swell | swelled | swollen |
| forget | forgot | forgotten | swim | swam | swum |
| freeze | froze | frozen | take | took | taken |
| get | got | gotten | tear | tore | torn |
| give | gave | given | throw | threw | thrown |
| go | went | gone | wake | woke | woken |
| grow | grew | grown | wear | wore | worn |
| hang | hung | hung | wring | wrung | wrung |
| hide | hid | hidden | write | wrote | written |
| hold | held | held | | | |

**FIGURE 4-4**  *Past and Past Participle Forms of Common Irregular Verbs*

## Practice 4-7

*Select the correct verb form from within the parentheses:*

1. The movement (elicit, elicited) the symptoms.

2. I had (spoke, spoken) to the nurse about the change.

3. The symptoms (occur, occurred) as a result of inadequate circulation.

4. The driver had (drive, drove, driven) the ambulance right up to the door.

5. The nurse (shook, shake, shaken) the bottle to mix the medication.

## CONFUSING AND TROUBLESOME VERBS

Some verbs are frequently confused with verbs that seem to mean the same thing. Even coming up with the correct forms for their principal parts can be troublesome. Errors are made frequently with these verbs, both orally and written. A brief explanation of some troublesome verbs may be helpful.

### Lie and Lay

*Lie* means "recline, rest, or stay," as in "I need to *lie* down for a while." *Lay* means "put or place," as in "*Lay* your head on the pillow." Here are the principal parts of those two verbs:

| Present | Past | Past Participle | Present Participle |
|---------|------|-----------------|--------------------|
| lie | lay` | lain | lying (reclining) |
| lay | laid | laid | laying (placing) |

## *Examples*

I *lay* the book on the table.

I *lie* down.

I *lay* down yesterday.

I *have lain* down.

 *Practice 4-8*

*Fill in the correct form of the verb* lie *or* lay *and state whether the action is to recline or to place:*

1. She has _____ in bed all day. _____

2. The sick patient _____ ill for days. _____

3. The M.A. had _____ the instruments out for the procedure. _____

4. Where did I _____ my lab coat? _____

5. The medications were _____ on the table. _____

### Rise and Raise

*Rise* means "to move upward by itself or to get up," as in "Temperatures *rise* in the afternoon." *Raise* means "to lift to a higher position," as in "*Raise* the cost of medicine by 2 percent." Here are the principal parts of these two verbs:

| Present | Present Participle | Past | Past Participle |
|---------|---------------------|------|------------------|
| rise | rising | rose | has risen |
| raise | raising | raised | had raised |

## Examples

We *raised* the treatment table an inch higher.

Medical costs *rise*.

Costs *rose* frequently last year.

Costs have *risen*.

## Practice 4-9

*Fill in the correct form of the verbs* rise *or* raise: *State whether the action is to lift to a higher position, to move upward by itself, or to get up.*

1. Did the patient's diet _____ the blood chemistry levels?

2. The potassium has _____ to normal levels.

3. The patient did not _____ enough sputum for the test.

4. Elevated cholesterol in the blood _____ the risk of coronary disease.

5. They _____ the level of medication needed for the test.

The key distinction between *lie/lay* and *rise/raise* is that *lay* and *raise* are transitive (the sentence has a direct object) and *lie* and *rise* are intransitive (the sentence has no object).

### May and Can

Errors are often made between the words *may* and *can*. *May* means permission or a degree of certainty. To use the word *may* is considered polite.

## Examples

You *may* leave at 4:30 p.m. [permission]

*May* I please borrow your stethoscope? [permission]

The report *may* be true. [degree of certainty]

*Can* means an ability or a possibility because certain conditions exist.

### Examples

You *can* see the pain in her face. [ability]

A puncture wound *can* cause tetanus. [ability]

I *can* perform the procedure if I get back on time. [possibility]

## Practice 4-10

*Select the correct word from within the parentheses:*

1. Call me if you think I (can, may) be of any help.

2. The nurse (can, may) perform that type of procedure.

3. The decision (may, can) determine the patient's quality of life.

4. You (may, can) be familiar with the characteristics of the disease.

5. I (may, can) work on the lab report if you (can, may) find the statistical data.

# Use of Verb Tenses in Sentences

Verb tenses express the time of action. Errors arise when the time elements in different parts of a sentence do not agree. For example, the use of verb tense in the following sentence is incorrect:

When we *are* tired, we *rested* at the hotel.

The sentence starts in the present tense, *when we are tired,* but according to the rest of the sentence the present action is complete in the past, *we rested at the hotel.* An action begun in the present cannot be completed in the past because it is still occurring. The sentence should read:

When we *are* tired, we *rest* at the hotel.

Similarly:

When Valerie *was* young, she likes to *visit* her grandmother. [incorrect]

When Valerie *was* young, she *liked* to *visit* her grandmother. [correct]

## Practice 4-11

*Correct the verb tenses in these sentences:*

1. The doctor will read the chart before he saw the patient. _____

2. If she is smart, she asked for a consultation. _____

3. Time flew quickly while we had cleaned the storage closet. _____

4. I would schedule an appointment if I have better insurance. _____

5. Aseptic hand washing is crucial if we wanted to prevent transmission of pathogens.

_____

# Voices of Verbs

Voice shows whether the subject of the verb is doing the action or receiving the action.

## ACTIVE AND PASSIVE VERBS

Verbs have two voices: active and passive. If the subject is doing the action, the verb is in the active voice. If the subject is receiving the action, the verb is passive.

| Example | Voice | Explanation |
| --- | --- | --- |
| Bob mailed the letter. | Active | *Bob*, the subject of the sentence, performs the action of the verb, *mailed*. The subject, *Bob*, is busy and *actively* in motion. |
| The letter was mailed by Bob. | Passive | The subject, *letter*, is the receiver of the action of the verb, *mailed*. The subject of the sentence *passively* receives the action. |

## Examples

John typed three reports a day. [active]

Three reports were typed by John. [passive]

The doctor disclosed the information. [active]

The information was disclosed by the doctor. [passive]

The students transmitted the disease. [active]

The disease was transmitted by the students. [passive]

The surgeon resected the tumor. [active]

The tumor was resected by the surgeon. [passive]

Compare the active and passive voices in the previous sentences. Which voice is heard more often when people speak? Which voice seems easier to speak and understand? Most grammarians agree that the active voice is easier to understand and has more energy. The active voice quickly tells who did what, not what was done by whom. Writers who use the grammar check on the computer will note that the use of the passive voice is discouraged. However, some grammarians feel that because the passive voice is grammatically correct, it has a place in the English language. The following example shows how the passive voice may simplify a sentence.

Active        Someone on the ethics committee made the decision on October 15.

Passive       The decision *was made* on October 15.

The words *someone on the ethics committee* is not necessary to the meaning of the sentence, unless the name of the actor is specifically requested.

## IDENTIFYING THE PASSIVE VOICE

Two elements help detect the passive voice: (1) a being verb and (2) a past participle. Another signal is the frequent appearance of the word *by* in sentences using the passive voice.

### Examples

Three reports a day *were* [being verb] *typed* [past participle] *by* John.

The information *was* [being verb] *disclosed* [past participle] *by* the doctor.

The disease *was* [being verb] *transmitted* [past participle] *by* the students.

Water *was drunk by* the thirsty patients.

The passive voice can be changed to the active voice simply by making the direct object the subject. In the passive sentence "Water was drunk by the *patients*," the direct object is *patients*. Make it the subject of the sentence to achieve active voice: "*Patients* drank the water."

## Practice 4-12

*Identify the voice as active or passive.*

1. The conditions are complicated by isolation precautions. _____

2. The medication was taken by the patients. _____

3. The nasogastric tube was used because the patient had esophageal sphincter problems. _____

4. Dr. Villes biopsied the growth. _____

5. The surgery began promptly at 7 a.m. _____

# Moods of Verbs

Mood is the manner in which the action of the sentence is performed. Mood depends on the attitude of the speaker or writer and the purpose of the sentence. Verbs have three moods: indicative, imperative, and subjunctive.

The purpose of the indicative mood is to state a fact or ask a question.

## Example

The medical assistant types reports.

The purpose of the imperative mood is to give instruction or commands, or to make requests. The subject of verbs in the imperative mood is always *you*, the person to whom the order is given. The *you* is often omitted from the sentence.

## Example

Type this report.

The purpose of the subjunctive mood is to express a command, preference, strong request, or a condition contrary to fact. The present subjunctive is formed in two ways: (1) by substituting *be* in place of *am, are*, or *is* and (2) by dropping the s ending from the third person singular, present tense verb. The past subjunctive is the same as the past tense except that the verb *be* uses *were* for both singular and plural subjects.

## Examples

The doctor requests that her report *be* typed within 24 hours.

The medical assistant wished she *were* able to type the report within 24 hours.

## Practice 4-13

*Indicate whether the verbs are in the indicative, imperative, or subjunctive mood:*

1. We urge that the doctor be given a second chance. _____

2. Heart disease is the leading cause of death. _____

3. Please remove the soiled linens immediately. _____

4. The cardiologist insisted that the EKG be done again. _____

5. Tell the people in the lab that the blood tests must be done today. _____

# Verbs Summary

| | | |
|---|---|---|
| Action verb | Expresses both physical and mental activity. | The doctor *operates* on patients. The patient *thought* he was in good health. |
| Being verb | Any form of the verb to be: *am, is, are, was, were, be, being, been.* | Erythromycin *is* the cure for bacterial pnuemonia. |

| | | |
|---|---|---|
| Main verb | A single verb in a sentence. | The x-ray *revealed* a fracture in the arm. |
| Helping verb | A verb that accompanies the main verb: *do, will, would, can, could, shall, should, may, might, must, have, has, had*. | The x-ray *may reveal* a fracture. Many *do believe* that disease is curable. |
| Linking verb | Connects a complement (predicate noun, pronoun, adjective). | The students *felt comfortable* about the changes. |
| | Common linking verbs: *being verbs, grow, seem, appear, stay, taste*. | The patient *appears* self-motivated. The diet seems well planned. |
| Transitive verb | Shows action and needs an object to complete its meaning. | You must remove the *sutures*. |
| Intransitive verb | A verb that has no object to receive the action. | The medical report is filed. |
| Gerund | Verb + *ing*; acts as a noun | The doctor is *operating*. |
| Infinitive | *To* + verb; acts as a noun, verb, adjective, or adverb. | The doctor wants *to operate*. |
| Person of a verb | Person speaking (first). | *I* love my medical terminology course. (singular) |
| | Person spoken to (second). | Do *you* need more medication? (singular or plural) |
| | Person spoken about (third). | *They* formed an ethics team. (plural) |
| Number of verb | Indicates singular or plural. | He *arrives* at the ER. (singular verb agrees with singular pronoun) |

## VERB TENSES

| | | |
|---|---|---|
| Present | Action happening now. | The nurse works now. |
| Past | Action completed in the past. | The nurse worked yesterday. |
| Future | Action will happen later. | The nurse will work tomorrow. |

See chapter figures for explanation of additional tenses.

## PRINCIPAL PARTS OF SPEECH
## REGULAR:

| | | |
|---|---|---|
| Past | Forms the past by adding *e* or *ed* to the *present* form of the verb (cure + d = cured). | The doctor *cured* the patient. |
| Past participle | Add a *helping verb* to form the *past* form (had + cured = had cured). | The doctor *had cured* the patient. |

| Present participle | Add *ing* to the *present* form of the verb (cure + ing = curing). | The medicine is curing the patient. |

## IRREGULAR:

| Past | came | The message *came* by telephone. |
| Past participle | had come | He *had come* to the end of the paragraph. |
| Present participle | coming | I'm *coming* to that conclusion. |

## VOICES OF VERBS:

| | Shows whether the subject does the action or receives the action. | |
| Active | The subject does the actions. | The *doctor* made the incision. |
| Passive | The subject receives the action. | The *incision* was made by the doctor. |

## MOODS OF VERBS

| | The manner in which verbs are expressed. | |
| Indicative | States a fact or asks a question. | Medical examinations are expensive. |
| Imperative | Makes a request, gives a command or instruction (subject is always the word you). | (you) Take these instruments and sterilize them. |
| Subjunctive | Expresses a command, preference, strong request, or condition contrary to fact. | The patient insists that all other treatments be exhausted before undergoing chemotherapy. |

# Medical Spelling

*Become familiar with the spelling of the following words:*

| | |
|---|---|
| accompany | compose |
| accumulate | diagnose |
| administer | deteriorate |
| bifurcate | deviate |
| calibrate | disclose |
| circulate | elicit |
| complicate | evaluate |
| complain | examine |

| | |
|---|---|
| incubate | radiate |
| introduce | recur, recurred, recurrence |
| intubate | refer |
| irrigate | resect |
| ligate | resuscitate |
| occur, occurred, occurrence | reveal |
| originate | stabilize |
| operate | sterilize |
| palpate | stimulate |
| perform | suture |
| pulsate | tolerate |
| puncture | transmit |

The skills of effectively using nouns, pronouns, and verbs are necessary in all types of medical writing. The medical record is one example of medical writing that requires concise sentences with clear subject–verb agreement, as it is written proof that a procedure was done or medicine given. Data gathered from medical records are used for diagnosing and assessing a patient's condition.

# The Medical Record

The medical record is the specific instrument of documentation that stores written information about a patient's health condition. It is also called the *clinical record* or *medical chart*. One purpose for the medical record is to contain all necessary information needed to provide quality patient care. It provides the evidence that the patient has received treatments, procedures, and medications, and it contains other vital information.

The medical record requires short, clear sentences with a specific noun as subject and verb as predicate. For example, The patient (noun subject) is (verb predicate) allergic to penicillin.

If a patient is allergic to penicillin and the medical record does not include this critical information, there could be a disaster. Should the patient be given penicillin, it could result in an anaphylactic shock that could be fatal. This simple illustration reflects the importance of documenting and charting medical information. Continuous and up-to-date documentation is vital for proper diagnoses and quality care.

The medical record may be used to gather statistical information for the research and evaluation of certain diseases. Two examples of this are knowing how many pertusis (whooping cough) cases are found in certain geographic areas or understanding the effects of cholesterol on the arteries. Analysis of data found in medical records often leads to better health care, choices of medications, medical procedures, or other important health decisions.

Another important use for the medical record is that it serves as a legal validation of patient care that insurance companies may need to substantiate claims. Attorneys may also access the record for litigation purposes.

In 1928, the American Medical Record Association (AMRA) was founded to improve the standards of documentation. In the early days of medical documentation, the patient's record consisted of one liners that gave very little information. Today, the medical record is a complex file of multiform documents. Some types of information found in medical records are

| patient demographic information | consent for treatment | plan for care |
| past and current diagnoses | medications | consultation reports |
| history and physical | dietary restrictions | doctors' orders |
| known allergies | laboratory tests | radiology reports |
| hospital discharge summaries | treatments | progress notes |

The Joint Commission on Accreditation of Healthcare Organizations (JCAHO) has the responsibility of accrediting health-care facilities. In order to achieve accreditation status, a facility's medical records must meet certain standards regarding entries, types of information documented, formats, correction procedures, abbreviations and symbols, completeness of data, timely recordings, dates, deadlines, signatures, and various legal documents.

State and local laws govern the retention of medical records. Some physicians keep them for an indefinite period of time. The physician or the facility owns the physical record itself. The patient owns the information in the medical record. For this reason, health personnel are responsible for safeguarding the confidentiality of the patient. Many employees are required to sign a confidentiality statement.

Certain features are essential when charting data in medical records. They include the following:

| | |
|---|---|
| Documentation | Only authorized individuals are responsible for documenting patient care. The record must contain all original reports. |
| Signature | Professionals must sign entries and reports to verify that care is given. Rules and regulations govern this area. |
| Abbreviations | Only approved medical abbreviations and symbols must be used. |
| Timeliness | All entries should be written as soon as possible. |
| Legibility | Records need to be legible. If possible, reports should be typed. |
| Accuracy | A mistake in an entry is corrected by drawing a single line through the error and writing the correction above it. The entry must be initialed and dated. Correction fluid is *never* used. |
| Writing Style | Entries into the medical record must be brief, accurate, and to the point. |
| Organization | Organization of medical records promotes efficiency and accuracy. Physicians and specialists usually select the organizational style of the medical record. A specialist who sees a patient occasionally will not need complex records. A specialist who sees a patient frequently needs a detailed format. |

> *Accurate and well-documented medical records are necessary if the medical office is to run smoothly.*

Appropriate documentation is very critical in medical records. If done incorrectly, it can have legal ramifications. Consider these rules:

1. Use short, accurate phrases and sentences.

2. If there is a space left blank, draw a line through it so no one can write in the space.

3. Proofread all entries.

4. Never use correction fluid to fix errors.

5. Never document before the fact.

6. Use only approved abbreviations.

7. Be absolutely sure you have the correct chart before writing.

8. State facts.

9. Record the date and time of entry.

# Practice 4-14

*Respond to these items:*

1. State three purposes for the medical record.

   _____

   _____

   _____

2. Name four items found in the medical record.

   _____

   _____

   _____

   _____

3. What is the meaning of JCAHO?

   _____

4. Who owns the information in the medical record?

   _____

5. Documenting and charting includes all of the following except _____

   a. patient's reaction to procedures        c. insurance bills

   b. medications                              d. tests

*Answer true or false to these statements:*

1. Opinions may be added to the medical record. _____

2. The American Medical Association (AMA) provides accreditation to medical facilities. _____

3. The medical record is a legal document. _____

4. Sentences but not phrases are used in the medical record. _____

# The Language of the Medical Record

The use of abbreviations is a standard practice in charting, reporting, and documenting medical information. They form the background and essence of the medical language and originate from a variety of sources.

## Examples

Observation regarding a patient's condition:

Pt. appears cyanotic.

Pt. appears anxious and apprehensive.

Documenting assistance in physiological functions:

Pt. I&O was recorded.

Pt. ↑ ambulation today.

Documenting assistance with pain or comfort measures:

Pt. was given pain meds.

Pt. given lamb's wool for comfort.

Documenting written or verbal orders:

Doctor ordered Pt. OOB t.i.d.

Dr. ordered P.T.q. day.

# The Health Insurance Portability and Accountability ACT

Protecting patients' privacy and confidentiality regarding healthcare information is a critical issue in all health-care environments. A Gallup survey done for the Institute for Health Freedom (www.forhealthfreedom.org/Publications) in 2000 found that most adults in the United States do no want third parties to access their health information. Seventy-eight percent of patients want their medical records confidential. Ninety-three percent did not want genetic information made available to researchers without their personal, written consent. Eighty-two percent objected to insurance companies having access to their medical records. The statistics are clear; patients want their medical information protected because it contains the most private and intimate aspects of a person's life.

The Health Insurance Portability and Accountability Act (HIPAA) was formed in 1996 to address privacy issues and provide national standards to ensure patient privacy and confidentiality. The purpose of this organization was to establish mandatory regulations and procedures to ensure privacy of patients' medical records and the confidentiality of transactions.

Maintaining confidentiality and protecting privacy about health-care information is critical in all environments. The increased use of technology to disseminate information through wire/wireless networks is a great advancement, but is also creates the potential for violations of privacy and confidentiality that could cause great harm. The transmission of individual health information through the airways in an electronic format requires strict guidelines. For these reasons, HIPAA enacted complex security measures to apply to all health-care providers to protect the privacy of patients' medical records.

The law also requires greater efficiency in health-care delivery systems by setting and enforcing standards that protect the electronic interchange of health information.

More in-depth coverage and information regarding HIPAA guidelines can be found through www.hhs.gov. Four primary HIPAA objectives are

1. to assure health insurance portability from one employer to another,

2. to reduce healthcare fraud and abuse,

3. to enforce standards for health information, and

4. to guarantee security and privacy of health information.

As of April, 2003, all health-care providers were required to comply with HIPAA regulations by

- writing privacy procedures,

- training employees regarding these policies and procedures,

- identifying a privacy officer who is responsible for HIPAA compliance,

- agreeing to extend privacy protection to third parties, and

- obtaining patient consent for most disclosure of health information.

The date established by HIPAA for health-care providers to implement and comply with HIPAA regulations was April 14, 2003. The Department of Health and Human Services (DHHS) at the Office for Civil Rights is authorized to enforce these regulations. Violations and failures to implement HIPAA regulations can result in fines ranging from $100 to $250,000 and/or imprisonment. Many regulations governs the privacy of patients' information, but it is important to stress that individuals have the right to access their own records. Examples of complying with HIPAA rules are listed below.

## Example 1

Many types of information, both personal and medical, comprise the identity of a patient. Examples of medical information are found in written documents, materials sent by fax or email, words spoken by patients, or data stored in a computer. All personal information that identifies a patient, such as a social security number and medical record number, must be secured and protected. Health professionals are obligated to protect any information that needs to be disposed of, either by locking it in shredding bins or placing it directly into the shredder.

## Example 2

Health-care facilities that initially treat patients need to know specific health information that is essential to the care of the patient. However, caution is required about sharing patient information among other health personnel. The disclosure of information needs to be limited to the minimum amount necessary to accomplish its purpose.

## Example 3

Once a patient has left the unit, there is no need to share health information about that patient, nor is there any need for initial caregivers to know subsequent health information. If the caregiver has continued interest in the patient, the caregiver may ask the patient how he or she is feeling.

## Example 4

Discussions about patients are prohibited outside the medical setting, within any public area of the health facility, or beyond workday hours. Curtains should be closed to protect a patient's physical privacy from visitors or other patients who pass through the unit or clinic.

# Practice 4-15

*Answer true or false to the following statements:*

1. HIPAA is strictly for nurses in the medical profession. _____

2. HIPAA was implemented in 1996. _____

3. Anyone who signs a release form has access to a patient's information. _____

4. One objective of HIPAA is to reduce health-care fraud and abuse. _____

5. The advancement of technology has set the stage for potential violation of privacy. _____

# Skills Review

*Following the completed example given as item 1, fill in the missing part of each verb. In the fourth column, state whether the verb is regular or irregular.*

| Present Tense | Past Tense | Past Participle | Regular/Irregular |
| --- | --- | --- | --- |
| 1. write | wrote | was written | irregular |
| 2. operate | | was operated | |
| 3. | ran | have run | |
| 4. see | saw | had seen | |
| 5. go | | have gone | |
| 6. fall | | | |
| 7. | cared | | |
| 8. | | have diagnosed | |
| 9. take | took | | |
| 10. | dictated | | |

*Identify the verbs in the following sentences as transitive or intransitive:*

1. The doctor hired an attorney to settle the claim. _____

2. The lawyer arrived late for the meeting. _____

3. The judge appeared impatient. _____

4. The lawyer presented his case to the judge. _____

5. The judge ruled in favor of the patient. _____

*Circle the verb phrase in each sentence:*

1. The decision was made.

2. By the end of this year, the book will have been printed.

3. Each new employee is required to have a physical.

4. Many patients are fearful and tense.

5. Hypertension has been called the silent disease.

*Circle the correct verb from within the parentheses:*

1. Everyone in the hospital (know, knows) Doreen is the best nurse.

2. Patients (appreciate, appreciates) good health care.

3. When I went to the hospital, I was (took, take, taken) to the emergency room.

4. The problem (is, are) we have no empty beds.

5. A young or older person (make, makes) choices in life.

*Simplify these sentences correctly:*

1. Sutures came in a variety of materials such as silk and catgut which is from sheep's intestines. _____

2. The type of sutures which the surgeon ties each stitch separately is called interrupted. _____

3. The diameter (gauge) of the suture material vary from fine (11-0) to very coarse (3). _____

4. The 6-0 suture is also called six aught and might be wrote 000000. It is very fine. _____-

5. Whole numbers such as 1, 2, 3, and 4 imply that the suture is very large diameter thread. This is very coarse suture material. _____

*Answer true or false to the following.*

1. A medical record can never be used for research on certain diseases. _____

2. Attorneys may use the medical record for litigation purposes. _____

3. Any type of abbreviations any symbols may be used in the medical record. _____

4. Information in the medical report is available for anyone who needs it. _____

5. If an activity isn't recorded in the medical documentation, it didn't happen. _____

6. Physicians may keep medical records forever. _____

7. One example of information found in the medical record is chemistry reports. _____

*Circle the correct spelling in each line:*

1. punchered      resucitate      sterilised      radiate
2. biforcate      pulsat      stabilised      irrigate
3. reconect      irigate      examine      operatted
4. transmitted      transmited      transmmitted      transmitted
5. incubatte      circulate      refferred      imapairr
6. diviate      deveate      deviate      deviatte
7. acompanied      accompannied      acomppanied      accompanied
8. vomet      originate      irigate      reconect
9. diteriorate      detteriorate      deteriorate      detereorat
10. examine      acumulate      administir      desclose

*Translate medical abbreviations using a medical dictionary or appendix.*

1. DPT _____
2. Dx _____
3. EEG _____
4. DRGs _____
5. DO _____
6. EOM _____
7. FBS _____
8. F.U.O _____
9. F/U _____
10. Fx _____

# Comprehensive Review

*Circle the correct word from within the parenthesis:*

First impressions are lasting impressions. Health-care professionals help (project, projects) a positive image to all people (who, whom) they encounter in the medical environment. Medical assistants with a good appearance (has, have) an effect on the patients they (meet, met) daily. The impression that a medical assistant (portrays, portray) to the patients (color, colors) the image of the physician and the care the patients expect.

Good grooming is essential in fostering good impressions. Good grooming (include, includes) a bath or shower daily, use of deodorant, and good oral hygiene. Hair should be (clean, cleaned), neatly styled, and above the collar. Shoes should be comfortable. Laces in shoes (need, needs) to be washed often.

The usual attire in the medical setting (is, are) uniforms, depending on the dress code of the medical facility. A uniform (give, gives) the impression of professionalism and (identify, identifies) the person as a member of the health-care team. Wear a clean uniform to work daily. In offices where a uniform is not (required, requires), the medical assistant is expected to show good taste in selecting and wearing a professional wardrobe.

The amount of jewelry (is, are) limited to an engagement ring, wedding band, or professional pin. Sometimes staff members (wear, wears) name tags to help patients (identify, identifies) the health-care provider by name.

A frequent problem that (surface, surfaces) with health-care workers (is, are) burnout. Medical assistants need to take care of (himself, herself, themselves). Good health habits (include, includes) frequent exercise, eight hours of sleep each night, and eating the right kinds of food.

Good appearance and good health habits (is, are) important habits to foster in health-care professionals.

*Write the correct word above the incorrect italicized word:*

The law maintains that each physician is responsible for *their* own negligence when someone is injured. A physician is also responsible for the negligent act *performs* by medical assistant employed in *their* office. An injured party generally *sue* the doctor because there is a better chance of collecting more money. A medical assistant is not licensed to practice medicine. One must be careful what he or she *discuss* with the patient. Patients may think the medical *assistants* remarks are those of the physician. These facts *illustrates* the importance of performing all actions with extreme care.

*Select the BEST answer that identifies the underlined words in each sentence.*

1. *Charting* and *documenting* are instruments that hold the medical team accountable for services rendered to patients.

   a. infinitive     b. gerunds     c. linking verbs     d. helping verbs

2. Data obtained from the medical record *does* help in the treatment of patients.

   a. action verb     b. intransitive verb     c. being verb     d. helping verb

3. Scientists *had found* critical evidence regarding medications and test results.

   a. present tense     b. past tense     c. past participle     d. present participle

4. A cohesive method is needed *to give* information to physicians and supportive staff.

   a. gerund     b. infinitive     c. linking verb     d. present participle.

5. Health care facilities *must follow* HIPAA standards for faxing health-care information.

   a. imperative     b. indicative     c. subjunctive     d. none of these answers

# CHAPTER 5

# Sentences

## PRACTICAL WRITING COMPONENT: CHARTING AND DOCUMENTING

**OBJECTIVES** *Upon completion of this chapter, the learner should be able to:*

❖ identify the four basic types of sentence structures

❖ recognize the four classifications of sentences according to their purpose

❖ identify the factors that cause ineffective sentences

❖ utilize the factors that contribute to the effectiveness of sentences

❖ spell various medical terms

❖ translate various medical abbreviations

❖ recognize different styles of charting in the Medical Records

The writing style used in the medical profession is unique. When medical personnel document data, it is usually written without regard to sentence structure. Information is jotted down in abbreviations, words, and symbols. However, when this information is translated into formal letters or reports, correct sentence structure is absolutely necessary.

## Examples

Medical documentation: Pt. is scheduled for TURP

Sentence translation: The patient is scheduled for transurethral resection of the prostate.

Medical documentation: Dx is CHF

Sentence translation: The diagnosis is congestive heart failure.

# Components of Sentences

A sentence expresses a complete thought. To be grammatically correct and express a complete thought, every sentence must have two basic parts: a subject and a predicate. The subject is the part about which or whom something is said. The predicate tells what the subject is doing or what is being done to the subject. The simple subject is the main noun or pronoun in the sentence; the simple predicate is referred to as the *verb*. Together a subject and predicate form an independent clause.

| Simple Subject | Simple Predicate (Verb) |
|---|---|
| Medication | cures. |
| Physicians | examine. |
| Payment | arrived. |

To find the subject of the sentence, locate the verb and ask the question *who?* or *what?* about it.

The verb is *cures*. *What* cures? Medication cures. *Medication* is the *subject*.

The verb is *examine*. *Who* examines? Physicians examine. *Physicians* is the *subject*.

The verb is *arrived*. *What* arrived? Payment arrived. *Payment* is the *subject*.

Subjects and predicates may be compound. A compound subject consists of two or more subjects connected by the conjunction *and* or *or*. A compound subject has the same verb. A compound predicate has two or more verbs linked by the conjunction *and, or,* or *but*. The compound predicate has the same subject.

| Compound Subject | Compound Predicate |
|---|---|
| *Medication and rest* cure. | Medications *cure or arrest diseases*. |
| *Physicians and nurses* document. | Physicians *document and dictate*. |
| *Payment and claims* were received. | Payment was *received and stamped*. |

## Practice 5-1

*Identify the subject of each sentence by asking who? or what? about the verb (predicate):*

1. The operation was cancelled. _____

2. The patient owns the information in the medical record. _____

3. The physician owns the medical record itself. _____

4. Entries in a medical record are unalterable. _____

5. A breach of confidentiality has legal implications. _____

# Sentence Structure

The three sentence structures are simple, compound, and complex.

## SIMPLE SENTENCES

A simple sentence has one independent clause and no dependent clause.

## Examples

Sutures are surgical stitches.

Patient records are known as charts.

CT scans take a series of pictures around the same plane.

## COMPOUND SENTENCES

A compound sentence contains two or more independent clauses but no dependent clause. They are joined with a coordinating conjunction, a semicolon, or a semicolon and conjunctive adverb.

## Examples

Medical asepsis involves procedures to reduce microorganisms, *and* hand washing is the first step in the process.

The risks for infection control were raised; the first case of vancomycin-resistant staphylococcus aureus was reported to the CDC.

The appointment schedule was booked solid; *therefore*, only emergencies were accepted.

## COMPLEX SENTENCES

A complex sentence has one independent clause and one or more dependent clauses.

## Examples

*After the procedure was done*, Christopher's major complaint was fatigue.

*When preparing for surgical asepsis*, the objective is to eliminate all microorganisms.

*Whenever a patient complains of chest pain*, the first drug given should be ASA.

## COMPOUND-COMPLEX SENTENCES

A compound-complex sentence has two or more independent clauses and one or more dependent clauses. Because they are long, and sometimes difficult to understand, they should be used sparingly.

## Examples

*After being treated with diet restrictions and medications for Crohn's disease, the patient survived, but he left the hospital with total parenteral nutrition.*

*With diabetes being an epidemic in our society, John controls his disease, but he risks complications with his weight and lack of exercise.*

# Practice 5-2

*Identify the sentences as either simple, compound, or complex.*

1. Many supplies in the doctor's office are disposable, and many are made of surgical steel for autoclaving. _____

2. When one is preparing for surgical asepsis, the objective is to eliminate all microorganisms. _____

3. Autoclaving is the most common method of sterilizing. _____

4. Keep charts neat. _____

5. Sterile solutions are often required during surgical procedures. _____

# Classifications of Sentences

Sentences are classified in four ways according to what they do: declarative, imperative, interrogative, and exclamatory.

### DECLARATIVE SENTENCES

Most sentences are declarative because they make known (*declare*) some type of information or statement. Declarative sentences end with a period (.).

## Examples

The medical assistant is responsible for filing.

The diagnosis is influenza.

A differential diagnosis is given when there are other possible diagnoses.

## Examples

*Because of medical staff absenteeism,* everything was behind schedule.

*If you want to stay healthy,* drink more water and exercise daily.

*Medical x-rays that indicate an abnormality in the neck require further review.*

*Medications in the locked closet* need to be distributed.

---

Edit, revise, and proofread each sentence until it is clear and complete.

---

## Practice 5-4

*State whether these sentences are complete or fragmented:*

1. Recording each patient's medication. _____

2. Common charting terminology. _____

3. Give 50 mg of morphine SC stat. _____

4. Use plastic gloves for aseptic reasons. _____

5. Decontaminate work surfaces. _____

## THE COMMA SPLICE

A **comma splice** occurs when two or more independent clauses are incorrectly connected by a comma.

## Examples

First we cleaned the incision, then we did the dry sterile dressing.

Migraines occur when the vessels are not filled with blood, the scalp feels the pain.

The patient can waive confidentiality, confidentiality can also be overruled through a court order or subpoena.

## THE RUN-ON SENTENCE

A **run-on sentence** occurs when two or more independent clauses are joined together without punctuation.

## Examples

First we cleaned the incision then we did the dry sterile dressing.

Migraines occur when the vessels are not filled with blood the scalp feels the pain.

The patient can waive confidentiality confidentiality, can also be overruled through a court order or subpoena.

**The run-on sentence and the comma splice can be corrected in the following ways:**

1. Connect the independent clauses by a comma and a coordinating conjunction.

   First we cleaned the incision, and then we did the dry sterile dressing.

   Migraines occur when the vessels are not filled with blood, and the scalp feels the pain.

   The patient can waive confidentiality, but confidentiality can also be overruled through a court order or subpoena.

2. The independent clauses can be put into two separate sentences.

   We cleaned the incision. Then we did the dry sterile dressing.

   Migraines occur when the vessels are not filled with blood. The scalp feels the pain.

   The patient can waive confidentiality. Confidentiality can also be overruled through a court order or subpoena.

3. A semicolon can connect the closely related clauses. Sometimes a conjunctive adverb is used.

   First we cleaned the incision; then we did the dry sterile dressing.

   Migraines occur when the vessels are not filled with blood; consequently, the scalp feels the pain.

   The patient can waive confidentiality; however, confidentiality can also be overruled through a court order or subpoena.

4. Make one of the dependent clauses into a dependent clause.

   After we cleaned the incision, we did the dry sterile dressing.

   Migraines occur when the vessels are not filled with blood, while the scalp feels the pain.

   Although the patient can waive confidentiality, confidentiality can also be overruled through a court order or subpoena.

## Practice 5-5

*Identify the following sentences as true or false:*

1. A run on sentence occurs when independent clauses are joined without punctuation. _____

2. The predicate of a sentence tells who or what about the verb. _____

3. A sentence forms a dependent clause. _____

4. A sentence fault disrupts the flow of ideas. _____

5. Independent clauses can form two sentences. _____

Poor punctuation is the only cause of run-on sentences. By not using a period, semi-colon, or conjunction, one sentence is permitted to run into another. Carelessness rather than a lack of understanding more likely causes this type of error.

## Examples

| | |
|---|---|
| Run-on | I took her vital signs I marked the results on the patient's chart. [No punctuation mark or coordinating conjunction used between the two complete sentences.] |
| Correct | I took her vital signs. I marked the results on the patient's chart. [A period separates the two sentences.] |
| Correct | After I took her vital signs, I marked the results on the patient's chart. [Revised to make a single sentence with a dependent and independent clause.] |
| Run-on | I took her vital signs, I marked the results on the patient's chart. [A comma is used in place of a period.] |
| Correct | I took her vital signs, and I marked the results on the patient's chart. [Added a coordinating conjunction.] |

# Effective Sentences

Writing for medical professionals is very different from other professions. A person's reason for writing greatly influences the tone or manner in which words are expressed. A novelist uses multiple words to create settings, establish moods, and express emotions. A historian concentrates on exact times, cultures, and the cause and effect of events. A poet uses metaphors, rhythm, and rhyme. Medical writers use abbreviations, codes, and phrases unique to their situations. Note the difference in style between a novelist and a medical professional:

**Novelist**

How glad she was to see her children! She wept for pleasure when she felt their little arms clasping her; their hard, ruddy cheeks pressing against her own glowing cheeks. She looked into their faces with hungry eyes that could not be satisfied with looking

[Kate Chopin, *The Awakening*]

**Medical Professional**

Patient experiences no motion in the back. Range of motion of the hips is within normal limits and painless. There is only a +1 dorsalis pedis on the right; otherwise, there are no peripheral pulses present. There is marked coldness of both feet.

[Diehl and Fordney, *Medical Typing and Transcribing*]

Many elements contribute to the effectiveness of good sentence structure. Four of these elements are covered in this chapter: parallel structure, conciseness, word choices, and positive statements.

## PARALLEL STRUCTURE

Parallel sentence structure requires that words, phrases, and clauses be expressed in the same grammatical construction. The elements or units of a sentence (words, phrases, and clauses) joined by a conjunction should be expressed in the same form. The sentence reads smoothly when the ideas are expressed in this cohesive way.

| | |
|---|---|
| a noun with a noun | *doctors* and *nurses* |
| an adjective with an adjective | *red* and *green* lights |
| an infinitive with an infinitive | *to* speak and *to* listen |
| a gerund with a gerund | *climbing* and *reaching* |

## *Examples*

| | |
|---|---|
| Nonparallel | Dr. Spencer is *trustworthy* and *a gynecologist*. [*Trustworthy* is an adjective and *gynecologist* is a noun.] |
| Parallel | Dr. Spencer is a *surgeon* and a *gynecologist*. [two nouns]. |
| Parallel | Dr. Spencer is trustworthy and honest. [two adjectives] |
| Nonparallel | The medical assistant's tasks are *transcribing* and *to file*. [*Transcribing* is a gerund and *to file* is an infinitive.] |
| Parallel | A medical assistant's tasks are *transcribing* and *filing*. [two gerunds] |
| Parallel | A medical assistant's tasks are *to transcribe* and *to file*. [two infinitives] |

# Practice 5-6

*Identify these sentences as parallel or nonparallel:*

1. The patient underwent an MRI, an X-ray, and blood test. _____

2. The patient education was interesting and of knowledge. _____

3. The doctor proofread the History and Physical quickly and thoroughly. _____

4. I want an appointment for next week, rather than putting it off until next month. _____

5. Ann purchased a computer, a color printer, and she also bought a modem. _____

## CONCISENESS

Conciseness is the hallmark of medical documentation. Conciseness is expressing a lot of information in a few words. More words are not necessarily better. Sentences should not be cluttered with unnecessary words.

## *Examples*

| | |
|---|---|
| Wordy | The black and blue mark is on the right lower leg. |
| Concise | The hematoma is on the right lower leg. |
| Wordy | If you think you want more information, don't hesitate to call. |
| Concise | Call me for more information. |
| Wordy | The purpose of this letter is to acknowledge the receipt of your medical payment. |
| Concise | Thank you for your remittance. |
| Wordy | We received your check for the full amount. |
| Concise | We received the balance in full. |
| Wordy | The patient has difficulty breathing. |
| Concise | The patient has dyspnea. |
| Wordy | To the best of my knowledge, we did all we could do for the patient. |
| Concise | We did all we could for the patient. |

---

*A sentence should contain no unnecessary words, a paragraph no unnecessary sentences, for the same reason that a drawing should have no unnecessary line and a machine no unnecessary part.*

William Strunk, Jr.

---

Wordy expressions can be replaced by concise words:

| | |
|---|---|
| as a result | therefore |
| at this time, at this point in time | now, currently |
| bring to a conclusion | conclude, end |
| cognizant of the fact | know |
| due to the fact that | because |
| during the month of | during |
| each and every | each |
| enclosed please find | I am enclosing |
| lend credence to the report | support the report |
| many eccentricities | many behaviors |
| peruse the document | read the document |

| | |
|---|---|
| I would appreciate it if | please |
| in regard to | regarding, concerning |
| in some cases | sometimes |
| in reference to the subject matter | regarding |
| in the near future | soon |
| it has come to our attention | we learned |
| it is incumbent on you | it is your duty |
| of primary importance | significant |
| please be advised that | know |
| regarding the matter of | regarding |

## Practice 5-7

*Make these sentences more concise:*

1. You are eligible for Medicare because of the fact of your age. _____

2. The pharmacy makes deliveries of customers' medications for a charge that amounts to $7.00 per delivery. _____

3. The group moves to negotiate acceptance of the physician's plan. _____

4. During the month of April, my health premiums increased by the amount of 5%. _____

5. Enclosed please find a check in the amount of $100. _____

To be concise also means to reduce the length of sentences. Writing shorter sentences means using fewer words. Ten or fifteen words per sentence is about average. Be careful of sentences that run longer than two typed lines. Shorten lengthy sentences by adding periods and making two or more sentences out of one. For example,

| | |
|---|---|
| Lengthy Sentence | The gallbladder was edematous and somewhat thick-walled, with a stone lodged in the cystic duct of the gallbladder, measuring about 1.0 cm in diameter, but there were no filling defects and there was good emptying of the contrast medium into the duodenum. |
| Revision | The gallbladder was edematous and somewhat thick-walled. It contained a 1.0-cm stone lodged in the cystic duct of the gallbladder, which had no filling defects. |

There was good emptying of the contrast medium into the duodenum.

---

*Eliminate unnecessary words. Write to express, not impress.*

---

On the other hand, too many short sentences could be boring:

| | |
|---|---|
| Short Sentences | Heather Adams is an 83-year-old woman. She also looks young for her age. She has a history of heart problems. She refused medication. It makes her dizzy. There are also occasional accidents from incontinence. Also diarrhea. X-rays were ordered. |
| Varied Sentences | Heather Adams is an 83-year-old woman with a history of heart problems. She refuses medication because it makes her dizzy. The patient experiences incontinence and diarrhea. X-rays were ordered. |

Another way to be concise is to change a dependent clause into either a phrase, an appositive, or a single word.

### Phrase (a group of words without a subject or predicate)

Working medical staff [gerund phrase]

After the operation [prepositional phrase]

To get an early start [infinitive phrase]

Troubled by headaches [participial phrase]

### Appositive (a word or group of words that renames)

John, who is the physical therapist = John, the physical therapist

### Single Word

That had been canceled = canceled

## Examples

| | |
|---|---|
| Clause | The biopsy *that came to the pathology laboratory* was not scheduled for today. |
| Phrase | The biopsy *from the pathology lab* was not scheduled for today. |
| Clause | *After you graduate*, you are eligible for the certification exam. |
| Phrase | *After graduation*, you are eligible for the certification exam. |
| Clause | Her two nurses, *one of whom is Joan and the other Bill*, took care of her. |
| Appositive | Her two nurses, *Joan and Bill*, took care of her. |

|  | |
|---|---|
| Clause | Allow the patient *who is angry* to express his feelings. |
| Single Word | Allow the *angry* patient to express his feelings. |

## Practice 5-8

*Keep the meaning of these sentences, but make them more concise:*

1. In chart notes, some doctors write in longhand that is hard to read. _____

2. The patient had herpes zoster at a young age and recovered nicely. _____

3. The patient is alert, holding the right section of his arm at times during the exam. _____

4. Prompt diagnosis and treatment comes from early recognition of signs and symptoms. _____

5. When original materials are used in a report, credit must be given to the author in a footnote. _____

## DICTION

Diction refers to the writer's choice of words and how those words are used in writing. Diction makes the difference between a clear style and a weak, vague style. The intended audience usually determines the type of diction. Among the types that have no place in medical documentation are unfamiliar words, slang, colloquialisms, and vagueness.

Some writers feel that using long or unfamiliar words makes a good impression. Although these words have their merit, medical documentation is not the place to impress.

## Examples

The patient's *idiosyncrasies* irritated her condition.

The patient's *behavior* irritated her condition.

*Peruse* the medical report before you make any comment.

*Read* the medical report before you make any comment.

Slang is a new or old expression that contains colorful words and expressions that take on new meaning. Phrases like *don't bug me, it's cool, in the swim,* and *off the wall,* are examples of slang. Colloquialisms are informal words and phrases used in everyday conversation: *globs, lots and lots, all revved up,* and *been there–done that.*

## Examples

The patient is *off the wall.*

Medical research *is not my thing.*

The new medical equipment is real cool.

Another trap to avoid in writing effective sentences is the use of vague words or phrases. Vagueness is expressing oneself unclearly. Like slang and colloquialisms, vague words have no place in medical documentation. Recording that a patient received medication without the name or dosage of the drug opens the door to all kinds of problems. Can you imagine the consequences if a medical assistant failed to document that a patient's *right* hand was the source of pain? Be specific with the facts. Assume nothing in medical reporting. Use specific words over vague words or wordy expressions.

## Examples

| | |
|---|---|
| Vague | The patient wasn't feeling well. |
| Specific | The patient complained of abdominal pain. His skin was cool, pale, and moist. |
| Vague | The medication was given before bedtime. |
| Specific | A.S.A. 500 mg was given H.S. |
| Vague | The head nurse supervised the project. |
| Specific | Ellen Barker, the head nurse, supervised the Ethics Project. |
| Vague | Call me some time during the day. |
| Specific | Call me between 1:00 and 2:00 p.m. on Wednesday. |

*The difference between the right word and the nearly right word is the same as that between lightning and the lightning bug.*

Mark Twain

## Practice 5-9

*Underline the sentence in each pair that provides specific information:*

1. A. Come to the office tomorrow.

   B. Make the appointment on Wednesday at 3:15 p.m.

2. A. The physician informed the Board of Directors about the financial situation.

   B. Last night, the patient had lots and lots of pain and discomfort.

3. A. You and I think along the same lines.

   B. The moral issue about confidentiality was discussed at the meeting.

4. A. Credit was given to Dr. Sullivan for his consultation report.

   B. Although many suggestions were good, some were very far out.

5. A. The patient could care less about what medication to take.

   B. I appreciate the effort you put into fund raising.

## POSITIVE STATEMENTS

To write more effective sentences, use positive statements instead of negative ones. Write what can be done rather than what cannot be done. A positive tone creates an environment of efficiency, acceptance, and professionalism. Notice how these negative sentences were changed to positive sentences:

| | |
|---|---|
| Negative | Your medication isn't due until 3 p.m. |
| Positive | Your medication is due at 3 p.m. |
| Negative | Why didn't you clean the wound before applying bacitracin? |
| Positive | Clean the wound well before applying the bacitracin. |
| Negative | The medication isn't in stock right now. |
| Positive | We expect to receive the medication tomorrow. |
| Negative | You did not sign the release form. |
| Positive | Please sign the release form. |

Negative sentences, like those used in the previous examples, contain some form of the word *not*. Other negative words are *nor, never,* and *no*. Some sentences may also convey a negative tone even without using a specifically negative word:

| | |
|---|---|
| Negative | Doctors are like God. |
| Positive | Doctors are human like everyone else. |
| Negative | Get it right the first time. |
| Positive | I'll take my time and do it well. |
| Negative | What if I lose my job? |
| Positive | If I lose my job, I'll find a better one. |

# *Practice 5-10*

*Change these negative sentences to positive ones:*

1. Most people never change. _____

2. My supervisor refused to give me a raise. _____

3. The doctor's office isn't open after 5 p.m. _____

4. You won't be satisfied with the quality of care in that hospital. _____

5. Don't think twice about calling the doctor. _____

# Sentence Summary

| Sentence | Subject (Simple or Compound) | Complete Subject | Simple Predicate (Verb) | Complete Predicate |
|---|---|---|---|---|
| My sister, Ethel, is a technician | Ethel (simple subject) | My sister, Ethel | is | is a technician. |
| Dental care is free to children. | care (simple subject) | Dental care | is | is free to children. |
| The hurricane and wind destroyed many houses and trees. | hurricane and wind (compound subject) | The hurricane and wind | destroyed | destroyed many houses and trees. |

## Sentence Structure

| Simple Sentence | Contains one independent clause. | The disease was contagious. |
|---|---|---|
| Compound Sentence | Contains two or more independent clauses. | The disease was contagious, but precautions were taken. |
| Complex Sentence | Contains one independent clause and one dependent clause. | Careful handwashing reduces the spread of contagious disease when done properly. |

## CLASSIFICATIONS OF SENTENCES

| Declarative | Makes a statement, is used more than any other type, and ends in a period: "This doctor seldom asks for a copayment." |
|---|---|
| Imperative | Gives a command, makes a request, and ends in a period. The subject *you* is understood: "Give the patient medicine." "Don't forget your appointment." |
| Interrogative | Asks a question and ends with a question mark: "What is my temperature?" "When are you flying to France?" |
| Exclamatory | Expresses strong feelings and ends with an exclamation point: "Get to the ER quickly!" |

## Ineffective Sentences

| Fragment | Does not express a complete thought and occurs when a phrase is considered as a sentence: "involuntary shaking," "under medical care," "who are known to have hemophilia." |
|---|---|

| Run-on | Omits punctuation between two sentences: "Chart notes are formal or informal physicians take them when they see a patient." "The abdomen is flat without scars bowel sounds are normative." "Make an entry in the chart do the entry correctly." |
|---|---|
| Comma Splice | Incorrectly uses a comma to connect two or more independent clauses: "The goal of organizing documents is to provide easy access to patient information, information is needed by many different health professionals." |

**Characteristics of Effective Sentences**

| Parallel structure | Two or more sentence elements of equal rank expressed similarly: "Water skiing is as challenging as to dive" [not parallel]. "Water skiing is as challenging as diving" [parallel]. |
|---|---|
| Conciseness | Avoiding wordiness and sentences that are too long: "We were sitting in seats that were close to the stage" [wordy]. "We were sitting close to the stage" [concise]. |
| Appropriate diction | Clear expression through the choice of words and how they are used in a sentence: "The meeting is in the afternoon" [vague]. "The team meeting is at 3:30 p.m." [precise]. |
| Positive statements | Affirmative expression: "I can't perform that procedure" [negative]. "I'll refer you to a physician who does that procedure" [positive]. |

# Medical Spelling

*Become familiar with the spelling of the following words:*

| | |
|---|---|
| assessment | fluoroscopy |
| cachexia | immunoglobulins |
| carcinogens | incontinence |
| chemotherapeutic | influenza |
| cytology | insomnia |
| dehiscence | integrity |
| dementia | interferon |
| diabetes | interstitial |
| diffusion | intoxication |
| dysplasia | manifestation |
| emesis | mediastinum |
| endogenous | narcolepsy |
| endoscopy | neurophysiologic |
| enteric | oxygenation |
| episodic | pathophysiology |
| evisceration | pediculosis |
| exacerbation | perceptual |
| fissure | pericarditis |

| | |
|---|---|
| rehabilitation | ultrasound |
| stenosis | vertilligo |
| syndrome | visceral |
| tolerance | |

# Charting and Documenting

When medical services are provided, information is jotted down in charts and documents. Facts recorded in charts and documents use abbreviations, words, and symbols that must be translated into complete sentences for letters and formal reports. The unique writing style associated with charting and documentation is covered in this section.

Charting and documenting are the instruments that hold the medical team accountable and responsible for the type of services rendered to patients. The rapid changes in the health-care industry require that accurate, detailed documentation by multilevel personnel involved in the care of patients be maintained at all times. Documentation provides critical evidence regarding patients' reactions, treatments, symptoms, tests, medication, and other vital information. Data obtained from charts and documents are used for diagnosing and assessing a patient's condition.

There are many types of charting. The method for your facility is the method that should be followed. Many institutions develop a combination of types of charting.

## TRADITIONAL OR NARRATIVE CHARTING

Narrative notes are phrases, clauses, and sentences without any specific structure. They are traditional notes that were used for many years and were lengthy, containing both important and unimportant information such as "pt. is comfortable, visitors today." For many years the narrative notes were thrown away after a patient was discharged and not kept as part of the permanent record.

Through the years, many factors motivated the need for changes in written documentation: legal requirements, Medicare reimbursement, insurance benefits, and billing and coding practices, to name just a few.

Because people perceive and interpret information differently, it was difficult to streamline charting and documenting. Concise and focused charting has been developed in more recent times. Today, narrative charting communicates only essential facts about the patient.

## Example

5-30-20XX     9 pm     Pt. c/o pain over the incision. Pain med administered. Pt. voided 150cc 5 hrs. after Foley cath was removed.

11pm     Pt still c/o pain. Dr. Villes notified.     D. Oberg, RN

5-30-20XX     12midnoc     Dr. Villes in to examine pt. Increased dosage of pain med.

L. Villmare, CMA

This type of information is often placed in the source-oriented medical record (SOMR). It is a simple system and requires the least amount of work and organization.

## SOAP

Lawrence Weed, M.D., instituted the problem-oriented medical record (POMR) method in 1969, at Case Western Reserve in Cleveland. The POMR organizes the patient's record in a comprehensive manner by charting the patient's problems in order of importance and how those problems are addressed. Some institutions still use this format. Others have incorporated part of the format to fit their own charting and documenting needs. The POMR has four parts:

1. *Data base.* The data consists of information from various sources that identifies the problem and is the basis for evaluating the patient's health.

2. *Problem list.* This is a chronological list of the patient's problems and reasons for seeing the doctor.

3. *Initial plan.* A treatment plan is developed to address each problem the patient has.

4. *Progress notes.* The written notes are called SOAP (Subjective-Objective-Assessment-Plan) notes. In this format, progress notes are dated, headed, and numbered for specific problems.

SOAP notes consist of:

S  A history and subjective data told to the physician by the patient or a family member, such as nausea, descriptions of symptoms, and feelings.

## Examples

*I have a pain in my leg.*

*Pt. c/o pain in the lower back.*

*Pt. c/o migraine headache.*

O  Objective data from the physician's physical exam of what is seen, heard, and touched.

## Examples

*results from tests and physical exam.*

*weeping, inflammation, vital signs.*

If, for instance, a patient comes to the ER and is complaining of being hot, and is perspiring and flushed, the entry might read like this:

*S—Pt. complains of temperature and diaphoresis.*

*O—V.S. taken: T-102, P-80, R-24, B.P. 150/80, diaphoretic.*

A  An assessment by the physician with diagnoses and impressions.

## Examples

*arthritis of the leg*

Dx: *emphysema*

*Pt. has chronic bronchiolitis.*

P    A treatment plan for medical problems, medications, consults, surgery, and patient education.

## Examples

*Take ASA q. 4 h. for pain.*

*Pt. to PT 3 X wk.*

## SOAPE

SOAP notes were later modified to include evaluation:

E    An evaluation stating how the patient responded to the illness and reacted to the treatment, medications, and medical care.

## SOAPIE

Another system added intervention and its evaluation:

I    An intervention is an approach to a particular problem.

E    The evaluation looks at the response of the intervention in terms of the illness and subsequent treatment.

Figure 5–1 is an example of SOAPIE charting.

## SOAPIER

Other components to the SOAP system of charting include intervention, evaluation, and revision.

I    Intervention considers the approach to a particular problem.

E    Evaluation looks at the patient's response to the treatment intervention.

R    Revision identifies changes that are prompted by the evaluation.

## PIE

PIE (Problem- Intervention- Evaluation) charting was introduced in 1984 at the Craven Regional Medical Center in North Carolina. With this method, problems are identified and addressed at least once on every shift. Teaching plans are incorporated in the progress notes. Notes must be read often to understand the evolution of the problems and the effectiveness of the treatment.

## Examples

P    Problem: *Pt hasn't had BM for 3 days.*

I    Intervention: *T.O. for MOM 30 ml. 8am.*

E    Evaluation: *Pt. had a BM in afternoon.*

Figure 5–2 is an example of PIE charting.

| | | Nurse's Progress Record |
|---|---|---|
| Date | Hour | Progress Notes |

10/14/01 | 0730 | Problem #2 Ketoacidosis

**S:** Client states "I feel sick all over." Client claims difficulty in breathing, abdominal pain + nausea.

**O:** Lungs clear, R 38/min, labored. Abdomen distended, bowel sounds underactive all 4 quadrants. Abdominal pain 5 on a 0-10 pain scale.

**A:** Alteration in nutrition + comfort R/T keto-acidosis. Blood glucose 458 mg/dl. Ketones strongly positive. pH < 7.3.

**P:** Maintain IV infusion of 0.9% NS c̄ regular insulin as ordered. NPO. Oral hygiene hrly. Maintain accurate I&O. Assess for rales, hypotension, cardiac dysrhythmias. Monitor blood glucose electrolytes. — L. White RN

10/14/01 | 0730 | **I:** Called Dr. Singh, blood glucose 458 mg/dl IV bolus regular insulin given as ordered. 1000ml 0.9% N.S. infusing @ 17/H central line #1 via infusion pump. 50 u regular insulin in 500 ml N.S. infusing @ 50ml/H central line #2 via infusion pump. EKG taken, placed on telemetry.

10/14/01 | 0835 | **E:** Lungs clear, R 24/min, non-labored. NSR abdominal pain 3 on a 0-10 pain scale. Urinary output 750ml hr. Blood glucose 360 mg/dl. — L. White RN

**FIGURE 5-1** *Sample SOAPIE Charting*

SENTENCES ❖ **125**

| Date | Hour | Progress Notes |
|------|------|----------------|

**Nurse's Progress Record**

10/14/01 0730 **P:** altered nutrition R/T ketoacidosis. Blood glucose 458mg/dl, ketones strongly positive, pH 7.2.

**I:** called Dr. Singh, blood glucose 458mg/dl IV bolus regular insulin given as ordered. 1000ml 0.9% N.S. infusing @ 1L/H central line #1 via infusion pump. 50u regular insulin in 500 ml N.S. infusing @50ml/H, central line #2 via infusion pump. EKG taken, placed on telemetry.

10/14/01 0835 **E:** Lungs clear, R 24/min nonlabored, NSR, abdominal pain 3 on a 0-10 pain scale. Urinary output 750 ml/H (0730-0830) Blood sugar 320mg/dl.
— T. White RN —

**FIGURE 5-2** *Sample PIE Charting*

An office may use SOAP notes, traditional narrative charting, or other types of charting. Medical offices, hospitals, and clinics usually develop their own methods of charting that best accommodate their particular situations. Data such as test results, abbreviations, and medical reports usually remain the same, but the organization of the documentation is unique to each locale. In any event, the ultimate goal of organizing documentation is to provide easier access to patient information, particularly in today's medical environment where so many different professionals access medical records.

## Practice 5-11

*Translate the following abbreviations and determine if the statement is subjective. Consult the abbreviation list.*

1. Pt. c/o SOB _____

2. Check I & O q.h. _____

3. Dx: URI _____

4. OOB adlib post op _____

5. U/A for RBC _____

6. D/C Coumadin STAT _____

*Respond to the following items:*

1. The term STAT means _____.

    a. immediately    b. by mouth    c. whenever necessary    d. stand by

2. An example of subjective information is _____.

    a. giving pain medication          b. a patient's complaint

    c. history of the problem          d. physical therapy

3. Dr. Lawrence Weed developed a medical record system called _____.

    a. HMRO                             b. the traditional method

    c. POMR                             d. chronological system

4. Which of the following is subjective?

    a. diagnosis    b. treatment    c. lab report    d. past surgical history

# Charting and Documenting Summary

The Medical Record

Specific instruments of documentation that store written information about a patient's health condition.

| | |
|---|---|
| Language of the Medical Record | Use medical terms and abbreviations for documenting medical information. |

**General Rules for Abbreviations:**

| | |
|---|---|
| Abbreviate acronyms—AIDS | Abbreviations are acceptable in formal reports if previously spelled out—tonsillectomy and adenoidectomy: T&A |
| Abbreviate chart notes | States have two letter abbreviations—MA, NY |
| Abbreviate chemical symbols | |
| Use lower case letters in Latin abbreviations | Certifications and registrations have no periods—RN, CMT, CMA |
| Measurement abbreviations have no periods | |
| In formal writing, days of the week and months of the year are not abbreviated—February 18, 20XX | A comma is not necessary when II or III follows a surname—John Archie IV |

**Types of charting**

| | |
|---|---|
| Traditional | A type of charting that uses phrases, clauses, and sentences without any specific structure. |
| Problem Oriented Medical Record (POMR) | Charting problems by order of importance. |
| SOAP | An acronym meaning: |
| | S—subjective data: feelings and description of symptoms. |
| | O—objective data: data from physical exam. |
| | A—assessment: diagnosis and impressions. |
| | P—plan: medication, treatments, consults, surgery. |
| SOAPE | E—evaluation: patient's response to treatment. |
| SOAPIE | I—intervention: an approach to a particular problem. |
| | E—evaluating that approach. |
| SOAPIER | I—intervention: approach to a problem. |
| | E—evaluating that approach. |
| | R—revision: changes prompted by the evaluation. |
| PIE | Problem–Intervention–Evaluation |
| | Problems are identified and addressed at least once on every shift. |

# Skills Review

*Complete these fragmented sentences:*

1. For medical coverage to continue. _____

2. Your medical insurance representative. _____

3. The results from your MRI. _____

4. An adjustment made to the patient's claim. _____

5. People with job-related illnesses. _____

*Select the best sentence from among the three choices:*

1. A. I see an arrhythmia on the telemetry call the cardiologist.

   B. I see an arrhythmia on the telemetry, call the cardiologist.

   C. I see an arrhythmia on the telemetry. Call the cardiologist.

2. A. The person is dyspneic, she needs oxygen.

   B. The person is dyspneic; she needs oxygen.

   C. The person is dyspneic she needs oxygen.

3. A. The biopsy is tomorrow I hope for good news.

   B. The biopsy is tomorrow, therefore, I hope for good news.

   C. The biopsy is tomorrow, and I hope for good news.

4. A. The hospital wing is closed repairs are being made.

   B. The hospital wing is closed because repairs are being made.

   C. The hospital is closed, repairs are being made.

5. A. A nurse expresses compassion when she works with her patients.

   B. A nurse expresses compassion when he works with his patients.

   C. Nurses express compassion when they work with their patients.

*Improve these sentences. (Many of them were obtained from actual doctor's reports.)*

1. The operation was successful and the patient left the operating room in excellent condition. _____

2. If you should have any questions or comments please don't hesitate to call me. _____

3. The patient moved slowly. She moved along the corridor, She used her walker. _____

4. After the operation, bring the patient to the next room over in the recovery room.

5. The problem was here yesterday and it will be here tomorrow unless you do something about it today. _____

6. If my secretary has not called you yet, please call her and schedule a 45 minute consultation. _____

7. This communication is to notify you that your results to your blood chemistry are normal. _____

8. The patient drinks several beers a day and occasionally a cigar or cigarette. _____

9. Hot compresses to the right hand. _____

10. Hygiene was carefully enforced. _____

*Translate these abbreviations and symbols using a medical dictionary or appendix.*

1. SC _____
2. SGPT _____
3. TB _____
4. ad lib _____
5. po _____
6. ADH _____
7. a.u. _____
8. BMR _____
9. BS _____
10. IV _____
11. ECHO _____
12. RBC _____
13. TPR _____
14. ROS _____
15. ESR _____
16. WBC _____
17. ELISA _____
18. GERD _____
19. GI _____
20. ⇌ _____

*Write either S for subjective, O for objective, or N if neither:*

1. Pt. c/o pain in the epigastric region _____
2. H&H lower this wk _____
3. TIA ten yrs ago _____
4. Dx: COLD _____
5. States Hx of COPD _____

*Translate the following and label O only if the statement is objective information:*

1. Pt. to go to P.T. via wheelchair q.o.d. _____

2. Pt. appears cyanotic. _____

3. Apply ice to the ankle for 24 hrs. _____

4. T-101° F _____

5. Pt. c/o sore throat. _____

*Write the symbol for these words:*

1. greater than _____

2. tablet _____

3. female _____

4. primary _____

5. right _____

6. left _____

7. without _____

8. of each _____

9. approximately _____

10. before _____

*Circle the correctly spelled word in each line:*

| | | | |
|---|---|---|---|
| 1. chemotherputic | chemotherapeutic | chemotheraputic | chemotherapuetic |
| 2. dihiscence | dehiscence | dehisence | dehissence |
| 3. evisceration | evicseration | evisserration | eviseraetion |
| 4. difusion | diffussion | diffusion | difuesion |
| 5. intoxcication | intoxsication | intoxecation | intoxication |
| 6. narcopsy | narrcolepsy | narkolepsy | narcolepsy |
| 7. dysplasia | dyspaysia | dysplaysia | displasia |
| 8. imunoglobulins | inmunoglobulins | immunoglobulins | immunoglobbulins |
| 9. incontenence | incontinence | incontanence | incontonance |
| 10. asessment | asesment | assessment | assesment |

*Translate medical abbreviations using a medical dictionary or appendix.*

1. sed. rt. _____

2. SOB _____

3. stat _____

4. Sx _____

5. sp. gr. _____

6. t.i.d. _____

7. TURP _____

8. U/A _____

9. URI _____

10. UTI _____

# Comprehensive Review

*Translate the abbreviations and symbols, and then construct them into complete sentences.*

1. Pt. arrived in PACU @ 13:10, V.S. stable T 98, BP 130/80, P 70, R 24.

_____

_____

_____

2. Lungs clear, no drg., pain level 5/10, no c/o N/V.

_____

_____

_____

3. PERRLA, IV infusing well @50ml/hr, EKG taken.

_____

_____

_____

# CHAPTER 6

# Punctuation

PRACTICAL WRITING COMPONENT:
MEDICAL REPORTS—HISTORY
AND PHYSICAL, CONSULTATION

## OBJECTIVES

*Upon completion of this chapter, the learner should be able to:*

❖ apply the appropriate punctuation marks to the ends of sentences

❖ recognize when to use periods other than at the ends of sentences

❖ use internal sentence punctuation correctly

❖ understand when to use parentheses, dashes, hyphens, apostrophes, italics, and quotation marks

❖ spell various medical terms

❖ translate various medical abbreviations and symbols

❖ recognize reports: history and physical, consultation

The purpose of punctuation is to make the written message easier to read and understand. To understand the importance of punctuation, read the following paragraph out loud:

> *Health-care professionals often work in teams a team that is committed to the task and makes full use of its members talents can achieve high levels of performance cooperation is needed for success in a spirit of cooperation people recognize the benefits of helping one another no one person has all the answers but each person has a piece of the puzzle once the pieces are shared the larger picture is clear and possible solutions are easier members need to feel that they are important and that they have something to contribute they claim ownership when they have a share in making decisions carrying out policies or solving problems members must trust and have confidence in one another trust is built when there is an atmosphere of honesty fairness sensitivity and respect a trusting environment helps members to feel comfortable enough to share their talents and reveal their opinions people who benefit most from high quality performance are the patients*

The previous paragraph shows how difficult it is to make sense out of a text when punctuation is missing. Knowing how to use punctuation correctly is a crucial skill, especially for medical assistants. Doctors who dictate information often do not include punctuation. Punctuation makes sentences clearer, and good writing requires it.

# Punctuation

The period, question mark, and exclamation point are referred to as end punctuation because they come at the ends of sentences. They mark the end of a complete thought.

## THE PERIOD

A period is used at the end of a declarative sentence that makes a statement. A period is also used at the end of an imperative sentence that gives a command. In both cases, think about the period as a stop sign.

## Examples

*Bradycardia indicates a low pulse.*

*Prepare the patient for a gastrointestinal (GI) exam.*

*Follow the doctor's orders.*

*Schedule an appointment for next week.*

### Other Uses for the Period

Use a period to separate dollars and cents and whole numbers with decimals (decimal point). Do not use a period after whole numbers not accompanied by decimal fractions.

## Examples

| | | | |
|---|---|---|---|
| *$6.50* | *3.50 mm* | *0.43 cm* | *$25 (not $25.00)* |
| *1290* | *16* | *21* | |

Use a period after most abbreviations.

## Examples

| | | | | | | | | |
|---|---|---|---|---|---|---|---|---|
| *Mr.* | *Mrs.* | *Ms.* | *Rev.* | *Sr.* | *Dr.* | *B.S.* | *B.A.* | *M.S.* |
| *M.Ed.* | *Ph.D.* | *Esq.* | *John F. Smith* | | *J.F. Smith* | *Jr.* | | |
| *a.m.* | *St.* | *Co.* | *Corp.* | | | | | |

Medically related abbreviations may appear in upper or lower case and with or without a period. Do not use periods with measurements.

## Examples

| | | | | | | |
|---|---|---|---|---|---|---|
| *i.e.* | *etc.* | *et al.* | *cf.* | *b.i.d.* | *a.c.* | *h.s.* |
| *mm* | *cm* | *kg* | *ml* | *l* | *gl* | *mcg* | *mg* | *oz* | *ft* |

A period is not placed after state abbreviations, zip codes, or acronyms. Acronyms are made up of the first letters in a series of words. They are sometimes pronounced as words.

## Examples

Boston, *MA*    *OH*    *CT*    *FL*    Douglas, *MA 01516*

*AMA*    *AAMA*    *CABG*    *AARP*    *OSHA*    *SIDS*

A period follows the letters and numbers in list or outline enumerations.

## Examples

1. Nouns
2. Pronouns
3. Verbs

  I. Medical Reports
    A. History and Physical
    B. Pathology
    C. Discharge Summary

## THE QUESTION MARK

A question mark is used after a direct question.

## Examples

*Where is the pain?*

*What is the diagnosis?*

*How much medication was ordered?*

*Do you know what the cure is for that disease?*

*"When can I go home?" asked the patient.*

## THE EXCLAMATION POINT

Use the exclamation point after a sentence that expresses strong feelings.

## Examples

*Ouch!*    *Call security!*

*CPR STAT!*    *Congratulations!*

*What a wonderful way to stay healthy!*

# Practice 6-1

*Place the appropriate punctuation marks at the ends of these sentences:*

1. The trachea functions as a passageway for air to reach the lungs

2. The symptoms are fever and headache

3. Is pruritus recorded as an objective symptom

4. The portion of the H&P where the physician uses hands and fingers during an examination is called palpation

5. The embolus traveled to the lungs

# The Comma

Within sentences, the comma is the most frequently used punctuation mark. It is also the punctuation mark that causes the most difficulty. Errors fall into two extreme categories: Commas are either disregarded, or they are used too frequently. The main purpose of the comma is to group words that belong together and separate words that do not. A comma also represents a brief pause when reading. The best rule to follow about commas is not to use it unless there is a reason to do so.

**RULE 1:** The comma is used to separate three or more items in a series.

## Examples

*Coryza, cough, and sore throat* are common in the winter.

Influenza is characterized by the sudden onset of *chills, headache, and myalgia.*

The five stages of grieving are *denial, anger, bargaining, depression, and acceptance.*

If items in a series are each linked by *and* or *or*, a comma is not used.

## Examples

The four blood types are A *and* B *and* AB *and* O.

You could give 10 mg *or* 20 mg *or* 40 mg of Demerol I.M. for the pain.

**RULE 2:** Use a comma to separate two or more adjectives that describe the same noun.

## Examples

*Purulent, rusty-colored sputum* was taken to the lab for testing.

The x-ray revealed *numerous, questionable nodules.*

**RULE 3:** A comma is used between two independent clauses joined by coordinating conjunctions (*and, but, or, nor, for, so, yet*).

## Examples

Medicare is administered by the Social Security Administration, *but the public welfare office handles Medicaid.*

Patients usually recover rapidly from influenza, *yet some patients experience lassitude for weeks.*

**RULE 4**: Place a comma between the day and year. If a date is used in a sentence, a comma goes between the year and the rest of the sentence.

## Examples

*February 28, 2009*

On *February 28, 2009,* the hospital will review its policies.

**RULE 5**: Use a comma between the city and state. When the city and state are used in a sentence, a comma is placed after the state.

## Examples

*Boston, Massachusetts*

Anesthesia was first discovered in *Boston, Massachusetts,* at Massachusetts General Hospital.

The American Association of Medical Assistants and the American Medical Association are located in *Chicago, IL.*

**RULE 6**: Use a comma to separate numbers that have four or more digits.

*3,000     30,000     300,000     3,000,000*

Exceptions include addresses and year numbers of four digits.

The address is *3600* Main Street.

**RULE 7**: Use a comma to separate appositives, nouns of direct address, titles that follow a person's name, and introductory words from the rest of the sentence.

## Examples

*Doctor,* please listen carefully to what I have to say.

Please listen carefully, *Doctor,* to what I have to say.

*Yes,* you may have a regular diet.

*However,* I do think you will have to curtail your intake of cholesterol.

A decrease in total dietary fat will help, *however.*

Dr. Villes, *a pathologist,* graduated from a medical school in Burlington, VT.

The pathologist, *Norm Villes, M.D.,* graduated from a medical school in Burlington, VT.

**RULE 8**: Use a comma to separate clauses and phrases that are unnecessary to the meaning of a sentence (nonessential, or nonrestrictive, clauses and phrases).

## Examples

The hospital, *unlike most facilities,* has a comprehensive evacuation plan. [*Unlike most facilities* is not necessary to the meaning of the sentence.]

The hourly pay, *in some circumstances,* increases over a period of time. [The sentence still makes sense when *in some circumstances* is omitted.]

Programs, *which are available on request,* are free of charge.

**RULE 9:** A comma follows the salutation in a friendly letter and the complementary close.

## Examples

*Dear Friend,   Hello,   Bill,*

*Yours truly,   Sincerely,   Best regards,*

**RULE 10:** Separate parenthetical expressions with a comma, depending on where they are placed in the sentence. Parenthetical expressions include

| | | | |
|---|---|---|---|
| *I believe (think, hope, see, etc.)* | | *I am sure* | *on the contrary* |
| *on the other hand* | *after all* | *by the way* | *incidentally* |
| *in fact* | *indeed* | *naturally* | *of course* |
| *in my opinion* | *for example* | *however* | *nonetheless* |
| *to tell the truth* | | | |

## Examples

The surgery was successful. *Therefore,* there is no need of further treatment.

The report, *I hope,* will give you many options about treatments.

The signs and symptoms, *in my opinion,* are indicative of angina pectoris.

An inadequate supply of oxygen to the myocardium, *for example,* is caused by arteriosclerosis.

**RULE 11:** Use a comma to separate a direct quotation.

## Examples

The doctor said, *"You must give up smoking."*

*"I really don't have the courage,"* the patient replied.

*"In that case,"* the doctor continued, *"you sign your own death warrant."*

**RULE 12:** A comma is used to set off contrasting statements that are introduced by the words *not, rather,* and *though.*

## Examples

Right now, *rather* than later, increase the medication.

I would describe her mood as thoughtful, *not* sullen.

*Punctuate these sentences:*

1. The divisions of the vertebrae are cervical thoracic lumbar sacral and coccygeal

2. A tickler file is a reference system of call-back appointment dates and future events

3. Prior to antibiotics her sinusitis caused headaches

4. The symptoms are vomiting drowsiness shock pallor diaphoresis and liver tenderness

5. The patient with the CABG needs blood work

6. The patient is instructed to wash the skin avoid scrubbing and keep hands away from the face

7. I don't believe it

8. The patient replied "I don't want my family to know"

9. Is there a history of myocardial infarctions in the family

10. After July 15 send my mail to Albany NY 02863

# The Semicolon

The semicolon is a punctuation mark that is stronger than a comma; that is, it indicates a more definite break in the flow of a sentence. Semicolons join items that are grammatically alike or closely related.

RULE 1: A semicolon is used instead of a comma and a coordinating conjunction (*and, but, or, nor, for, yet, so*) to separate two independent clauses.

## Examples

The physician shall respect the law; he shall recognize the responsibility to change any law that is contrary to the best interest of the patient.

Almost all victims of violence go to emergency centers; many have no health insurance.

Many people are homeless because they were discharged from a mental institution; most are without proper follow-up health care.

If a coordinating conjunction is present, commas are used to separate independent clauses. The clauses can also be rewritten as two sentences.

## Examples

The cost of health care in the U.S. is out of control; 37 million have no health insurance and 35 million are underinsured.

The cost of health care in the U.S. is out of control, yet 37 million have no health insurance and 35 million are underinsured.

The cost health care in the U.S. is out of control. Thirty-seven million have no health insurance and thirty-five million are underinsured.

**RULE 2:** Use a semicolon between independent clauses when the second clause begins with a transitional expression such as:

| | | |
|---|---|---|
| *for example* | *for instance* | *otherwise* |
| *that is* | *besides* | *therefore* |
| *accordingly* | *moreover* | *consequently* |
| *nevertheless* | *furthermore* | *however* |
| *instead* | *hence* | *namely* |

## Examples

Every medical office has its unique pathology format; *however,* the data required is the same.

The arterial blood gas reports are good; *therefore,* we can begin the process of weaning from the ventilator.

The cardiac rate was rapid and regular; *consequently,* there are no extrasystoles.

The patient was afebrile after admission; *nevertheless,* he became febrile with recurrent episodes of pain in the left side of the chest.

**Note:** A comma sets off one independent clause: "*The medical report is completed,* all ten pages." A semicolon sets off two independent clauses: "The medical report is completed; mail it first class."

**RULE 3:** Use a semicolon with a series of items that have one or more commas.

## Examples

Those present at the meeting were Dr. M. P. Carr, my family physician; Mrs. P. Archy, my lawyer; Bob, my husband; and Valerie, my daughter.

I sent copies to Burlington, Vermont; Concord, New Hampshire; and Boston, Massachusetts.

# Practice 6-3

*Punctuate these sentences:*

1. I wanted a response from Dr. Ville a forensic pathologist from Boston but as of today I have received none

2. Call Dr. Sarah the surgeon Kim Yonta the lawyer and Chris Ville the medical insurance representative

3. Val visited the medical library on Tuesday she also did further research on Saturday

4. The importance of determining the comparability of the two drug groups is evident for example eleven deaths are due to surgery five to acute myocardial infarction and six to embolic complications

5. Some redness pain and swelling appeared in the right ankle consequently ice packs were applied

# The Colon

The colon is a sign that more information follows. The information may be expressed in a series of words, phrases, or clauses.

**RULE 1:** A colon is used to introduce a list or series of items.

## Examples

The pathology report consists of the following; the patient's name, medical record number, tissues submitted, findings, impressions, and possible treatment.

The only explanations I can give are these: the patient didn't follow directions, forgot to take the medication, or stopped taking it because of side effects.

I made a list of the things we need: forceps, 4-0 catgut sutures, gauze sponges, and surgical scissors.

I made a list of the things we need:

1. forceps

2. 4-0 catgut sutures

3. gauze sponges

4. surgical scissors

**RULE 2:** A colon is not used if a verb or preposition immediately precedes a series of items. Whatever precedes a colon should be a complete sentence.

# Examples

The health team consists *of* physicians, nurses, a physical therapist, and a nurse aide. [preposition]

We *need* forceps, 4-0 catgut sutures, gauze sponges, and suture scissors. [verb]

RULE 3: A colon is used between hours and minutes to express time.

6:15          8:30 a.m.          8 a.m. (Do not use zeros for on-the-hour time.)

RULE 4: A colon is used in business letters.


# Examples

Dear Dr. Villes:

To Whom It May Concern:

Re: Medical Report #1234235

C: President Vernon
Valerie Christopher

# Practice 6-4

*Punctuate these sentences:*

1. SOCIAL HISTORY The patient neither smokes nor drinks

2. Is my appointment at 11 30 or 1 30

3. Many medical assistants were at the Cancer Conference Chris Luke John Valerie and Sarah

4. Tissues involved

   1 Node from the left lung

   2 Right mediastinal nodes

   3 Carina

   4 Left lung

5. Discharge diagnoses

   A Excision of benign cyst of left lung

   B Emphysema

   C Klebsiella pneumoniae infection

6. Fibrous tissue extending out from the vitreous was covered with many vessels

7. To Whom It May Concern

8. Digitalis therapy was begun because of dyspnea chest pain and swelling of the legs

9. The cases were arterial insufficiency diabetes gangrene glomerulonephritis and anemia

10. Marked interstitial edema was present with diffuse mononuclear infiltrate composed of lymphocytes and plasma

# Parentheses

**RULE 1:** Parentheses surround information that is added but unnecessary and unrelated to the main thought of the sentence.

## Example

The nurses from the second floor *(Lisa, Kurt, Nancy, and Ramon)* make a great team.

**RULE 2:** Parentheses are used around an abbreviation or acronym that follows the spelled out version, or vice versa.

## Examples

The medical assistant *(MA)* is responsible for typing the report.

OSHA *(Occupational Health and Safety Association)* provides valuation information to hospitals.

**RULE 3:** Use parentheses around numerals or italic letters that designate enumerations of list items within a sentence.

## Examples

The instructions are *(a)* more fluids, *(b)* A.S.A. 2 tabs prn, and *(c)* bedrest.

The instructions are (1) more fluids, (2) A.S.A. 2 tabs prn, and (3) bedrest.

# The Dash

The purpose of the dash (—) is to set off unnecessary items from the rest of the sentence. The reason for using the dash, rather than any other punctuation mark, is to give more emphasis to words. The dash may be applied singly or in pairs. However, it is rarely seen in medical documentation.

## Examples

I have 30 years—*very rewarding ones*—of medical practice.

The forms are to be written exclusively by physicians—*not nurses, not therapists, not social workers, and not aides.*

# The Hyphen

The hyphen is covered in Chapter 7, under "Predicate and Compound Adjectives." Because punctuation is so important in medical documentation, a short introduction is included here.

**RULE 1:** Use a hyphen between compound words used as an adjective when the adjective precedes the noun.

## Examples

| | | |
|---|---|---|
| *all-day* surgery | *102-year-old* man | *grayish-black* tissue |
| *follow-up* | *one-by-one* | |

A *well-developed, well-nourished* young man.

A *34-year-old* male was admitted to the West Wing.

When a compound modifier follows the noun, it is not hyphenated.

The young man was *well developed*.

Compound words that have become commonly used are not hyphenated.

| | | |
|---|---|---|
| *earache* | *gallbladder* | *nosebleed* |

**RULE 2:** Use a hyphen with numbers 21 to 99 and with written fractions.

*thirty-five days ago*          *one-third of the hospital rooms*

**RULE 3:** Use a hyphen with a prefix added to a word that begins with a capital letter.

*mid-March*          *un-American*

**RULE 4:** Some adjective forms are always hyphenated, whether before or after the nouns they modify.

*self-conscious*          *cross-referenced*

**RULE 5:** Use a hyphen in some compound words used as nouns.

*mother-in-law*     *check-up*     *work-up*     *ex-employer*

Always consult the dictionary when in doubt about hyphenation.

# The Apostrophe

Another punctuation mark often used in medical reporting is the apostrophe. An apostrophe is used to show ownership (referred to as the possessive form of a noun).

The apostrophe was covered in detail in Chapter 2 in Figure 2-5.

# Italics

Italic print is used for emphasis, words used as terms, or words used as words. If italic print is not available, underlining is used.

## Examples

All surgical equipment *must* be sterilized before use.

The term *officious* could be applied to his tone in the letter.

*Friendly* and *polite* are not synonymous.

Italics are also used in the following instances:

- Titles of books, magazines, and newspapers

*New England Journal of Medicine*

*New York Times*                    Gray's Anatomy

*Lancet*                            *Taber's Cyclopedic Medical Dictionary*

Harvard Health Letter          *JAMA*

- Movies, television, radio, plays, and operas

Mozart's Requiem

Did you watch *ER* on television last night?

- Foreign expressions

*mea culpa*: my fault

*fait accompli*: carried out with success

respondeat superior: "Let the master answer."

*res ipsa loquitur*: "Let the thing speak for itself."

- All biological names

*Clostridium difficile*              Staphylococcus aureus

*Streptococcus pyogenes*           *Escherichia coli*

Pseudomonas aeruginosa          *Salmonella enteritidis*

*Haemophilus influenza*            *Campylobacter jejuni*

# Quotation Marks

Quotation marks are used to enclose the exact words of the speaker. Quotations are often used when it is necessary to quote the exact words of the patient or a family member.

## Examples

Robert said, "*I have pain in my chest.*" [The period goes inside the quotation mark.]

"*I go to physical therapy at 3 p.m.,*" said Sheila. [The comma goes inside the quotation mark.]

"*Take the patient to room 205,*" Robert said, "*while I bring the chart to the desk.*" [Note the interruption of the quotation.]

"*What was the FBS?*" asked Dr. Oberg. [Note the question mark inside the quotation mark.]

"*I would advise caution,*" said the physician, "*because your condition is serious.*"

Quotation marks are also used to enclose a part of a completed published work or to indicate that words or phrases are being used in a special way.

## Examples

Chapter 9 is titled "Punctuation."

The title of the seminar is "Stress Management."

Write "confidential" on the envelope.

**Practice 6-5**

*Punctuate these sentences:*

1. The chapter entitled Punctuation is the most important chapter in the book.

2. Quick said John get the defibrilator!

3. We got the article out of the New England Journal of Medicine.

4. The vertebrae are composed of thirty three bony segments.

5. Yogurt is a form of curdled milk caused by Lactobacillus bulgaricus.

6. The preoperative medication is due forty five minutes before surgery.

7. The side effects of the medication are 1 headaches 2 possible vomiting and 3 diarrhea.

8. The speaker was very self conscious.

9. Yellow fever is caused by the bite of the female mosquito Aedes aegypti.

10. JAMA and the Lancet published the study.

# Punctuation Summary

**Period***

| | |
|---|---|
| After a statement | You looked better after your treatments. |
| With abbreviations | Dr. R. Williams    a.m.    $50 |
| Not with abbreviations of measurements | 3.5 mm    ft    gal |

* The period, question mark, and exclamation point are referred to as end punctuation because they come at the ends of sentences.

**Question Mark**

| | |
|---|---|
| After a question | At what time is the operation scheduled? |
| | How old were you on your last birthday? |

**Exclamation Point**

| | |
|---|---|
| After an exclamatory sentence | Your house is on fire! |
| | Get help in here right away! |

**Comma:** Used to group words that belong together, separate words that do not belong together, and provide a brief pause.

| | |
|---|---|
| In a series | The recovery rooms are painted in aqua, light blue, lavendar, and white. |
| Between two adjectives before a noun | A confidant, trustworthy nurse is hard to find. |
| | I'm looking for an inexpensive, comfortable car. |
| Before *and, but, or, nor, yet* following an independent clause | I have good medical coverage, but it expires when I leave my job. |
| Around unnecessary clauses and phrases | Computers, used correctly, can save time. To the best of my knowledge, the situation no longer exists. |
| | Looking ahead, we can prepare for the event. |
| Following introductory elements | Well, we can do it again to make sure. |
| Around parenthetical expressions | In fact, I did pass with honors. |
| Around appositives | If you believe that, John, you can believe anything. |

Other uses

| | |
|---|---|
| Following the salutation of a friendly letter | Dear Mom, |
| Following a complimentary close | Sincerely yours, |
| Between city and state | Chicago, Illinois 68594 |
| Between date and year | October 11, 20XX |
| To separate quotations | "I came by car," replied the salesman. |
| In numbers of four or more digits | 600,000 |
| Preceding a title after a person's name | Dr. William Borden, Ph.D. |

**Semicolon:** Used to indicate a more definite break than a comma in the flow of a sentence and to join items that are grammatically alike or closely related.

| | |
|---|---|
| Between independent clauses not joined by a coordinating conjunction (*and, but, or*) | I saw red; I was so angry. |
| Between independent clauses joined by *however, hence, that is, therefore,* etc. | Computers are faster; therefore, use them for scheduling appointments. |

| Separating elements in a series that contain commas | Cities and countries participating are Rome, Italy; London, England; and Ottawa, Canada. |

**Colon:** Used to indicate that more information is coming.

| Preceding a series, list, or outline that is introduced by a complete sentence. | Consider the following: less expensive, better quality, and good returns on investment. |
| Between minutes and hours in expressions of time | 9:15 p.m. |
| Following the salutation of a business letter | Dear Mr. President: |

**Parentheses:** Used to mark off explanations.

| Around added information unrelated to the main thought | The physicians (all eight of them) donated services to the needy. |
| Around words added to clarify the sentence | The AMA (American Medical Association) is a powerful organization. |
| Around numbers or letters that designate enumerations of list items within a sentence | The best things to do are (1) take a fever reducer, (2) get plenty of rest, and (3) drink a lot of fluids. |

**Dash:** Used to set off unnecessary items from the rest of the sentence.

| Adds emphasis | She won the prize—a trip to Disney World. |

**Hyphen:** Used between elements of compound words or numbers and to divide words into syllables.

| Compound words, syllables | state-of-the-art equipment |
| With written numbers 21 to 99 | twenty-five years ago |
| In written fractions | one-half the population |
| Between a prefix and the base word | un-American |
| | self-explanatory |

**Apostrophe:** Used to show ownership.

| Forms the possessive | Singular: patient's disease, boss's policy |
| | Plural: patients' diseases, bosses' policies |

**Italics:** Used in place of an underline to point out or emphasize.

| For names of books, magazines, works of art, biological names, foreign expressions | I subscribe to the *PMA*. |
| | *E. coli* is normal flora in the G.I. tract. |

**Quotation marks:** Used to enclose the exact words of a speaker.

| Around a direct quotation | The doctor said, "Be sure to take your medication." |

| | |
|---|---|
| Around all segments of an interrupted quotation | "Be sure to take your medicine," said the doctor, "or you won't get well." |
| Around parts of published works | The article "The Pathology of Germs" can be found on the Internet. |
| Around words or phrases used in a special way | The president's diagnosis was so "confidential" that even reporters weren't aware of it. |

# Medical Spelling

*Become familiar with the spelling of the following words:*

| | |
|---|---|
| afebrile | myalgia |
| anesthesia | myocardium |
| angina | neuromuscular |
| arteriosclerosis | nodules |
| buccal | norepinephrine |
| cholesterol | opaque |
| curette | papilla |
| defibrillator | penicillin |
| digitalis | percussion |
| earache | purulent |
| embolus | Salmonella |
| febrile | Staphylococcus |
| filtration | Streptococcus |
| forceps | tracheostomy |
| hematology | thrombus |
| infiltrate | ventilate |
| insufficiency | vitreous |
| interstitial | well-developed |
| Kaposis' sarcoma | well-nourished |
| keratitis | Xylocaine |

As shown in the first part of this chapter, punctuation marks (. ? ! , ; : ' " ") can either clarify or confuse the meaning of a sentence or abbreviation. To misplace one of these small but important symbols can create confusion or frustration for the reader; just think of what might happen if your bank misplaced a comma or decimal point in your account records!

For this reason, punctuation marks must be given special attention in all forms of medical writing. Medical reports, such as a history and physical report, are just one example of medical writing in which punctuation is key to understanding.

# History and Physical Reports

A history and physical (H&P) report is usually dictated after a new patient is admitted to a hospital or comes to a clinic, office, or health facility. The H&P is a collection of data about past events in relation to a patient's present illness. Its purpose is to aid in understanding the whole patient, past and present, in order to form a treatment plan based on how the patient can be helped in the future.

The format of the report varies from place to place and is usually generated by the medical facility's Form Committee. Regardless of the format, however, the type of information sought is universal.

The historical component is an account of the patient's systems and organs based on information rooted in the past, such as family and social histories, previous hospitalizations or treatments, allergies, chronic illness, and the patient's chief complaints. The physical component of the H&P is not historical. It is the physician's current evaluation of the patient's systems and organs.

A sample H&P follows:

---

**HISTORY AND PHYSICAL EXAMINATION (H&P)**

**Patient Name:** Roger Parks

**Hospital No.:** 11009

**Room No.:** 812

**Date of Admission:** 12/01/20XX

**Admitting Physician:** Steven Benard, M.D.

**Admitting Diagnosis:** Rule out appendicitis.

CHIEF COMPLAINT: Abdominal pain.

HISTORY OF PRESENT ILLNESS: The patient is a 31-year-old white man with acute onset of right lower quadrant pain waking him up from sleep at approximately 3 a.m. on the morning of admission. The pain worsened throughout the day, radiating to his back and becoming associated with dry heaves. The patient states that the pain is constant and is worsened by walking or movement. The patient states his last bowel movement was on the previous evening and was normal. The patient is anorectic. He also gives a 1-year history of lower abdominal colicky pain associated with diarrhea. He was seen by his local medical doctor and given a diagnosis of irritable bowel syndrome; however, the pain is worse tonight and is unlike his previous bouts of abdominal pain. The patient also has had associated fever and chills to date.

PAST HISTORY: SURGICAL: No previous operations.

ILLNESSES: None. Hospitalization for epididymitis 10 years ago. He is ALLERGIC TO PENICILLIN. It makes him bloated.

MEDICATIONS: None.

SOCIAL HISTORY: Carpenter. Lives with his wife and two children. He does not drink or smoke.

FAMILY HISTORY: Insignificant for familial inflammatory bowel disease except for the fact that his mother has colonic polyps. Father living and well. No siblings.

REVIEW OF SYSTEMS: Noncontributory.

PHYSICAL EXAMINATION: This is a 31-year-old white man with knees raised to his abdomen and complaining of severe pain. VITAL SIGNS: Admission temperature 99.6F; four hours after admission it was 102.6F. HEENT: Normocephalic, atraumatic, EOMs intact, negative icterus, conjunctivae pink. NECK: Supple. No adenopathy or bruits noted. CHEST: Clear to auscultation and percussion. CARDIAC: Regular rate and rhythm. No murmurs noted. Peripheral pulses 2+ and symmetrical. ABDOMEN: Bowel sounds initially positive but diminished. He has positive cough reflex, positive heel tap, and positive rebound tenderness. The pain is definitely worse in his RLQ. RECTAL: Heme negative. Tenderness toward the RLQ. Normal prostate. Normal male genitalia. EXTREMITIES: No clubbing, cyanosis, or edema. NEUROLOGIC: Nonfocal.

LABORATORY DATA: Hemoglobin 14.6, hematocrit 43.6, and 13,000 WBCs. Sodium 138, potassium 3.8, chloride 105, $CO_2$ 24, BUN 10, creatinine 0.9, and glucose 102. Amylase was 30. UA completely negative. LFTs within normal limits. Alkaline phosphatase 78, GGT 9, SGOT 39, GPT 12, bilirubin 0.9. Flat plate and upright films of the abdomen revealed localized abnormal gas pattern in right lower quadrant. No evidence of free air.

ASSESSMENT: Rule out appendicitis. Some concern of whether this could be an exacerbation of developing inflammatory bowel disease. Due to the patient's history, increasing temperature, and localizing symptoms to his right lower quadrant, the patient needs surgical intervention to rule out appendicitis.

—————————————

Steven Benard, M.D.

SB:xx

D:12/01/20XX

T:12/01/20XX

M.A. Novak and P.A. Ireland, *Hillcrest Medical Center Beginning Medical Transcription Course*, 6th ed. Albany, NY: Delmar Thomson Learning, 2005, pp. 16–17.

# Consultation Report

When a consultation has been requested to obtain a second opinion on a problem or diagnosis, a consultation report is prepared for the referring physician. It contains such data as present medical history, x-ray and lab results, and the consulted physician's impressions, recommendations, evaluations, diagnoses, and treatment.

Promptness in providing information is very important. The consultation report format may be a letter or a specially prepared form with the date and reason for consultation.

It is also proper to include a thank you for the referral. The report is dictated by the consulting physician and transcribed in the medical office or through outside services.

A sample consultation report follows:

---

**REQUEST FOR CONSULTATION**

**Patient Name:** Marty Gibbs

**Hospital No.:** 11532

**Consultant:** Patrick O'Neill, M.D., Plastic Surgery

**Requesting Physician:** Diane Houston, M.D., Internal Medicine

**Date:** 11/25/20XX

**Reason for Consultation:** Please evaluate extent of burn injuries.

BURNING AGENT: Coals in fire pit.

I have been asked to see this 5-year-old Caucasian male who appears in mild distress due to upper extremity burn after having fallen into hot coals in his back yard.

Using the Lund Browder chart,[4] the severity of burn is first and second degree. The total body surface area burned includes right lower arm 3%, right hand 1%. The joints involved include the right elbow, right wrist, right hand.

TREATMENT PLAN:   Splinting right hand.

Positioning: Elevation with splint on.

Range of motion: Good mobility.

Pressure therapy: Will follow for induration, for pressure fracture.

GOALS:   1.  Reduce risk of contractures of involved joints by positioning, splinting, and maintaining range of motion.

2.  Reduce scar tissue formation by using Jobst bandages, pressure therapy, and splinting.

3.  Obtain maximum mobility and strength of upper extremities.

4.  Maximize independence in activities of daily living. Activity as tolerated.

5.  Provide patient and family education regarding high-calorie, high-protein diet.

Thank you for asking me to see this delightful boy. I will follow him at the burn clinic in 2 weeks.

_____

Patrick O'Neill, M.D.

PO:xx

D:11/25/20XX

T:11/28/20XX

[4]See page 221: The Lund Browder Chart.

---

M.A. Novak and P.A. Ireland, *Hillcrest Medical Center Beginning Medical Transcription Course*, 6th ed. Albany, NY: Delmar Thomson Learning, 2005, pp. 21–22.

# Medical Reports Summary

| | |
|---|---|
| History and Physical | A report containing data about past events in relation to a patient's present illness. |
| Consultation | A report containing data such as present medical history, x-ray, lab results, consulted physician's impressions, recommendations, evaluations, diagnoses, and treatments. |

# Skills Review

*Punctuate these sentences if necessary:*

1. Because new drugs are pure chemicals they are dispensed by weight

2. Four common routes of antibiotic are intravenous intramuscular oral and local

3. If you do not receive your raise by the first of the year be sure to inform the personnel department

4. Objects should never be placed inside a cast to relieve itching relief comes by applying a cold pack over the cast where the itch is located

5. A patient is instructed on how to care for the cast limit activities use devices such as crutches or a cane and perform prescribed exercises

6. Coryza is a general term for a cold or inflammation of the respiratory mucous membranes

7. OTC medications are available for cough headache and fever

8. The large intestines are about 1.5 m long and are divided into 4 parts the ascending the transverse the descending and the sigmoid colon

9. Diabetes meaning *passing through* is a general term for excessive urination and is usually referred to as diabetes mellitus

10. ADMITTING DIAGNOSIS Rule out cholecystitis cholelithiasis

*Punctuate and capitalize these sentences:*

Health care professionals often work in teams a team committed to the task makes full use of its members talents and can achieve high levels of performance cooperation is needed for success in a spirit of cooperation people recognize the benefits of helping one another no one person has all the answers but each person has a piece of the puzzle once the pieces are shared the larger picture is clear and possible solutions are easier members need to feel that they are important and that they have something to contribute they claim ownership when they have a share in making decisions carrying out policies or solving problems members must trust and have confidence in one another trust is built when there is an atmosphere of honesty fairness sensitivity and respect a trusting environment helps members to feel comfortable enough to share their talents and reveal their opinions people who benefit most from high quality performance are the patients.

# Skills Review

*Use "H&P" (history and physical) or "C" (consultation) to answer each statement.*

1. Usually requested to obtain a second opinion. _____

2. Dictated after a patient is admitted for a surgical procedure. _____

3. Prepared for the referring physician. _____

4. Current evaluation of the patient's systems and organs. _____

5. Specific knowledge about a system of the body. _____

*Circle the correctly spelled word in each line.*

| | | | |
|---|---|---|---|
| 1. ceratitis | keratitis | karatitis | kerratitis |
| 2. kolesterol | cholisterol | cholesterol | cholestirol |
| 3. interstitiol | interstichial | interstiel | interstitial |
| 4. myalgia | mialgia | myalgea | myolgia |
| 5. artiriosclerosis | arteriscelrosis | arteriosclerosis | arterioclerosis |
| 6. Strepcoccus | Stretcocucus | Steptococcus | Streptococcus |
| 7. bukkal | bucal | buccal | buccle |
| 8. insuficiency | insufficiency | insifficency | insphiciency |
| 9. Xylocaine | Xylocane | Xylicaine | Zylocaine |
| 10. pencillin | penicillin | penecillin | pinicilin |

*Translate these medical abbreviations using a medical dictionary or appendix.*

1. ung. _____

2. TIA _____

3. T&A _____

4. S/P _____

5. TMJ _____

6. t/o _____

7. ≈ _____

8. tinct _____

9. UE _____

10. + _____

# Comprehensive Review

*Rewrite, type, and punctuate the following paragraphs.*

John miller a 31 year old adult came into the office of dr beth winters on February 12 20XX at 815 complaining of acute abdominal pains the pains were exacerbated by any type of body movement the patient has a long history associated with diarrhea a condition diagnosed as irritable bowel syndrome the patient said the pain was unlike any previous troubles of abdominal pain

_____

_____

_____

_____

_____

_____

_____

_____

_____

_____

_____

a physical examination showed these factors 102° temperature and no adenopathy or bruits noted bowel sounds were initially positive but diminished films reveal localized abnormal gas pattern in the right lower quadrant

_____

_____

_____

_____

_____

_____

_____

# CHAPTER 7 *Adjectives*

## PRACTICAL WRITING COMPONENT: MEDICAL REPORTS—RADIOLOGY, PATHOLOGY, DISCHARGE SUMMARY AND OPERATIVE

**OBJECTIVES** *Upon completion of this chapter, the learner should be able to:*

❖ recognize and understand various types of adjectives

❖ be aware of adjective placement to ensure clearer sentences

❖ recognize suffixes that form descriptive adjectives

❖ use adjectives to make comparisons

❖ spell various medical terms

❖ translate various medical abbreviations

❖ recognize sentences that contain misplaced modifiers

❖ understand the use of eponyms in medical documentation

❖ describe reports: radiology, pathology, discharge summary, and operative

## Types of Adjectives

In previous chapters, three important parts of speech were explained: nouns, pronouns, and verbs. These words are important because the noun (or pronoun, which takes the place of a noun) and verb constitute the main part of a sentence. A sentence must have a noun or implied pronoun (*you*) as the subject and a verb in order to express a complete thought; otherwise, there is no sentence. However, additional words or parts of speech are used to make sentences clearer and more enjoyable to read and write. These additional words—adjectives and adverbs—complement, describe, add meaning to, or explain the noun and verb (Figure 7-1).

This chapter explains the part of speech called an adjective. (Adverbs are covered in Chapter 8.) An adjective is a word that describes a noun or pronoun. It adds to the

| Noun | Verb | Additional Clarifying Words |
|---|---|---|
| Nurses | observe | Nurses observe *reactions to treatments.* |
| Doctors | operate | Doctors operate in *emergency situations.* |
| He | speaks | He speaks *with authority about accreditation.* |
| MAs | transcribe | MAs transcribe *medical reports* |

**FIGURE 7-1** *Adding Meaning to Sentences*

meaning of the noun by giving more information about it. In the sentences that follow, notice how the adjectives further clarify the nouns they modify:

The *new* members of the team will arrive next week.

The doctor gives a *thorough* examination.

*Hospital* policies often require *legal* consultation.

These grades show knowledge of *body* systems.

Your *license* renewal is due *this* month.

## LIMITING ADJECTIVES

Adjectives describe four important facts about nouns and pronouns by answering the questions *which one? how many? how much?* and *what kind?* Adjectives that answer the first three questions are called limiting adjectives because they limit the nouns to a definite or indefinite amount. Common limiting adjectives are *a, an, all, any, both, each, every, few, many, more, most, much, no, some, such, this, that, these, those, the, one* (or any other number), and *possessive nouns* and *pronouns* used as adjectives.

## Examples

| | | |
|---|---|---|
| *some* diseases | *two* patients | *this* streptococcal |
| *many* meetings | *each* day | *the* myocardial infarction |
| *a* necrotic tumor | *an* exam | *my* medication |
| *our* office | *your* license | *their* medical records |

*All* pathological findings should be recorded.

*These* charts are going to the Medical Records Department.

*Their* system works best for that individual practice.

Adjectives that tell *what kind* are called descriptive adjectives and are covered in the next section.

## A and AN

*A* and *an* are limiting adjectives called indefinite articles. When deciding between the use of *a* or *an*, consider the sound of the word that follows the article rather than its spelling. The *a* is used before words that begin with a consonant sound, a long *u* (as in "university"), and an *o* with the sound of a *w* (as in "one"). The *an* is used before words that begin with all other vowel sounds. *The* is a limiting adjective called a definite article.

## Examples

| | | |
|---|---|---|
| *a* uric acid test | *a* cross-section | *an* inguinal hernia |
| *an* unsuccessful medication | *an* antidiuretic pill | *an* asset |
| *an* honor | *a* uniform | *an* eight-hour day |
| *an* abdominal incision | | |

### Singular and Plural

A limiting adjective must agree with the noun or pronoun it limits. Limiting adjectives used with singular nouns are *a, an, each, every, either, this, that, neither*, and *one*.

## Examples

| | | | |
|---|---|---|---|
| *an* order | *either* instrument | *neither* doctor | *one* calculus |
| *every* patient | *this* bed | *every* report | *each* stitch |

Limiting adjectives used with plural nouns are *few, several, many, these, those*, and *two* (or any number other than one).

## Examples

*These* reports need to be filed tomorrow.

*Several* reports must be transcribed by tomorrow morning.

The limiting adjectives *all, any*, and *some* can be either singular or plural.

| | | |
|---|---|---|
| *all* data | *some* information | *any* problems |

Some limiting adjectives may change into other parts of speech, depending on how they are used in a sentence. One example is the adjective *many*. It can be used as an adjective or a pronoun. If the word modifies a noun or pronoun, it is an adjective. If the word functions alone as a subject, direct object, indirect object, or object of a preposition, it is a pronoun.

## Examples

| | |
|---|---|
| Limiting Adjective | *Many* medical assistants are taking the certification exam. [*Many* describes the noun *assistants* and is used as an adjective.] |
| Pronoun | *Many* of the medical assistants are taking the certification exam. [*Many* is used alone as a subject pronoun.] |

## INTERROGATIVE AND PROPER ADJECTIVES

Two limiting adjectives, *which* and *what*, are called interrogative adjectives because they ask *direct* or *indirect* questions. In the first case, a question is asked directly by the person wanting the answer. An additional step is added with the *indirect* question. The question is asked for someone else. *Which* is used when the speaker wants someone to make a choice among alternatives.

## Examples

| | |
|---|---|
| Direct Questions | *What* time is it, Bill? |
| | *Which* room is available for the patient? |
| Indirect Questions | The nurse wants to know *which* hours she will be working. |
| | The nurse wants to know *what* time the doctor is expected. |

A proper adjective has its source within a proper noun, such as the word *Italian*, which comes from the proper noun *Italy*. Like the proper noun, the proper adjective begins with a capital letter.

| | | |
|---|---|---|
| *Italian* spaghetti | *Spanish* influence | *American* citizen |

Eponyms are also proper adjectives. An eponym comes from the surname of a person after which something is named, as in *Foley* catheter or *Mayo* scissors. Because eponyms are important in medical documentation, more information is provided in a separate section later in this chapter.

## PREDICATE AND COMPOUND ADJECTIVES

Adjectives may also be used as predicate adjectives. Like their noun counterparts, predicate adjectives come after *linking* verbs.

## Examples

Smoking is *dangerous* to your health. [*Dangerous* is in the predicate, follows the linking verb *is*, and describes the noun *smoking*.]

Health fairs are *educational*.

The word "compound" means to combine two or more elements. Compound adjectives combine two or more describing words that act as a single describer. When the compound adjective comes before the noun it describes, it is usually hyphenated for clarity. When the compound adjective comes after the noun it describes, a hyphen is not usually used.

## Examples

The hospital has *state-of-the-art* technology. [before the noun]

The technology at the hospital is *state of the art*. [after the noun]

She had *second-degree* burns on her upper extremities. [before]

The burns on her upper extremities were *second degree*. [after]

A number plus a noun of single measurement (*16-unit*) is hyphenated when it comes before the noun. The number and noun are not hyphenated when they follow a noun.

# Examples

The hospital is a *six-story* building.    The hospital has *six stories*.

The *one-inch* wound needed sutures.    The wound with sutures was *one inch*.

Fractions are hyphenated when they are spelled out:

*two-thirds, one-half*                    *Two-thirds* of the faculty were women.

Some frequently used adjectives are not hyphenated because they are considered one word.

childbirth        earache        nosebleed        painless

In a series of adjectives with the same root word, omit all but the last root word.

# Examples

Incorrect        The medicine will take 5-*bottle*, 10-*bottle*, and 12-*bottle* sizes.

Correct        The medicine will take 5-, 10-, and 12-*bottle* sizes.

Correct        The report will have a four- to six-*week* delay.

A comma is placed between two or more adjectives that express different concepts about the noun they describe.

# Examples

The *young, polite* intern expressed good bedside manners.

The ambulance was a *large, colorful* vehicle.

The ambulance was a *large, well-equipped* vehicle.

# Practice 7-1

*Choose the correct limiting adjective from within the parentheses:*

1. (Many, A) nurse works on the third floor.

2. (A, An) nurse likes to work on the first shift.

3. (One, Two) elevators are available for ambulatory patients.

4. The doctor ordered (these, this) medications a week ago.

5. (Several, Each) alarm goes off when the emergency door is opened.

*Hyphenate the adjectives where necessary.*

1. The laboratory uses state of the art technology.

2. The doctor made many off the record comments.

3. Mary's medical record is up to date.

4. Ready to wear uniforms are popular with nurses.

5. A well known physician will do the operation.

## DESCRIPTIVE ADJECTIVES

Descriptive adjectives modify nouns or pronouns by describing their characteristics or qualities. Descriptive adjectives are perhaps the easiest type of adjective to understand. They provide clarity by adding specifics about the nouns they describe.

## Examples

The *tall* nurse wore a *white* uniform.

The *streptococcal* infection spread through the *respiratory* system.

The *medical* assistant took the *patient's medical* history.

*Physical* assessment is an *essential* aspect of *medical* care.

The *Trendelenburg* position is used in cases of shock, in some *abdominal* surgery, and for patient's with *low blood* pressure.

Many descriptive adjectives have common endings or suffixes:

| Ending | Examples |
|---|---|
| *able* | cap*able*, reli*able* |
| *an* | Americ*an* |
| *ian* | Canad*ian* |
| *al* | cervic*al*, occipit*al*, or*al*, |
| *ant* | const*ant* |
| *eal* | periton*eal* |
| *ical* | patholog*ical* |
| *ar, ary, ent* | muscul*ar*, preval*ent*, pulmon*ary*, transi*ent*, independ*ent* |
| *ese, ful* | Chin*ese*, wonder*ful*, care*ful*, cheer*ful* |
| *iac* | card*iac*, cel*iac*, man*iac* |
| *ial* | influent*ial*, part*ial* |
| *ible, ic, tic* | leg*ible*, chron*ic*, epigastr*ic*, thorac*ic*, necro*tic*, hydrochlor*ic* |
| *ior* | infer*ior*, anter*ior*, super*ior* |
| *ive, ly* | posit*ive*, friend*ly*, comprehens*ive*, manipulat*ive* |
| *ous* | delici*ous*, muc*ous*, anxi*ous* |
| *oid, ose* | muc*oid*, epiderm*oid*, adip*ose* |
| *ual, y* | punct*ual*, tid*y*, chill*y* |

A noun may also be used as an adjective. Nouns become adjectives when they are used to describe other nouns.

## Examples

The *uniform* store went out of business. [The noun *uniform* becomes an adjective because it describes the noun *store*.]

The patient's *blood* pressure is rising slowly.

## Practice 7-2

*Identify the descriptive adjectives in each sentence*:

1. The nurse is a likeable and friendly person. _____

2. Clinical examination showed external bleeding. _____

3. Allied health professionals must be responsible employees. _____

4. General procedures should be followed for hospital admission. _____

5. Triangular bandages are used in first aid. _____

# Placement of Adjectives

The placement of adjectives in a sentence is important to its meaning. To write clearer sentences, place adjectives near the nouns they describe.

❖ Before the noun: The *doctor's* report was filed correctly. The patient had a *radical* mastectomy.

❖ After the noun: The report, *exceptional* in detail, provided the necessary information. The doctor, *alert* to physical signs, diagnosed the problem.

❖ After a linking verb: Just as there is a predicate noun, so, too, there is a predicate adjective. The predicate adjective is found after a linking verb and describes a subject noun or pronoun.

He is *apprehensive*. [*Apprehensive* describes the subject pronoun *he* and follows the linking verb *is*.]

Shock is *serious*. [*Serious* follows the word *is* and modifies the noun *shock*.]

❖ At the beginning of a sentence: *Alert* to physical signs, the doctor diagnosed the problem. *Paleness, perspiration*, and *dizziness* are some of the symptoms of this disease.

In a group of adjectives that contains a limiting adjective and one or more descriptive adjectives *that all modify the same noun*, place the limiting adjective first. If there is a noun adjective, it is placed immediately before the noun it modifies.

| Limiting Adjective | Descriptive Adjective | Noun Modified | |
|---|---|---|---|
| The | first aid | classes | begin tomorrow. |
| That | bleeding gunshot | wound | was an accident. |

# Modifiers and Placement

Modifiers enhance and clarify the meaning of a word. Place the modifier as close as possible to the word it modifies.

A misplaced modifier is out of place and does not modify the word it is meant to modify.

## Examples

The doctor had six patients *only* yesterday.

The doctor *only* had six patients yesterday.

The doctor had six patients yesterday *only*.

Consider these sentences with misplaced modifiers:

| | |
|---|---|
| Misplaced | A medical assistant almost completed all of her procedures. |
| Revised | A medical assistant completed almost all of her procedures. |
| Misplaced | The patient in her peritoneal cavity had fluid accumulations. |
| Revised | The patient had fluid accumulation in her peritoneal cavity. |
| Misplaced | An ambulance is parked behind the hospital which is out of emergency I.V. fluid. |
| Revised | An ambulance, which is out of emergency I.V. fluid, is parked behind the hospital. |
| Misplaced | Give the head injury the anesthetic. |
| Revised | Give the anesthetic to the patient with the head injury. |
| Misplaced | Here are some suggestions to improve your illness from the cardiologist. |
| Revised | Here are some suggestions from the cardiologist to improve your illness. |
| Misplaced | Demerol was received by the patient of 100 milligrams intramuscularly for the pain. |
| Revised | The patient received 100 milligrams of Demerol intramuscularly for the pain. |

Although many misplaced modifiers result in humor, some could have serious consequences, particularly in legal situations. The court often requests medical records in malpractice cases. Sentences open to various interpretations provide a field day in court that could result in high financial losses.

The way to detect misplaced modifiers is to identify them and rearrange them near the word or words they modify. Read the following paragraph and note the possibilities for misinterpretation:

*Patient is a 40-year-old, white female who came to the ER with chest pain at 3:30 a.m.* (Who came to the ER, the patient or the pain?) *The patient called me stating the chest pain was acute prior to the ER visit.* (Did the patient call the doctor before the visit, or was the pain acute before the visit?) *The pain moving toward the neck was located in the right substernal area.* (Was the pain located in the neck or the right substernal area?) *Now under control with insulin, she has a history of diabetes.* (Is the chest pain or diabetes under control with insulin?) *Her mother died of myocardial infarction at 45.* (Did the infarction die at 45 or the mother?)

Here is the paragraph rewritten for clarity:

*The patient is a 40-year-old, white female with chest pain who came to the ER at 3:30 a.m. Prior to the ER visit, the patient called me stating the chest pain was acute. The pain was located in the right substernal area and was moving toward the neck. She has a history of diabetes now under control with insulin. The patient's mother died at 45 from myocardial infarction.*

## Practice 7-3

*Revise and simplify these sentences:*

1. The computer is in Dr. Villa's office that doesn't work. _____

2. Buy medicine from the pharmacy with a generic brand. _____

3. The hospital provides comfort for people with central air conditioning.

   _____

4. The nurse dropped the report I wrote in the wastebasket. _____

5. He was described by a psychotherapist with multiple problems. _____

# Degrees of Adjectives to Express Comparison

Degrees of adjectives help describe the quality of a person, place, thing, or idea in comparison to another person, place, thing, or idea. Because qualities vary, adjectives have three different degrees of comparison: the positive, comparative, and superlative.

### POSITIVE

The positive degree describes nouns *without* making a comparison. The adjective is in its *base* form.

## Examples

The hospital has *capable* doctors.

Ms. Archer is a *fast* transcriber.

This report is *good.*

Mr. Oberg is *reliable.*

## COMPARATIVE

Comparative adjectives compare two persons, places, things, or ideas. They are formed in two ways:

1. Add *r* or *er* to the positive or base form of the word. If the word ends in *y*, change the *y* to *i* and add *er*.

## Examples

| | | |
|---|---|---|
| young to young*er* | fat to fat*ter* | tall to tall*er* |
| happy to happ*ier* | healthy to health*ier* | smart to smart*er* |

The operation was *tougher* than the last one.

This report is *longer* than the pathology report.

Ms. O'Conner is a *faster* transcriber than the secretary.

2. Add the word *more* or *less* to adjectives of two syllables that do not end in *y* and to adjectives of three or more syllables.

## Examples

difficult to *more difficult*    successful to *more successful*

The left ventricle is *more muscular* than the right ventricle.

The patient's medical record is *more reliable* than this letter.

Irregular adjectives are covered later in this chapter under "Other Comparisons."

## SUPERLATIVE

Superlative adjectives are used to compare three or more persons, places, things, or ideas. They usually end in *st* or *est* and are formed in two ways:

1. Add *st* or *est* to the base form of a one-syllable adjective and two-syllable adjectives ending in *y*. If the word ends in *y*, change the *y* to *i* before adding *est*.

## Examples

This lab report is the *longest* one of all the reports.

Your appointment is the *earliest* in the day.

2. Insert the word *most* or *least* before the base form of adjectives of two syllables that do not end in *y* and to adjectives of three or more syllables.

## Examples

Mr. Jones is the *most reliable* medical assistant in the hospital.

The *least important* appointment on the schedule needs to be cancelled.

Dr. Villes is the *most competent* physician in his field.

Some adjectives are irregular. See "Other Comparisons."

The superlative degree may be used for emphasis when there is no obvious comparison.

As a nurse, you are the *greatest.*

## Practice 7-4

*Indicate the comparative and superlative degrees of these adjectives:*

1. weak      _____      _____

2. difficult      _____      _____

3. painful      _____      _____

4. dry      _____      _____

5. hearty      _____      _____

## OTHER COMPARISONS

Some commonly used adjectives are irregular when they form the comparative and superlative degrees:

| Positive | Comparative | Superlative |
|---|---|---|
| bad | worse | worst |
| good | better | best |
| little | less | least |
| many/much | more | most |

Consult a dictionary if you are unsure about the correct word to use.

One of the most common mistakes made in comparisons is using the *double comparison,* or combining *er* with the base word and using *more,* or combining *est* and using *most.*

## Examples

| Incorrect | more poorer | most poorest |
|---|---|---|
| Correct | poorer or more poor | poorest or most poor |

Other common mistakes involve the misuse of the words *than* and *as* when making a comparison. *Than* introduces a second person, place, thing, or idea into the comparison.

## Examples

The right arm is less cyanotic *than* the left arm.

Telecommunications is faster *than* sending mail.

In expressing both positive and comparative degrees in one sentence, use the word *as* after the positive adjective and the word *than* after the comparative adjective.

## Examples

Your method of filing is *as* well organized, but more complex *than* our method.

The medicine is *as* effective, but less expensive *than* the brand name.

Additionally, do not confuse the word *than* with the word *then*. *Than* is used when comparing modifiers. *Then* means *at that time*.

## Examples

Your epigastric pain isn't better *than* yesterday's pain?

The incision was made and *then* the retractors were used.

## Practice 7-5

*Identify the correct comparative degree needed for each sentence:*

1. colorful      This hematoma is the _____ of all your bruises.

2. bad      The peptic ulcer is _____ than ever.

3. difficult      The comprehensive exam was _____ than last semester's

     final.

4. good      John is _____ but Mark is _____.

5. competent      The intern is _____, but the specialist is _____.

# Troublesome Adjectives

Some adjectives need special attention in their use.

| | |
|---|---|
| Farther | Refers to distance or a remote point: "Worcester is *farther* east than Springfield." |
| Further | Means additional or to a greater extent: "*Further* information is needed before the operation is scheduled." |
| Later | Refers to the second of two events that occur in chronological order: "The medical assistant reserved a flight *later* in the day." |
| Latter | Refers to the second of two things presented together: "The doctor could use OR 1 or OR 2, but decided on the latter." |
| Last | Refers to the final item in a list or series: "The *last* payment is due in January." |

| Latest | Refers to the most recent of something in chronological order: "The answering machine is the *latest* model produced." |
| --- | --- |
| Loose | Means free, not tied to something: "Wear *loose* clothing in a wheelchair." |
| Lose | Means to part with something unintentionally: "The physician did not want to *lose* his stethoscope." |

# Eponyms

Eponyms are used frequently in medical documentation. An *eponym* is the name of something derived from and identified with a real or mythical person. A medical eponym is the real surname of an individual who is connected with a particular treatment, operation, or instrument. It is very important to spell these eponym adjectives correctly. When in doubt about correct spelling, consult a medical dictionary.

Eponyms are capitalized but the nouns associated with them are not: Parkinsonism fibers, Bartholin's glands, tetralogy of Fallot, Cheyne-Stokes respirations, Bell's palsy, Babinski's sign, APGAR score, Trendelenburg's position, Epstein-Barr virus, Buck's extension, bundle of His, Fowler's position, DeBakey prosthesis.

Words derived from eponyms need not be capitalized: parkinsonism, fallopian tube, eustachian tubes.

## Practice 7-6

*Identify the eponyms in each sentence:*

1. Adam Smith in the pediatric ward has a tetralogy of Fallot. _____

2. What is the newborn's APGAR score at one minute? _____

3. Teenagers are sometimes prone to the Epstein-Barr virus. _____

4. Place the patient in a semi-Fowler's position. _____

5. Bell's palsy may sometimes go away within six months. _____

# Adjectives Summary

| Adjective | Describes a noun or pronoun. | |
| --- | --- | --- |
| Limiting | Limits the noun or pronoun to a definite or indefinite amount. Answers how many, how much, which one. | a, an, all, any, both, each, every, few, many, more, most, much, no, some, such, that, those, this, these, numbers, possessive nouns, and pronouns. |

| | | |
|---|---|---|
| Interrogative | Asks a question. | which, what. |
| Proper | Finds its source in a proper noun. | American citizen. Russian immigrant. |
| Compound | Combines two or more describing words as a single modifier. | state-of-the-art computer (before noun). The computer is state of the art (after noun). over-crowded bus. 5-, 10-, 15-cent stamps. |
| Predicate | Describes a subject and comes after a linking verb. | The needle is *sharp*. The x-rays are *clear*. |
| Descriptive | Describes the quality of the person, place, thing, or idea of the noun. | red, large, generous, energetic, partial, beautiful, organized, hungry, poetic, powerful. |

# Degrees of Comparison Summary

| | Degree | | | |
|---|---|---|---|---|
| **Number of Syllables** | **Positive (base, describes without making a comparison)** | **Comparative (compares two or more)** | **Superlative (compares three or more)** | **Rule** |
| One syllable | young, new, light | younger, newer, lighter | youngest, newest, lightest | Add *er* or *est* to base. |
| Two or more syllables | healthy, gentle, expensive, fascinating | healthier, more gentle, more expensive, more fascinating | healthiest, most gentle, most expensive, most fascinating | For words ending in *y*, change *y* to *i* and *er* or *est*. Otherwise, use *more* and *most*. |
| Irregular adjectives | good | better | best | |
| | bad | worse | worst | |
| | little | less | least | |
| | many | much | most | |

# Medical Spelling

*Become familiar with the spelling of the following words:*

| | |
|---|---|
| abdominal | cyanotic |
| anterior | clinical |
| antidiuretic | comprehensive |
| apprehensive | dorsal |
| bronchial | epithelial |
| calculus, calculi | excessive |

fetal

frontal

gastrointestinal

hepatic

infection

inguinal

intravenous

lateral

muscular

mucous

myocardial infarction

nasogastric

necrotic

pathological

pelvic

peptic ulcer

peritoneal

pleural

proximal

respiratory

retractor

skeletal

streptococcal

superficial

thoracic

tonsillar

uric acid

urinary

Adjectives play an important role in medical writing, by helping to describe patient conditions and medical procedures and to express degrees of comparison important to medical reports. For example, a patient's temperature may be *higher* than expected, or a patient may show *favorable* signs of recovery. Adjectives are also helpful in distinguishing types of reports; for example, radiology reports may often contain terms ending in *scopy* or *graphy*. All medical reports contain descriptions of various medical conditions and treatments, so understanding the use of adjectives is essential when writing reports.

# Radiology Report

A radiology report describes the results of a diagnostic procedure using radiowaves or other forms of radiation. Examples of such procedures are x-rays, CT scans, MRIs, upper GI series, and ultrasonograms. These medical procedures provide visual images to aid in diagnosis.

# Pathology Report

A pathology report contains a description of tissue samples removed from the body. The removal of a tissue sample for examination is called a *biopsy*. The *pathologist* is the person who studies the tissue samples and generates the pathology report.

The focus of the pathology report is twofold:

1. Macroscopic findings (also called gross description, gross examination). This component describes how the specimen looks to the naked eye. It describes the size, general color, and texture.

2. Microscopic findings (also called microscopic description). This component describes how tissue looks when examined under a microscope.

The report usually ends with a diagnosis of the findings or an impression.

The pathology report is the examination of specific tissues. The pathology report becomes a permanent part of the patient's medical record. A sample pathology report is provided.

RADIOLOGY REPORT

**Patient Name:** Marietta Mosley

**Hospital No.:** 11446

**X-ray No.:** 98-2801

**Admitting Physician:** John Youngblood, M.D.

**Procedure:** Left hip x-ray.

**Date:** 08/05/20XX

PRIMARY DIAGNOSIS: Fractured left hip.

CLINICAL INFORMATION: Left hip pain. No known allergies.

Orthopedic device is noted transfixing the left femoral neck. I have no old films available for comparison. The left femoral neck region appears anatomically aligned. At the level of an orthopedic screw along the lateral aspect of the femoral neck, approximately at the level of the lesser trochanter, there is a radiolucent band consistent with a fracture of indeterminate age that shows probable nonunion. There is bilateral marginal sclerosis and moderate offset and angulation at this site.

Fairly exuberant callus formation is noted laterally along the femoral shaft.

IMPRESSION:
1. No evidence for significant displacement at the femoral neck.

2. Probable nonunion of fracture transversely through the shaft of the femur at about the level of the lesser trochanter.

_____
Neil Nofsinger, M.D.

NN:xx
D:08/05/20XX
T:08/05/20XX

M.A. Novak and P.A. Ireland, *Hillcrest Medical Center Beginning Medical Transcription Course*, 6th ed. Albany, NY: Delmar Thomson Learning, 2005, p. 18.

# Discharge Summary

The discharge summary is a report that is required for all patients who leave the healthcare facility. It is a summary of the patient's condition during his or her stay at the facility. Data in the discharge summary include the following:

❖ Reason for admittance

❖ History of present illness

❖ Social history

❖ Physical exam and laboratory data

❖ Events that occurred during the patient's stay

❖ Follow-up instructions

❖ Discharge medications

The report concludes with the condition of the patient at the time of discharge and the discharge prognosis. A sample discharge summary follows.

---

**PATHOLOGY REPORT**

**Patient Name:** Sumio Yukimura

**Hospital No.:** 11449

**Pathology Report No.:** 98-S-942

**Admitting Physician:** Donna Yates, M.D.

**Preoperative Diagnosis:** Cholelithiasis.

**Postoperative Diagnosis:** Cholelithiasis.

**Specimen Submitted:** Gallbladder and stone.

**Date Received:** 06/05/20XX

**Date Reported:** 06/06/20XX

GROSS DESCRIPTION: Specimen received in one container labeled "gallbladder." Specimen consists of a 9-cm gallbladder measuring 2 cm in average diameter. The serosal surface demonstrates diffuse fibrous adhesion. The wall is thickened and hemorrhagic. The mucosa is eroded, and there is a single large stone measuring 2 cm in diameter within the lumen. Representative sections are submitted in one cassette.

GROSS DIAGNOSIS: Gallstone.

KM:xx
D:06/05/20XX
T:06/05/20XX

MICROSCOPIC DIAGNOSIS: Gallbladder, hemorrhagic chronic cholecystitis with cholelithiasis.

_____
Robert Thompson, M.D.

RT:xx
D:06/06/20XX
T:06/06/20XX

---

M.A. Novak and P.A. Ireland, *Hillcrest Medical Center Beginning Medical Transcription Course*, 6th ed. Albany, NY: Delmar Thomson Learning, 2005, p. 20.

**DISCHARGE SUMMARY**

**Patient Name:** Joyce Mabry

**Hospital No.:** 11709

**Admitted:** 02/18/20XX

**Discharged:** 02/24/20XX

**Consultations:** Tom Moore, M.D., Hematology

**Procedures:** Splenectomy.

**Complications:** None.

**Admitting Diagnosis:** Elective splenectomy for idiopathic thrombocytopenic purpura and systemic lupus erythematosus.

HISTORY: The patient is a 21-year-old white woman who had noted excessive bruising since last June. She was diagnosed as having thrombocytopenic purpura. At the same time, the diagnosis of systemic lupus erythematosus was made. The patient continues with the bruising. The patient had been treated with steroids, prednisone 20 mg; however, the platelet count has remained low, less than 20,000. The patient was admitted for elective splenectomy.

LABORATORY DATA ON ADMISSION: Chest x-ray was negative. Electrocardiogram was normal. Sodium 138, potassium 5.2, chloride 104, $CO_2$ 25, glucose 111. Urinalysis negative. Hemoglobin 14.8, hematocrit 43.5, white blood cell count 15,000, platelet count 17,000, PT 11.5, PTT 27.

HOSPITAL COURSE: The patient was taken to the operating room on February 19 where a splenectomy was performed. The patient's postoperative course was uncomplicated with the wound healing well. The platelet count was stable for the first 3 postoperative days. The patient was transfused intraoperatively with 10 units of platelets and postoperatively with 10 additional units of platelets. However, on the fourth postoperative day the platelet count had risen to 77,000, which was a significant increase.

The patient was discharged for follow-up in my office. She will also be seen by Dr. Moore, who will follow her SLE and ITP.

DISCHARGE DIAGNOSIS: Idiopathic thrombocytopenic purpura and systemic lupus erythematosus.

DISCHARGE MEDICATIONS:
1. Prednisone 20 mg q.d.
2. Percocet 1 to 2 p.o. q. 4 h. p.r.n.
3. Multivitamins, 1 in a.m. q.d.


_____<br>Carmen Garcia, M.D.

CG:xx
D:02/25/20XX
T:02/26/20XX

M.A. Novak and P.A. Ireland, *Hillcrest Medical Center Beginning Medical Transcription Course*, 6th ed. Albany, NY: Delmar Thomson Learning, 2005, pp. 23–24.

# *Operative Report*

The operative report is a comprehensive description of a surgical procedure performed on a patient. The report includes specific details about preoperative, operative, and post-operative experiences such as specimens removed and sent to pathology, diagnosis, type of operation performed, names of surgeons and assistants present, type of anesthesia, instruments used, drain packs, closure, sponge count, suture materials and thickness, any unusual circumstances or complications, and estimated blood loss.

The report may be in narrative form or divided into subheadings, such as "anesthesia," "incision," "findings," "procedures," and "closing." The report details end with the patient going to the recovery room. The operative report must be dictated and filed in medical records as soon as possible after surgery. A sample operative report follows:

---

OPERATIVE REPORT

**Patient Name:** Kathy Sullivan

**Hospital No.:** 11525

**Date of Surgery:** 06/25/20XX

**Admitting Physician:** Taylor Withers, M.D.

**Surgeons:** Sang Lee, M.D., Taylor Withers, M.D.

**Preoperative Diagnosis:** Urinary incontinence secondary to cystourethrocele.

**Postoperative Diagnosis:** Urinary incontinence secondary to cystourethrocele.

**Operative Procedure:** Total abdominal hysterectomy with Marshall-Marchetti correction.

**Anesthesia:** General endotracheal.

DESCRIPTION: After an abdominal hysterectomy had been performed by Dr. Withers, the peritoneum was closed by him and the procedure was turned over to me.

At this time the supravesical space was entered. The anterior portions of the bladder and urethra were dissected free by blunt and sharp dissection. Bleeders were clamped and electrocoagulated as they were encountered. A wedge of the overlying periosteum was taken and roughened with a bone rasp. The urethra was then attached to the overlying symphysis by placing two No. 1 catgut sutures on each side of the urethra and one in the bladder neck. The urethra and bladder neck pulled up to the overlying symphysis bone very easily with no tension on the sutures. Bleeding was controlled by pulling the bladder neck up to the bone. Penrose drains were placed on each side of the vesical gutter. Blood loss was negligible. The procedure was then turned back over to Dr. Withers, who proceeded with closure.

_____
Sang Lee, M.D.

SL:xx
D:06/25/20XX
T:06/26/20XX

---

M.A. Novak and P.A. Ireland, *Hillcrest Medical Center Beginning Medical Transcription Course*, 6th ed. Albany, NY: Delmar Thomson Learning, 2005, p. 19.

# Medical Reports Summary

| | |
|---|---|
| Radiology | A report describing the results of a diagnostic procedure using radio waves or other forms of radiation. |
| Pathology Report | A report containing a description of tissue samples removed from the body. |
| Discharge Summary | A report summarizing the patient's condition while at a health-care facility. |
| Operative Report | A report describing a surgical procedure performed on a patient. |

## Skills Review

*Identify any adjectives in these sentences:*

1. A streptococcal infection is serious. _____
2. Protein repairs tissues damaged by disease. _____
3. A good trait for a nurse is compassion. _____
4. A pathologist studies diseased tissues. _____
5. Gangrene is obstruction of blood flow resulting in necrotic tissue. _____

*Fill in the specific kind of adjective requested on the left.*

1. Limiting _____ staff members work on weekends.
2. Descriptive   Insurance covers only _____ benefits.
3. Interrogative _____ report do you want faxed?
4. Predicate   The hospital logo was _____.
5. Proper   All _____ citizens must have a social security number.

*Write medical adjectives having these suffixes:*

1. al   _____
2. ian   _____
3. ior   _____
4. able   _____
5. cal   _____
6. ic   _____
7. ous   _____
8. ual   _____
9. iac   _____
10. ary   _____

*Circle the correct word within the parentheses in each sentence:*

1. Medicine is (most, more) competitive (then, than) it was ten years ago.

2. The hospital is one of the (busy, busier, busiest) facilities in the country.

3. Dr. Ray is (good, better, best), but Dr. Taft is (good, better, best).

4. The medical terminology book (further, farther) explains the meaning of words.

5. Over a period of time, (fewer, less) numbers of people applied for the job.

*Write true or false next to the following statements:*

1. Adjectives answer what kind and how many. _____

2. A noun can be used as an adjective. _____

3. The letters *est* are a sign of the comparative degree. _____

4. The letters *er* are used to describe three or more persons, places, things, or ideas. _____

5. *This*, *that*, *these*, and *those* are examples of descriptive adjectives. _____

*Grammar Exercise: Underline each error in the paragraph and write its correction above the word.*

Based on the evaluation, the patient will be addmitted to the hospital. The patient was placed on a high dose of NSAID. The report concerning the patients abdominal xray were obtained. The patient requiered an intervanous before reaching the hospital. The patients' condition will probably give some pain. This pain can be relieved by over the counter medication. Please call the ofice if there are any questions.

*Rewrite these sentences to make them logical:*

1. On the second day the knee was better and on the third day it completely disappeared.

   _____

2. The patient left the hospital feeling much better.

   _____

3. The patient has chest pain if she lies on her left side for over a year.

   _____

4. The patient has been depressed ever since she began seeing me ten years ago.

   _____

5. By the time he was admitted, his rapid heart had stopped and he was feeling better.

   _____

*Use these words to complete the sentences.*

| macroscopic findings | pathologist | microscopic findings |
| pathology report | biopsy | discharge summary |
| follow-up instructions | paramedic | laboratory |

1. The part of the pathology report that describes how tissue looks to the naked eye is _____.

2. The report that documents what happens during hospitalization is _____.

3. The person who examines diseased tissue is a _____.

4. A special report that examines the cause of disease is a _____.

*In which medical report may these statements be found?*

1. Hospitalized for epididymitis 10 years ago. _____

2. Bleeders were clamped and electrocoagulated as they were encountered. _____

3. Fairly exuberant callus formation is noted laterally along the femoral shaft. _____

4. No evidence for significant displacement at the femoral neck. _____

5. DIAGNOSIS: Gallbladder, hemorrhagic chronic cholecystitis with cholelithiasis. _____

6. I have been asked to see a five-year-old Caucasian male who appears in mild distress due to upper extremity burn after falling into hot coals in his back yard. _____

7. She will be seen by Dr. Moore, who will follow her SLE and ITP. _____

8. Penrose drains were placed on each side of the vesical gutter. _____

*Translate medical abbreviations using a medical dictionary or appendix.*

1. not equal to _____

2. ♀ _____

3. one half _____

4. ♂ _____

5. central nervous system _____

6. biopsy _____

7. diagnosis _____

8. # _____

9. coronary artery disease _____

10. ℞ _____

*Circle the adjectives in the sentences below:*

1. The mucosa is eroded, and there is a single, large stone.

2. The patient was admitted for elective splenectomy.

3. Blood loss was negligible.

4. The test showed no evidence of significant displacement at the femoral neck.

5. The patient's postoperative course was uncomplicated.

*Circle the correctly spelled word in each line:*

| | | | |
|---|---|---|---|
| 1. bronchal | bronchial | bronkial | branchiol |
| 2. cephelic | cefalic | cephalich | cephalic |
| 3. epithelel | epithelial | epathelial | epathelil |
| 4. gastrointestianl | gastrointistinal | gastrointestinal | gastraintistinal |
| 5. mocous | mucos | mucous | nocous |
| 6. pleural | plueral | pleurel | pluerel |
| 7. streptococcal | streptocaccal | stretococcal | streptocacal |
| 8. comprihensive | conprehensive | comprehensive | comprehinsive |

| | | | |
|---|---|---|---|
| 9. urinery | uranary | urenery | urinary |
| 10. pathlogical | pathilogical | pathological | patholgical |

# Comprehensive Review

*Underline the adjectives in each sentence. Identify the adjective as limiting, interrogative, proper, compound, predicate, or descriptive.*

1. The wall is thickened and hemorrhagic.

2. The patient was taken to the operating room on February 19, where a splenectomy operation was performed.

3. What significant evidence shows displacement at the femoral neck?

4. Functional endoscopic sinus surgery (FESS) was performed by the Mass Eye and Ear specialists.

5. The perioperative nurse should have an empathetic and compassionate ability to care for patients.

*Write five sentences involving a medical situation. Use one of each type adjective (interrogative, proper, compound, predicate, or descriptive).*

1. _____

2. _____

3. _____

4. _____

5. _____

# CHAPTER 8

# *Adverbs*

## PRACTICAL WRITING COMPONENT: FACSIMILE, PHONE MESSAGES, MINUTES OF A MEETING

**OBJECTIVES** *Upon completion of this chapter, the learner should be able to:*

❖ recognize and use adverbs effectively

❖ distinguish between the use of adjectives and adverbs

❖ change adjectives into adverbs

❖ use adverbs to make accurate degrees of comparisons

❖ avoid the use of double negatives

❖ place adverbs appropriately

❖ spell various medical terms

❖ translate various medical abbreviations

❖ understand the fax, phone message, and minutes of a meeting

## *Recognizing Adverbs*

Learning about parts of speech may be confusing at times because there are so many exceptions to the rules of grammar. However, some parts of speech have similar characteristics that help simplify understanding of their usage. As mentioned in Chapter 2, pronouns take the place of nouns and are used in many similar ways: as subjects, direct objects, and indirect objects. The same kind of relationship exists between adjectives and adverbs in that an adverb does to a verb, adjective, or other adverbs what an adjective does to a noun. The main function of both adjectives and adverbs is to describe. Adjectives describe nouns; adverbs most commonly describe verbs:

| Noun Modifier | Verb Modifier |
|---|---|
| *coronary* embolism | *usually* found |
| *axillary* crutches | *commonly* used |
| *electrical* connection | spoke *eloquently* |

Adjectives and adverbs can be distinguished by the different types of questions they answer.

| **Adjectives Answer:** | **Adverbs Answer:** |
|---|---|
| Which one | How |
| What kind | Where |
| How many, how much | When |
| | How many times |
| | To what extent |

❖ Adverbs tell *how:* "The details in the chart were described *accurately.*"

❖ Adverbs tell *where:* "The wound bled *locally.*"

❖ Adverbs tell *when:* "The operation was performed *yesterday.*"

❖ Adverbs tell *how many times:* "The nurse cleaned the wound *twice.*"

❖ Adverbs tell *to what extent:* "Insurance costs increased *dramatically.*"

---

## Examples of Adverbs

| | | | |
|---|---|---|---|
| actually | early | maybe | seriously |
| afterward | easily | most | somewhere |
| again | enough | never | soon |
| ago | entirely | next | still |
| almost | especially | now | surely |
| already | everywhere | obviously | there |
| always | extremely | occasionally | today |
| anymore | fast | often | together |
| anywhere | finally | once | tomorrow |
| apparently | fortunately | orally | too |
| carefully | generally | perhaps | up |
| certainly | hard | quite | very |
| clinically | here | quietly | well |
| completely | immediately | rarely | where |
| constantly | just | regularly | yesterday |
| downward | later | seldom | yet |

---

If you are confused about whether a word is an adjective or an adverb, determine the part of speech that the word describes. If the word modifies a noun, it is an adjective. If the word modifies a verb, it is an adverb. Note, however, that the same word may be either an adjective or an adverb depending on its use in a sentence:

The nurse gave a *daily* report. [*Daily* is an adjective modifying the noun *report.*]

The nurse administered pills *daily*. [*Daily* is an adverb modifying the verb *administered.*]

## Practice 8-1

*Select the adverb in each sentence and identify the question it answers (how, when, where, how many times, or to what extent):*

1. He is extremely frustrated that he cannot use his dentures. _____

2. The cholesterol levels were checked regularly. _____

3. Implants were removed surgically. _____

4. The pain lessened after the patient took the medication. _____

5. The patient took the medication today. _____

# Adverbs as Modifiers

An adverb is a word that modifies (describes) a verb, verb phrase, adjective, or other adverb. Adverbs that describe verbs are the easiest to identify.

## Examples

The patient has recovered *nicely* from the procedure. [*Nicely* modifies the verb *recovered* and answers the question *how*.]

He was casted in the office *yesterday*. [*Yesterday* modifies the verb *casted* and answers the question *when*.]

The medical assistant wrapped the burned area *twice* a day. [*Twice* modifies the verb *wrapped* and answers the question *how many times*.]

Adverbs can also describe adjectives and other adverbs. Examples of adverbs that perform this function are *very, too, rather, fairly, truly, extremely, unusually, exceptionally, somewhat,* and *especially*. Determining whether the adverb modifies an adjective or adverb depends on how the word is used in a sentence.

## Examples

The medical team performed an *especially* safe operation. [*Especially* modifies the adjective *safe*.]

The incision healed *fairly* rapidly. [*Fairly* modifies the adverb *rapidly*.]

## Practice 8-2

*Identify the adverb(s) in each sentence and state whether the adverb describes a verb, adjective, or other adverb:*

1. This elevator services only surgical patients. _____

2. The hospital generally accepts the H&P prepared by the medical office. _____

3. Cranial nerves II-IV appear grossly intact. _____

4. The patient tolerated the procedure well. _____

5. The doctor will probably review the consultation later. _____

# Frequency Adverbs

Specific adverbs exist that describe an amount of time, from full time to no time at all. Some of them are *always, usually, often, sometimes, seldom, rarely,* and *never.*

## Examples

I *always* remember.    I *sometimes* remember.

I *usually* remember.    I *rarely* remember.

I *often* remember.    I *never* remember.

The patient *often* reacts to medication.

The report is *usually* filed on Mondays.

We *always* test the blood for HIV.

# Degrees of Adverbs to Express Comparison

Adverbs, like adjectives, have three degrees of comparison: positive, comparative, and superlative.

## POSITIVE

The positive degree shows no comparison. It is the base form of the adverb.

The progress note was written *clearly.*

## COMPARATIVE

The comparative degree is used to compare two persons or things that perform the same action. Adverbs ending in *ly* form the comparative by adding the word *more* or *less* immediately before the adverb. Other adverbs form the comparative by adding *er* to the base word.

## Examples

The progress note was written *less clearly* than the other one.

James finished the transcription, but Pat did hers *faster.*

## SUPERLATIVE

The superlative degree is used to compare more than two persons or things that perform the same action. To form the superlative degree of adverbs ending in *ly*, add *most* or *least* immediately before the adverb. Other adverbs are also formed by adding *est* to the base form.

## *Examples*

The final progress note was written *least clearly* of all.

The nurse scored the *highest* in the class.

The hospital admitted patients *most cordially*.

## OTHER COMPARISONS

Some verbs do not form their comparative and superlative degrees according to the rules stated in the previous paragraphs. They are irregular:

| | | |
|---|---|---|
| Positive | *little* | Dr. Mary Ann cares *little* about covering the emergency room. |
| Comparative | *less* | Dr. Bill is *less* likely than she to cover the emergency room. |
| Superlative | *least* | Of all the physicians, Dr. Joseph is the *least* likely to cover the emergency room. |

Other common irregular adverbs are listed below:

| **Positive** | **Comparative** | **Superlative** |
|---|---|---|
| badly | worse | worst |
| well | better | best |
| much | more | most |

When using the words *more* or *most*, do not make the mistake of also adding the suffix *er* or *est* to adverbs.

| | |
|---|---|
| Incorrect | Bill worked *more harder* than expected. |
| Correct | Bill worked *harder* than expected. |
| Incorrect | Migraines are the most painfulest of headaches. |
| Correct | Migraines are the most painful of headaches. |

# *Practice 8-3*

*Select the correct word in the parentheses:*

1. Oral medications are (more, most) acceptable than intramuscular medications.

2. Certified mail is the (good, better, best) way to send documents at the post office.

3. Telecommunication such as a fax machine and computer-to-computer e-mail is the (fast, faster, fastest) method of communication.

4. More medical supplies are (available, more available, most available) on the Internet.

5. The test results are (good, better, best) than they were yesterday.

# Changing Adjectives into Adverbs

Medical words can be expressed as adjectives and adverbs.

## Examples

The *medical* prognosis for that patient is serious. (Adjective)

The prognosis for that patient is *medically* serious. (Adverb)

1. Simply add *ly* to the adjective: clinical, clinical*ly*; medical, medical*ly*; physical, physical*ly*; progressive, progressive*ly*; anterior, anterior*ly*; posterior, posterior*ly*; pathological, pathological*ly*.

2. Adjectives that end in *y* preceded by a consonant are made into adverbs by changing the *y* to *i* and adding *ly*: easy, eas*ily*; happy, happ*ily*.

3. Adjectives ending in *le* are made into adverbs by changing the ending to *ly*: probable, probab*ly*; acceptable, acceptab*ly*; justifiable, justifiab*ly*.

4. Adjectives ending in *ll* are made into adverbs by adding *y*: full, full*y*; dull, dull*y*.

5. Adjectives ending in *ic* are usually made into adverbs by adding *ally*: historic, historic*ally*; diagnostic, diagnostic*ally*.

6. Some adverbs have special spellings: tru*ly*, public*ly*, whol*ly*.

 **Practice 8-4**

*Change the following words into adverbs:*

1. safe _____

2. successful _____

3. oral _____

4. continual _____

5. painful _____

# Negative Adverbs

A negative, the oppositive of affirmative, is a word that expresses a denial or a refusal. A negative contradicts what is said.

> John lives in Boston. [affirmative]
>
> John does not live in Boston. [negative]

Regular negative adverbs are *no, not, never, nowhere, none, hardly, rarely, barely, scarcely,* and *seldom*. Be aware that the word *no* is also a negative *adjective*. Words like *nobody, nowhere, nothing,* and *no one* are negative *pronouns*. The prefixes *dis-, in-, non-,* and *un-* are also indicators of negatives.

## Examples

> She *never* goes to the doctor. [adverb]
>
> The treatment room has *no* surgical tape. [adjective]
>
> *Nobody* can tell me the information I want. [pronoun]
>
> *Nothing* should stand in the way of improving your health. [pronoun]
>
> I did *not* attend the meeting. [adverb]
>
> *Unpack* the medical supplies that just arrived. [prefix]
>
> The doctor *dis*charged the patient before the weekend. [prefix]

### NOT AS A CONTRACTION

The adverb *not* is often joined to verbs to create a new word. The new word is called a contraction. To form a contraction, an apostrophe (') replaces the letter *o* in the word *not (n't)*. Because the abbreviated form of *not* is implied in the contraction, it is considered a negative word.

## Examples

| are not | *aren't* | cannot | *can't* | could not | *couldn't* |
|---------|----------|--------|---------|-----------|------------|
|         |          |        |         | would not | *wouldn't* |
| did not | *didn't* | does not | *doesn't* | do not | *don't* |
| has not | *hasn't* | have not | *haven't* | had not | *hadn't* |
| is not | *isn't* | must not | *mustn't* | should not | *shouldn't* |
| was not | *wasn't* | were not | *weren't* | will not | *won't* |

Many people use the contraction *ain't* in their speech. This word is unacceptable in the English language and should not be used, especially in formal writing. Actually, contractions in general are usually avoided in formal writing.

### DOUBLE NEGATIVES

Another grammatical error that should be avoided is the use of two negatives in a sentence. In such a case, the second negative cancels the first negative and turns the whole sentence into an affirmative. An example is the sentence, "I haven't no money." If you do not have *no* money, it means you have some money.

| Incorrect | The policy *didn't* offer *no* deductible. |
| Correct | The policy offered *no* deductible. |
| | The policy didn't offer *any* deductible. |
| Incorrect | The medical assistants *didn't* have *no* money. |
| Correct | The medical assistants have *no* money. |
| | The medical assistants *didn't* have *any* money. |

## Practice 8-5

*Correct these double-negative sentences:*

1. The insurance company can't pay none of its bills. _____

2. The nurse won't have no difficulty telling the patients. _____

3. The DRGs used by Medicare haven't had no effect on billing. _____

4. The medication couldn't scarcely work after two hours. _____

5. She doesn't want none of my help. _____

# Placement of Adverbs

If adverbs and adjectives are not placed near the words they describe, they can provide the reader with a good laugh. For example, the sentence "She promised him that she would marry him frequently," should read, "She frequently promised him that she would marry him." Which is the intended meaning: how many times did she promise to marry him, or how many times did she actually marry him?

Adverbs that modify adjectives or adverbs are placed immediately before the words they describe:

| Awkward | Luke said that he was going to the office emphatically. |
| Better | Luke emphatically said that he was going to the office. |

Adverbs that modify verbs can be placed in many positions in a sentence:

The doctor listened *intently* to the patient's symptoms.

The doctor listened to the patient's symptoms *intently*.

## Practice 8-6

*Place the adverb from the first column in its best position in the sentence:*

1. always          Sue has a yearly physical.

2. ever            Have you had an operation on your gallbladder?

|   |   |   |
|---|---|---|
| 3. | seldom | The office opens earlier than 9 a.m. |
| 4. | usually | Medical assistants work very hard. |
| 5. | probably | For this reason, nurses need help. |
| 6. | highly | Students are acclaimed when they qualify for medical school. |
| 7. | immediately | Get her to the operating room. |
| 8. | especially | On busy days, the medical assistant works later. |
| 9. | courageously | The patient signed a health care proxy. |
| 10. | rarely | Doctors make mistakes in diagnosing obvious diseases. |

# Troublesome Adverbs

The following words are often confused.

| | | | |
|---|---|---|---|
| *awhile*: | The doctor paused *awhile* during the difficult surgery [adverb] | *a + while*: | There was silence in the ER [noun] for *a while*. |
| *well*: | The patient feels *well*. [adjective] | *good*: | The woman had a *good* doctor. [adjective] |
| *really*: | I was *really* expecting a bonus. [adverb] | *real* | The patient had a *real* greenstick fracture. [adjective] |
| *surely*: | You can *surely* count on me for help when you are ill. [adverb] | *sure*: | The diagnosis is a *sure* thing. [adjective] |

# Adverbs Summary

| Definition | A word that describes a verb, adjective, or other adverb. | The operation was *successfully* completed. |
|---|---|---|
| Question answered | *How? where? when? how many times? to what extent?* | Treatments have to be administered *often*. (how many times) |
| | | The answer may be found *here*. (where) |
| Placement | Immediately near adjective, anywhere with verb. | What is needed are *extremely* safe guidelines |
| Comparative and superlative | | |
| One syllable | Add *er, est*: fast, faster, fastest. | This method is *faster* than the other one. |
| Two syllables | Add *more, most*: more | She replied most *impatiently*. |
| Three syllables | impatiently, most impatient. | |
| Irregular | *Well, better, best* *Badly, worse, worst* | This is the *worst* I have ever felt. |
| Avoid double comparatives | Do not use *er* or *est* endings with more and most: more easy, *not* more easier; most easy, *not* most easiest. | Avoid at all cost. |
| Avoid double negatives | Do not use two negatives in a sentence (*not, rarely, seldom, hardly, scarcely, barely*). | Avoid at all cost. |

# Medical Spelling

*Become familiar with the spelling of the following words:*

| | |
|---|---|
| abnormally | laterally |
| absolutely | locally |
| accurately | nutritionally |
| analysis | occasionally |
| apparently | orally |
| axillary | particularly |
| carefully | physically |
| chronically | possibly |
| clinically | posteriorly |
| confidentially | potentially |
| currently | primarily |
| developmentally | radically |
| dorsally | relatively |
| emotionally | significantly |
| immediately | specifically |
| initially | temporarily |
| insufficiently | timely |
| intramuscularly | tomorrow |
| intravenously | ventrally |
| involuntarily | yesterday |

In medical writing, when you describe where and how a procedure was done, how often a treatment was administered to a patient, or to what extent medication is working on a patient's condition, you are using adverbs. Adverbs help to answer questions of how, where, when, and to what extent an action was performed. In the medical setting, sending faxes, taking phone messages, or transcribing the minutes of a meeting may call for this same kind of information and so are good ways to learn the importance of adverbs.

# Facsimile

Written communication often includes more than letters and memos. A facsimile, or fax machine, is an electronic device that transmits documents, drawings, and photographs as exact reproductions. The fax is standard equipment in the medical office today and is an excellent way to disseminate valuable medical information among medical facilities and professionals.

In formal professional situations, a cover sheet should accompany any electronically transmitted message or document. Medical offices usually have their own cover sheet format that includes all necessary information, as follows:

One Morey Place
Anywhere, MA 01102
(555) 555-4727 Phone
(555) 555-444 FAX

**V**
**M**
**C**

*VILLES MEDICAL*
*CENTER*

**FAX** Cover Sheet

To: *Carol LeClaire*             From: *VMC*

FAX: *555-555-4444*             Date: *6-30-20XX*

Phone: *555-4279*             Pages: *7*
                              (Including cover sheet.)

Comments

*The pathology report you requested on Carlos Rodriguez is enclosed.*

FIGURE 8-1     *Sample Fax Cover Sheet*

- the name, phone number, and fax number (or extension, if applicable) of the sender.

- the name, title, department, company, and fax number of the recipient.

- the date the fax is sent and the number of pages.

- any written instructions, messages, or other information.

Figure 8-1 is an example of a fax cover sheet.

# Phone Messages

Most medical offices have an office phone message form that staff members complete when someone cannot be reached by phone. The form is designed to contain all the necessary information without having to write too much. Pertinent information consists of the caller's name and phone number; the name of the person who called; the date, time, and purpose of the call; a short message; and the name of the person who took the message. Figure 8-2 is an example of a phone message form.

The important thing to remember about phone messages is to deliver them promptly. The efficiency and professionalism of the medical office require that persons receive information in a timely manner. Be sure the handwritten message is legible.

To: *Dr. Valerie Christopher*

Date: *2-18-00*         Time: *9 am*

### WHILE YOU WERE OUT
### PHONE MESSAGE

M   *Mark Villes, M.D.*

Of   *Villes Medical Center*

Phone   *555-5551*         *Ext 222*

_____ Telephoned        _____ Called to see you.

✓ Please call back        _____ Returned your call.

_____ Will call again.        _____ Urgent

MESSAGE

*Called regarding a metting on March 31 at 5 p.m.*

*Beverly Berc, CMA*

**FIGURE 8-2**   *Sample Phone Message*

# Minutes of a Meeting

Medical personnel may be expected to type the minutes of a meeting. Minutes are an official (and sometimes legal) summary record of events and decisions that occur during the meeting. Asking *who, what, where, when,* and *why* about the meeting simplifies the process. All questions need not be answered. These questions are only a tool for getting at the important information. Record only what is done at a meeting and not what is said.

| | |
|---|---|
| Who | Who attends the meeting? Who is absent? Who is responsible for carrying out tasks? Who chairs the meeting? Who is secretary? Who distributes the minutes? Who reminds people of the next meeting? |
| What | What happens at the meeting? What decisions are made? What is the meeting about? What is the agenda of this meeting or the next meeting? |
| Where | Where is the meeting? Where is the next meeting? |
| When | When is the meeting? When is the follow-up meeting? When does this decision take effect? |
| Why | Why does the group make the decision? Why are some people absent? |

Like other forms of written communication, a structured model of writing minutes is necessary to ensure a consistent style. Minutes are usually summarized in three components: a heading, a body, and a conclusion (Figure 8-3).

VMC Villes Medical Center
Officer Staff Meeting
Conference Room
October 11, 20XX
2–3 p.m.

Present: Rose William, Office Manager
Norbert Oberg, RN
Thomas Buick, Medical Assistant
Marcia Taft, Secretary

1. The purpose of the meeting was to discuss the distribution of the HIPAA brochures as they pertain to the office staff.

2. Two specific procedures were decided.

3. The brochure will be given to each patient during an office visit.

4. Patients must sign a 506 form verifying receipt of the brochure.

5. These procedures will be evaluated at the December office meeting.

Next Meeting
October 15, 20XX
2–3 p.m.
Conference Room

**FIGURE 8-3** *Minutes of a Meeting*

| Heading | Name of organization |
| --- | --- |
| | Purpose of meeting |
| | Date, time, and place of meeting |
| | Chairperson and secretary |
| | Names of those present and absent |
| | Approval of previous meeting's minutes |
| Body | Paragraph(s) on subject matters regarding decisions, rulings, events, data |
| Conclusion | Time and place of next meeting |
| | Agenda |
| | Chairperson and secretary |

## Practice 8-7

*Answer true or false to the following:*

1. A cover sheet is not necessary when faxing a message or document electronically.

2. If phone messages are recorded, they don't need to be delivered promptly. _____

3. Minutes of a meeting are a summary of events and decisions that occur during the meeting. _____

4. A fax machine is standard equipment in the medical office today. _____

5. Everything that is discussed at a meeting should be included in the minutes of the meeting. _____

# Facsimile, Phone Message, and Minutes of a Meeting Summary

| Type of Communication | Definition | Format/Structure |
|---|---|---|
| Fax | An electronic device that transmits documents, drawings, and photos as exact reproductions | Cover sheet with name, phone number and fax number of sender; name, company, and fax number of recipient; date and number of pages; any message |
| Phone message | A message from a caller to some-one not present to receive the call | Name of person who called; caller's name, phone number; date, time, purpose of call; message, name of person who took message |
| Minutes of a meeting | A summary of events and decisions that occur at meetings: | |
| | Heading | Name of organization<br>Purpose of meeting<br>Date, time, and place of meeting<br>Chairperson and secretary<br>Names of those present and absent<br>Approval of previous meeting's minutes |
| | Body | Paragraph(s) on subject matters regarding decisions, rulings, events, and data |
| | Conclusion | Time and place of next meeting Agenda<br>Chairperson and secretary |

# Skills Review

*Add to the sentence the type of adverb that is described in the parentheses:*

1. The patient ate his meal. (adverb telling how) _____

2. A low-fat diet was ordered. (adverb telling when) _____

3. The patient ambulated to the door and back. (how) _____

4. The pain increased. (how) _____

5. The patient was bleeding. (how) _____

*Identify the modifiers and state whether they are adverbs or adjectives:*

1. The extensive surgery took hours. _____

2. Xylocaine was used locally. _____

3. The chronic pain was treated with morphine. _____

4. The incision was made laterally. _____

5. The medication was given orally. _____

*Give the comparative and superlative forms of these adverbs:*

1. fast      _____     _____

2. badly     _____     _____

3. lovingly    _____     _____

4. poor      _____     _____

5. carefully   _____     _____

*Rewrite these sentences, if necessary.*

1. The doctor won't order no laxative.

_____

2. The patient's temperature hasn't hardly risen all day.

_____

3. The operation wasn't never cancelled.

_____

4. Nothing couldn't hardly stop the bleeding.

_____

5. This sphygmomanometer won't never be useful again.

_____

*Circle the correct word within the parentheses:*

1. The nurse hadn't told (anybody, nobody) about the patient.

2. OSHA standards protect employees who may be (occupational, occupationally) exposed to infectious material.

3. There is exposure to blood or other (potential, potentially) infectious material.

4. The answer to the problem was (probably, probable) easy to solve.

5. Remove all protective clothing (immediate, immediately) upon leaving the work area.

*Indicate whether these statements are true or false:*

1. The most important procedure in any type of written communication is to follow all steps in the writing process. _____

2 To send an e-mail is more expensive than using the telephone. _____

3. A cover letter is not necessary when sending a fax. _____

4. Phone messages may be written in longhand. _____

5. Make the e-mail short, complete, and accurate. _____

*Circle the correctly spelled word in each line:*

| | | | |
|---|---|---|---|
| 1. chronicaly | kronically | chroncally | chronically |
| 2. portnetally | potentiantly | potentially | protentially |
| 3. signifcanntly | signifikantlly | significantly | sigfically |
| 4. intervenously | intrevenously | intervously | intravenously |
| 5. primarely | primarily | premarily | primerily |
| 6. developementally | deveolpmentally | developmentally | defelopmentally |
| 7. imediately | immediately | imediately | immedeately |
| 8. confidentally | confedintialy | confidentilly | confidentially |
| 9. dorsally | dorsilly | dorsaly | dorsully |
| 10. latirally | laterally | latarally | lateraly |

*Translate medical abbreviations using a medical dictionary or appendix.*

1. KUB _____

2. LE _____

3. LP _____

4. mEq _____

5. LUQ _____

6. MI _____

7. mg _____

8. NKA _____

9. NPO _____

10. NSAID _____

# Comprehensive Review

The office medical assistant received a phone call from Tom Dwyer at Oxford Laboratories stating that he had a change of plans and cannot attend the meeting on this coming Friday morning. He also asked that your employer, Morgan Jones, call him immediately to reschedule another meeting.

*Use the form below to write a phone message to your employer. Include and underline at least three adverbs.*

To _____

Date _____ Time _____

WHILE YOU WERE OUT

PHONE MESSAGE

M _____

Of _____

Phone _____

Telephoned _____          Called to see you _____

Please call back _____          Returned your call _____

Will call again _____          Urgent _____

MESSAGE

_____
_____
_____
_____

*Write a different adverb in each circle to modify the verb.*

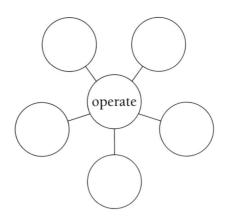

*Then write a sentence for each one, using words that apply in a medical situation.*

1. _____

2. _____

3. _____

4. _____

5. _____

# CHAPTER 9

# Prepositions and Conjunctions

---

## PRACTICAL WRITING COMPONENT: RESEARCH MANUSCRIPT, GRANT

**OBJECTIVES**  *Upon completion of this chapter, the learner should be able to:*

❖ recognize prepositions, compound prepositions, and prepositional phrases

❖ use prepositional phrases as modifiers

❖ understand problematic prepositions

❖ recognize coordinating, correlative, and subordinating conjunctions

❖ spell various medical terms

❖ translate various medical abbreviations

❖ consult various resources for medical research

❖ understand the format for writing a manuscript and grant proposal

## Prepositions

A preposition shows how a noun or pronoun is related to another word or group of words in a sentence. It is a connective word that joins a noun or pronoun to the rest of the sentence. Prepositions are used very often in speaking and writing. A prepositional phrase is nonessential and can be removed entirely from a sentence.

### Examples

Sociology is the study *of* the origins *of* society.

Anatomy is the science *of* the structure *of* the body and the relationship *of* its parts.

"Physio-" refers *to* nature. Physiology is the study *of* the functions and activities *of* the living body.

Radiopaque means impenetrable *to* x-rays. X-rays do not go *through* metals.

Dr. Jack and Dr. Jill went *up* the hall *to* fetch a liter *of* I.V. fluid.

Dr. Jack fell *down* the hall and broke his arm. Dr. Jill came tumbling *after* him.

The words in italics, the prepositions, show the relationship to the nouns and pronouns in the sentences.

Some prepositions help to show location or place: *between, below, near, on, against, in,* and *through.*

# Examples

Lateral is situated away *from* the midline *of* the body.

Intercostal is *between* the ribs.

Subcostal means *below* a rib.

Decline means *to* go down *to* something lower.

Dorsal means *toward* or situated *on* the back side.

The medical report is *on* the table.

*In* the anatomical position, the body is facing forward *with* the arms *at* the sides and the palms *toward* the front.

A few prepositions show a relationship of time: *before, during, since,* and *until.*

# Examples

*Before* performing the examination, wash your hands carefully.

The intern fell asleep *during* the lecture.

I can't pay my medical loans *until* I get a job.

*During* the delivery of the Rh-negative baby, some of the baby's blood cells containing antigens may escape *into* the mother's bloodstream.

Other prepositions show different kinds of relationships between a noun or pronoun and another word: *about, among, by, for, from, like, of, to,* and *with.*

# Examples

Rh immune globulin is given *to* the mother *to* help prevent the antigen–antibody reaction.

Antibiotics inhibit the growth *of* microorganisms.

Biopsy is the examination *of* tissue *from* the body.

The biopsy was taken *from* the lymph node.

A professional relationship exists *among* doctors and health-care professionals.

Some prepositions indicate direction: *around, beside, under, through, across, over, toward,* and *to.*

# Examples

The sterile drape was placed *over* the Mayo stand.

The cast is molded *around* the contours of the body.

Place the tourniquet *around* the arm three or four inches *above* the venipuncture site.

The physical therapist put the patient *through* range of motion exercises.

## Common Prepositions

| | | |
|---|---|---|
| about | between | on/onto |
| above | beyond | out/outside |
| across | by | over |
| after | concerning | past |
| against | despite | round |
| along | down | regarding |
| amid | during | since |
| among | except | through, throughout |
| around | for | till |
| as | from | to, toward |
| at | in/into | under, underneath |
| before | inside/outside | until |
| behind | like | unto |
| below | near | up/upon |
| beneath | of | with/without/within |
| beside/besides | off | |

## COMPOUND PREPOSITIONS

Compound prepositions are two or three words that are used so frequently together that they function like one-word prepositions.

## Commonly Used Compound Prepositions

| | | |
|---|---|---|
| according to | in addition to | in terms of |
| along with | in back of | in support of |
| apart from | in connection with | next to |
| as for | in contrast to | on account of |
| as regards | in defense of | on behalf of |
| as to | in front of | out of |
| aside from | in place of | together with |
| because of | in reference to | with reference to |
| by way of | in regard to | with regard to |
| contrary to | in spite of | with respect to |
| due to | instead of | |

## PREPOSITIONAL PHRASES

A prepositional phrase begins with a preposition and ends with a noun or pronoun that is its object.

## Examples

| | |
|---|---|
| by next Wednesday | under the fascia |
| through the bloodstream | for the patient |
| at work | regarding the long-term prognosis |

# Practice 9-1

*Underline the prepositional phrases:*

1. Throughout the exam, Mrs. Griffs was very cooperative and without pain.

2. The liver removes bilirubin from the blood.

3. Vitamin K aids in the clotting of blood and is responsible for the production of prothrombin.

4. Vitamin D aids in the building of bones and the body's use of calcium and phosphorus.

5. The normal pulse rate for toddlers and very young children is 80 to 100 pulsations per minute.

As a word of caution regarding compound prepositions, avoid using two or three words when a single word will suffice.

## Examples

| | |
|---|---|
| Compound | Place the patient's medication *next to* the file. |
| Singular | Place the patient's medication *beside* the file. |
| Compound | Medical supplies are kept *inside of* the cabinet. |
| Singular | Medical supplies are kept *in* the cabinet. |
| Compound | Rose is doing well *in spite of* her sickness. |
| Singular | Rose is doing well *despite* her sickness. |
| Compound | Rubber gloves are placed *down under* the shelf. |
| Singular | Rubber gloves are placed *under* the shelf. |

Compound     Medical assistants' uniforms are made *out of* synthetic materials.

Singular     Medical assistants' uniforms are made *of* synthetic materials.

# Practice 9-2

*Underline the compound preposition and its object:*

1. According to the physician, the patient can exercise in spite of his injury.

2. Because of the cancer metastasis, the patient will be discharged.

3. Dr. Villes spoke in support of the consultation.

4. I thank you on behalf of my staff for your dedicated service.

5. With respect to the involved personnel, this has been a team effort.

## Prepositional Noun/Pronoun Modifiers

As a preposition and the accompanying word or words that form the prepositional phrase are often used to modify a noun or pronoun. Such phrases are usually found in one of two positions: after the word being modified or after a linking verb.

# Examples

An *assistant* to the doctor made the travel arrangements to the conference.

The purpose of splinting prevents *motion* of the injured part.

The medical *report* is on the table.

He *is* in the waiting room.

# Practice 9-3

*Underline the prepositional phrase, and circle the noun it modifies:*

1. An insurance company charges a premium for its coverage.

2. A patient with emphysema uses the Fowler's position.

3. The autoclave in the treatment room is working.

4. All employees in the medical office must observe asepsis.

5. Hypertension is a major contributor to heart attacks.

## Prepositional Verb Modifiers

Prepositional phrases can also modify verbs and answer the questions *how? when? where?* and *to what extent?*

## Examples

The tricuspid valve is located *in the heart.* [where?]

The medication must be taken *with meals.* [when?]

The surgeon dictates the surgical procedure *in great detail.* [to what extent?]

Prepositional phrases that modify verbs can occupy different positions in the sentence, thus enabling the writer to emphasize different points.

## Examples

*At last,* the patient agreed to undergo treatment.

The patient agreed *at last* to undergo treatment.

The patient agreed to undergo treatment *at last.*

Good writing focuses on the reader rather than the writer. Starting a sentence with the word *I* can easily be avoided by beginning the sentence with a prepositional phrase instead.

## Examples

*On Friday,* I spoke to the x-ray technician.

*In spite of the work involved,* I want to write the article for the medical journal.

## Practice 9-4

*Underline the prepositional phrase, and circle the verb it modifies:*

1. Personality remains stable during normal aging.

2. Repression occurs when painful thoughts are forced into the unconscious.

3. Tissues that are removed in surgery are sent to pathology.

4. Illness is denied through defense mechanisms.

5. Viruses live within other cells and can be seen only by electron microscopes.

*Circle all of the prepositions in this paragraph:*

"I will follow that system of regimen which, according to my ability and judgment, I consider for the benefit of my patients, and abstain from whatever is deleterious and mischievous. I will give no deadly medicine to anyone if asked, nor suggest any such counsel; and in like manner I will not give to a woman a pessary to produce abortion. With purity and with holiness I will pass my life and practice my art. I will not cut persons laboring under the stone, but will leave this to be done by men who are practitioners of the work. Into whatever houses I enter, I will go into them for the benefit of the sick, and I will abstain from every voluntary act of mischief and corruption; and, further, from the seduction of females or males, of freemen and slaves. Whatever, in connection with my professional practice, or not in connection with it, I see or hear, in the life of men, which ought not to be spoken of abroad, I will not divulge, as reckoning that all such should be kept secret." (Taken from the Hippocratic Oath)

## PROBLEMATIC PREPOSITIONS

Prepositions that often cause difficulty in writing are *between* and *among*, and *beside* and *besides*. *Between* refers to two people, things, or groups and *among* refers to more than two:

Information *between* a patient and a physician is highly confidential.

*Among* all the students in the class, she was the one who worked in the OR.

*Beside* means "next to" and besides means "in addition to" or "except":

The oxygen tank is *beside* the bed.

There is another insurance company *besides* that HMO that offers the benefits.

*Practice 9-5*

*Identify the correct word within parentheses:*

1. (Beside, Besides) radiation, the patient must also have chemotherapy.

2. This information is shared (among, between) the doctor and the patient.

3. The medication was placed (beside, besides) the glass of water.

4. Hospital physicians are (among, between) the personnel who attended the meeting.

5. Corridors (between, among) the first and second floor must be locked.

Other prepositions that often are misused are *to, different from, in,* and *into.* The problem with the preposition *to* is that it sounds like the words *two* and *too. To* is a preposition meaning toward something, *two* is a number and a noun, and *too* is an adverb meaning "also":

John went *to* the science lab.

*Two* opinions are needed by the insurance company.

I'd like more medical information, *too.*

Confusion exists about the use of the preposition *from* after the word *different.* The preferred expression is *different from* rather than *different than.*

Use *different from* when it means the same as "differs from something else":

The recommendation was *different from* ours.

Use *different than* with the comparative degree of adjectives and adverbs:

Mr. Jones's training was *different than* Mr. Smith's.

The preposition *in* refers to a location or movement within an area:

The file is *in* Dr. Villes's office.

The preposition *into* means "entry, introduction, insertion, superposition, or inclusion":

The doctor and lawyer entered *into* a mutual agreement, and then the patient came *into* the conference room.

# Practice 9-6

*Identify the correct word to be used from within the parentheses:*

1. The supervisor wanted the nurse to look (in, into) the causes of the injury.

2. A heart operation is very (different than, different from) a lung operation.

3. Medical personnel entered (in, into) a discussion about cancer treatment.

4. Isopropyl alcohol is used to clean the surface of the skin, (to, too, two).

5. Put the specimen (in, into) the container.

## PREPOSITIONS AT THE END OF A SENTENCE

Many English instructors maintain that a sentence ending with a preposition is weak. However, it is an acceptable practice to do so in certain situations, such as when the preposition is part of the previous verb and when the end preposition emphasizes a strong point.

## Examples

I am sending you some reports to look *at*. Read them *through*.

The medical team can be counted *on*.

The side effects were too much to contend *with*.

Where did the cancer metastasize *from*?

In formal writing, it is best to try to place the preposition anywhere but at the end or to rewrite (but without being awkward).

## Examples

Medicare is for patients 65 years of age or *over.*

Medicare is for patients *over* 65 years of age. (better)

The subject of death and dying is difficult to talk *about.*

Death and dying is a difficult subject *about* which to talk. (awkward)

Chris is the person I work *with.* I work *with* Chris. (better)

What is the book *about?* The book is *about* what? (awkward)

Where is this medication shipped *to?* Where is the medication shipped? (better)

## Practice 9-7

*Rearrange the preposition within the sentence or otherwise revise for clarity:*

1. These symptoms are something I never heard *of.* _____

2. Cathy feels it necessary to drain the water *off.* _____

3. I changed the dressing *after* physical therapy. _____

4. What are you in the hospital *for?* _____

5. The anesthesiologist put the patient *under?* _____

# Conjunctions

A conjunction is another part of speech that joins words or parts of sentences. There are three types: coordinating, correlative, and subordinating.

### COORDINATING CONJUNCTIONS

The coordinating conjunctions *and, but, or,* and *yet* are used to join two single words or groups of words of the same kind or of equal construction.

## Examples

Dr. Hebert *and* Dr. Balin prepared for surgery. [The conjunction *and* joins two proper nouns, *Dr. Hebert* and *Dr. Balin,* to form a compound subject.]

Ask Kate *or* Jane to cover the main desk. [The word *or* connects or joins the two indirect objects, *Kate* and *Jane.*]

His speech was short *but* effective. [*But* connects the equal construction of the two predicate adjectives, *short* and *effective*.]

She said she'd be late, *yet* she arrived on time. [*Yet* connects the group of words relating the similar constructions, *she'd be late* and *she arrived on time*.]

## CORRELATIVE CONJUNCTIONS

Correlative conjunctions consist of two elements used as pairs to connect parallel structures.

| | |
|---|---|
| both … and | *Both* the doctor *and* the nurse were present. |
| not only … but also | The machine *not only* copies materials *but also* sorts. |
| either … or | *Either* I *or* my assistant will be in the ER. |
| whether … or | I'm going *whether* you are *or* you're not. |
| neither … nor | *Neither* the doctor *nor* the nurse could contain the patient on the stretcher. |

## SUBORDINATING CONJUNCTIONS

The subordinating conjunction begins an adverb clause and joins the clause to the sentence. This type of conjunction is covered in detail in Chapter 10 on clauses and phrases.

## Practice 9-8

*Identify the conjunction and state whether it is coordinating or correlative:*

1. Give Valerie or Christopher a call at the hospital. _____

2. Both chemotherapy and radiation are needed for this type of cancer._____

3. Runny nose and general malaise are symptoms of a cold. _____

4. You can make a dental appointment either now or later. _____

5. Either set the fracture now or bring the patient for a CT scan. _____

# Prepositions and Conjunctions Summary

| | | |
|---|---|---|
| **Prepositions** | Shows how a noun/pronoun is related to another word or group of words in a sentence; a connective word that joins a noun/pronoun to the rest of the sentence: "The letter continues *on* the next page." | |
| Compound prepositions | Two to three words that function like one preposition. | I'm calling *in regard to* the package I received *by way of* Federal Express. |

| Prepositional phrases | Begins with a preposition and ends with a noun or pronoun that is its object. | The procedure took place *in the operating room.* |
|---|---|---|

Prepositional modifiers:

| Noun/pronoun modifiers | Found after the word modified or after a linking verb. | The reason *for the meeting* is obvious. The reports are filed *under the letter S.* |
|---|---|---|
| Verb modifiers | Modifies a verb and answers *how? when? where? and to what extent?* | The answer is found *in the last chapter.* (where) The medication is taken *before going to bed.* (when) |
| Problematic prepositions | Between—refers to two. Among—refers to more than two. <br><br> Beside— next to. <br><br> Besides—in addition to. To—the preposition. Two—the number. Too—also. Different from is the preferred expression over different than. | This information is just *between* us. Patience is listed *among* the qualities. Stand *beside* me during the announcement. *Besides* the book there is a map. Go *to* the OR STAT! *Two* problems exist in the report. I'm going, *too.* This treatment is *different from* the last one. |
| Prepositions at the end of a sentence | An acceptable practice when preposition is part of a previous verb or emphasizes a strong point. Try to avoid it at the end in formal writing. | This is one thing you have to attend *to.* |
| **Conjunctions** | Joins words or parts of sentences | |
| Coordinating | Joins two single words or groups of words of the same kind or equal construction: *and, but, yet.* "Vitamin D is found in liver, butter, *and* green vegetables." "The wound is healing, *yet* it still needs to be covered." | |
| Correlative | Pairs of words used to connect parallel structures: <br><br> *both . . . and:* "*Both* Ben *and* his wife are sick." <br><br> *not only . . . but also:* "The doctor is *not only* a surgeon *but also* an instructor." <br><br> *either . . . or:* "The patient comes in *either* today *or* sometime next week." <br><br> *whether . . . or:* "*Whether* the scrubs are green *or* yellow is up to you." <br><br> *neither . . . nor:* "*Neither* the x-ray *nor* other tests revealed any problem." | |
| Subordinating | Begins an adverb clause and joins it to the sentence: "*Before* she left the doctor's office, she paid her copayment." | |

# Summary of the Parts of Speech

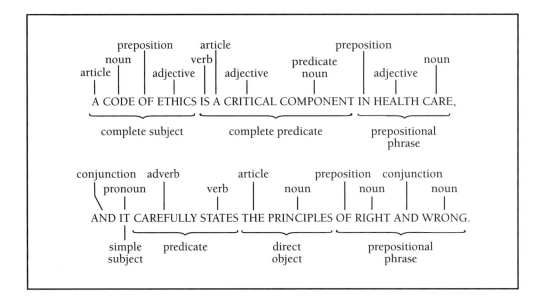

# Medical Spelling

*Become familiar with the spelling of the following words:*

| | |
|---|---|
| antiemetic | manipulation |
| antihistamines | metastasis |
| asepsis | nausea |
| asphyxia | palpitation |
| autoclave | percussion |
| bilirubin | postprandial |
| cyanotic | prothrombin |
| deficiency | pruritus |
| diaphoresis | regime |
| diaphragm | regimen |
| electrode | sanitization |
| eliminated | semi-Fowler's |
| fascia | specimen |
| flatulence | sterilization |
| Fowler's position | syncope |
| fumigation | technique |
| hazardous | Trendelenburg |
| hypertension | urticaria |
| isopropyl | vertigo |
| lithotomy | viruses |

Prepositions and conjunctions are short words or phrases that help connect ideas within sentences in order to establish larger ideas; for example, "the patient experienced *both* physical injury *and* psychological trauma, which calls for closer analysis." This kind of structure can be especially useful when writing more formal documents, such as research papers, manuscripts, and grant writing.

# Research, Manuscripts, Grants

The diversity of writings in the medical profession is vast, ranging from a single one-page information sheet to a research paper containing multiple pages. The most common types of medical writings are listed bellow.

*Journal article:* writing on a specific topic that details background, methods, results, and conclusions; usually appears in a newspaper, journal, or magazine.

*Manuscript:* a written or typewritten version of a book or other work submitted for publication.

*Report:* a formal account of proceedings presented in detail.

*Document:* an original written or printed page that furnishes evidence or information.

*Abstract:* a short piece of writing that clearly summarizes larger works; covers procedures, results of studies or experiments, and conclusions.

*Research paper:* an investigation into a topic to obtain facts or theories.

*Grant proposal:* a request for a sum of money to research special projects.

# Research

Research is necessary in all types of medical writing. Research is a diligent and systematic investigation into a topic to discover facts and theories. Change occurs rapidly in the development of diseases, health conditions, treatments, and technologies. Continuous research is an integral process to the advancement of medical discoveries. One- or two-year-old data are considered outdated. Here are some available resources.

❖ Medical libraries

❖ Internet

❖ Medical periodicals

❖ Public health department

❖ Healthcare organizations

❖ Hospitals and clinics

❖ Interviews with medical personnel

❖ Computer technology

❖ Clinical studies

When researching medical literature, focus on finding the answers to these analytical questions:

What is the objective of the study?

Was the hypothesis tested?

Were convincing factors used to justify the study?

Were laboratory tests used?

What were the significant results?

Did the conclusions match the results?

What new questions resulted?

# *Manuscripts*

Medical professionals may not be required to write original materials. However, they are routinely responsible for the mechanics, editing, and organization of multiple pages of data.

## GENERAL FORMAT GUIDELINES

Undoubtedly, the most challenging piece of writing to organize is the manuscript. The manuscript is a document intended for publication, either as an article in a periodical, a chapter in a book, or a complete book. When publication is under consideration, the publisher usually provides format guidelines. The main parts of a manuscript as follows:

| | |
|---|---|
| Title Page | Title |
| | Names of authors |
| | For whom the manuscript is written |
| | Name of the department, affiliation. |
| | Date of submission |
| Abstract | Brief summary of the article (100–150 words) |
| Introduction | Specific problem under study |
| | Background to clarify topic |
| | Rationale and purpose of the manuscript |
| Methods | How the study was conducted |
| | Procedure |
| Results | Tables and figures |
| | Statistics |
| Discussion | Evaluation and interpretation of results |
| Other Experiments | Integration of results |
| References | Supportive interpretations cited |
| Appendix | Supplementary information |

## APA WRITING STYLE

Manuscripts written about topics in the medical field should follow the American Psychological Association (APA) style of writing. Anyone writing a manuscript should secure a copy of the *Publication Manual of the American Psychological Association.*

A copy can be obtained from

American Psychological Association
Book Order Department
P. O. Box 92984
Washington, DC 20090-2984

Telephone 800.374.2721          FAX 202.336.5502

Web site: www.apa.org/books/ordering

Consider these basic APA guidelines when organizing and editing a manuscript:

❖ Standard white bond paper, 81/2 by 11 inches

❖ One inch margins on top, bottom, left, and right sides

❖ Lines typed unjustified, or uneven (ragged) at the right margin

❖ Pages numbered consecutively in upper right-hand corner, using Arabic numerals

❖ Pages arranged in the following order:

Title page (page 1)

Abstract is on a separate page (page 2)

Text starts a new page (page 3)

References

## Title Page

On the title page, the main title is typed in uppercase and lowercase letters. If the main title is more than one line, use a double space between the lines. An abbreviated version of the title is called a running head, which may be used for identification of the article on subsequent pages. The name of the author and affiliation appear on separate lines. If the author of the manuscript is not affiliated with an institution, the city and state of the author is used instead (see Figure 9-1).

## Abstract Page

The word "abstract" is centered on the abstract page (Figure 9-2). A running head is used, and the text is one paragraph in block form, double-spaced.

## Text Page

On the first page of text (Figure 9-3), the title is centered, one double space below the short title. The first line of the text is one double space below the main title.

Secondhand Smoke   1

Respiratory Health Effects of

Secondhand Smoke

Dr. Corner Weinman

Villes Medical Center

**FIGURE 9-1**   *Manuscript Title Page*

## Reference Page

A reference list is a list (Figure 9-4) of all sources cited in a manuscript. (In contrast, a bibliography lists further readings or other works not specifically cited in the text.) References are placed in alphabetical order by the author's last name. The first names are abbreviated. The first line of an item is indented and subsequent lines are flush with the left margin. All typing is double spaced.

## Citations

When facts, opinions, and ideas of others are referred to in a manuscript, it is necessary to acknowledge the source. If a writer quotes or paraphrases a fact or idea in a text, the author's last name, the year of publication, and, if applicable, a page number are cited parenthetically.

## *Examples*

Furthermore, Parker (1988) found that . . .

Diseases have been reported to increase (Momfort, 1989).

Secondhand Smoke   2

Abstract

The overall percentage of people affected by secondary smoke has reached

alarming proportions according to this study . . .

**FIGURE 9-2**   *Manuscript Abstract Page*

Secondhand Smoke   3

Respiratory Health Effects of

Secondhand Smoke

The first recorded use of tobacco appeared over a thousand years ago

on Mayan stone carvings. History also records that Columbus saw natives

roll, light, and smoke tobacco . . .

**FIGURE 9-3**   *First Page of Text of Manuscript*

Secondhand Smoke   30

Reference

MgGinnis, J.M. (1997). Health progress in the United States. *Journal of the American Medical Association, 46*(4), 130–132.

Lo, B. (2000). Behind closed doors: Promises and pitfalls of ethics committees, *New England Journal of Medicine, 28*(2), 150–167.

**FIGURE 9-4**   *First Page of Reference List of Manuscript*

In a study conducted in this city, Wahlen and Pyne (2000) found that . . .

Dr. Villes determined that the cause was due to "inadequate diet" (Smith 1997, p. 189).

The *Publication Manual of the American Psychological Association* covers text reference citations and reference lists in great detail.

# Grant Writing

Health facilities, like most other community service organizations, seek funding from private foundations and corporations, or from government programs for various projects or specific medical research endeavors. Funding source requirements differ in length and format. However, the same types of information are generally required. A simple, basic format and logical approach to planning and writing a grant is explained in this chapter.

Further information about grants may be obtained from these sources:

www.tgci.com/publications/puborder

www.synapseadaptive.com

www.techwriteinc.com

www.revisions-grants.com

A simple format for writing a grant follows:

1. Proposal Summary

2. Introduction

3. Problem Statement

4. Goals and Objectives

5. Methods

6. Evaluation

7. Future Funding

8. Budget

9. Appendix

## PROPOSAL SUMMARY

The proposal summary briefly summarizes the whole proposal text. It is the first thing a grant reviewer reads, either in the few opening paragraphs of a letter or as a larger section within a more formal proposal. The summary provides the first impression, so it should be good.

## INTRODUCTION

The introductory component reinforces the connection between the requesting organization and the granting organization. The requesting organization uses this section to build its credibility, which may be more significant than the rest of the proposal. Include these important points:

❖ History of the organization

❖ Uniqueness of the agency

❖ Significant accomplishments

❖ Scope of financial support

❖ Successful related projects

❖ Support received from other individuals and organizations

## PROBLEM STATEMENT

The section stating the problem deals with specific societal issues outside the organization that could be addressed if funds were granted (issues of homelessness, children with AIDS, violence among youth). Make sure the problem is realistic and that the proposed solution can be achieved in reasonable time with reasonable funds. Demonstrate knowledge of the problem with data and quotation from experts nationally and locally.

## GOALS AND OBJECTIVES

Goals are general statements that offer the reader a broad picture of the problematic issue. Because goals are broad, they cannot be measured as stated.

## Examples

Reduce teenage smoking.

Enhance reading skills of children with learning disability.

Objectives are specific, measurable outcomes of the program and the promises made to improve the conditions in the problem statement.

## Examples

Reduce teenage smoking by 20%.

Within one year, children with learning disabilities will increase their reading ability by two grade levels.

The specifics of the objectives should realistically estimate the amount of benefit expected from a program. One way to define specific objectives is to project where the agency could be a year or two in the future.

## METHODS

The methods section explains what strategies need to be implemented to bring about the desired results. This section gives the reader a picture of exactly how things will work and look. Justify the methodology by stating why certain strategies were chosen over others.

## EVALUATION

An evaluation serves two purposes. The first is that it measures the results of the proposal. The second is that it can also provide information to make changes or adjustments in the program as it moves along. To do this, the evaluation plan is implemented at the time the program starts.

Having an outside organization perform the evaluation is an option. An outside evaluation gives a more objective viewpoint and adds more credibility to the proposal.

## FUTURE FUNDING

The future funding component explains what happens to the program after the grant money is spent, unless it is a one-time request. Present a plan that assures there is life after the grant is completed.

## BUDGET

A budget is a list of expenditures during a given period. Funds to run a program fall into three categories:

1. Personnel: salaries and wages for full or part-time staff, including fringe benefits, consultants, and contract fees. These expenses may be determined by comparing salaries to similar services elsewhere. In-kind services should be listed; that is, matching support contributions by the requesting agency.

2. Nonpersonal expenses: rent for space, lease or purchase of equipment, travel, hotel, meals, printing, and professional association membership or dues.

3. Indirect costs: costs not readily identifiable but necessary to the operation of the whole fall into this category, such as phone costs and general supplies.

## APPENDIX

An appendix is a collection of supplementary materials provided at the end of the proposal. (Refer to the appendixes at the end of this book as examples.) Grantors may stipulate what to include in this section, but here are some common elements:

| | |
|---|---|
| Financial audit | List of board of directors |
| Nonprofit status | Organizational plan |
| Timelines | Letters of support, endorsement |
| Resumes | Job descriptions |

❉ ❉ ❉

Many agencies that rely on grants for support often contract the services of a professional grant proposal writer. Otherwise, proposals are written by the personnel of the requesting organization. The role of medical assistants, however, is to organize information given to them into an acceptable grant format. See Figure 9-5 for a sample grant proposal.

## Proposal Summary

The purpose of this one-time grant is to seek $8,000 from the Davis Foundation to present a Teen Smoke-Out Program at Barry High School, in collaboration with the Villes Medical Center. The general goal of the program is to reduce smoking among students by at least 20% (30 students). The methodologies used to achieve this goal are to sponsor four two-hour seminars by a physician, to disseminate educational materials among students, to conduct a peer support group twice a month, and to offer individual counseling sessions as needed. Evaluation procedures are conducted to determine the effectiveness of the program in order to integrate it into the school's core curriculum in subsequent years.

## Introduction

Nicotine is the most addictive drug used by teenagers today. Two facilities, the Villes Medical Center and Barry High School, are collaborating to address this issue.

The Villes Medical Center, established over 25 years ago, provides a variety of medical services within the state and beyond. The Center is especially successful in providing smoking-cessation programs within educational settings. More than 87 elementary and high schools have benefited from the expertise of the Center's qualified staff. Grants, service fees, and private donations support the Center.

Barry High School is a public facility offering college, business, and technology courses to prepare students for life and work. Enrollment is approximately 500 students, with a student–teacher ratio of 1 to 15. The philosophy of the school is the total development of the student in body, mind, and spirit, that each may reach his or her full human potential.

## Problem Statement

Smoking is the most serious health risk among teens today. More than 3,000 teens become smokers daily. In a given year, teens smoked 28 million cigarettes. More than 5 million teens will prematurely die because they chose to smoke. Teens who smoke are more likely to use alcohol, marijuana, and cocaine.

According to a recent health survey given at Barry High School, three out of ten students smoke—150 out of a total of 500 students. Barry High School, in collaboration with the Villes Medical Center, decided to do something to reduce smoking among teens. The request of $8,000 in grant funds from the Davis Foundation is for that purpose.

## Goals and Objectives

The goals of the grant are to

1. Educate the student population on the effects of smoking.
2. Reduce the smoking rate of teens at Barry High School.

**FIGURE 9-5** *Sample Grant Proposal*

The goals are to be achieved through these objectives:

1. Provide four two-hour educational Teen Smoke-out Seminars.
2. Reduce the number of teenage smokers by 20% in one year.
3. Provide an incentive to entice students to quit smoking.
4. Inform parents and elicit their support through the home.

## Methods

Strategies of the program consist of the following:

1. Present four seminars on smoking by a physician from the Villes Medical Center to freshman, sophomore, junior, and senior classes during their respective assembly periods. Topics are the health effects of smoking, reasons for teen smoking, societal and individual costs of smoking, and smoking prevention. Seminars will occur in October, December, February, and April.
2. Establish a bimonthly support group facilitated by a Barry High School counselor and the Villes Medical Center smoking cessation counselor.
3. Give two additional credits in health science to smokers who commit themselves to the group process.
4. Offer individual counseling to group members as needed.
5. Provide program information to parents and ask for their support.

## Evaluation

The program will be evaluated in three ways:
1. Give the health survey again to determine the number of students who quit smoking.
2. Have students fill out an evaluation sheet after each seminar.
3. Ask for continuous feedback from the bimonthly support group.

## Future Funding

This grant is for one year. Seminars will be videotaped and integrated into the core curriculum in subsequent years.

## Budget

Educational Materials
    Videos/Movies    $1,500
    Text: <u>Tobacco Biology and Politics,</u> by Stanton A. Glantz, Ph.D.    2,500
    Pamphlets, Brochures, Charts, Modules, Information Sheets    600

**FIGURE 9-5** Continued

| Personnel | | |
|---|---|---|
| Physician | | 1,200 |
| Group Counselor | | 1,000 |
| Individual Counselor | | 1,000 |
| Travel | | 200 |
| | TOTAL | $8, 000 |

| In-kind Contributions | | |
|---|---|---|
| Program Coordinator | | 2,000 |
| Barry High School Counselor | | 1,000 |
| Facility Space, Maintenance | | 700 |
| Secretarial Services | | 300 |
| | TOTAL | $4,000 |

## Appendix

Copy of Seminar Evaluation Sheet
Resumes of Participating Personnel
Brochures: Villes Medical Center, Barry High School, May I Introduce Myself? I Am a Cigarette

**FIGURE 9-5**   Continued

## Practice 9-9

*Answer true or false to the following statements:*

1. An appendix is a collection of supplementary materials provided at the end of a proposal. _____

2. The section of the grant that deals with specific issues is the evaluation. _____

3. Activities that take place to achieve the objectives of a grant are called references. _____

4. A systematic investigation into topics to discover facts and theories is referred to as research. _____

5. An abstract is a brief summary. _____

# Research, Manuscripts, Grants Summary

**Research**

Investigation into a topic to discover facts and theories.

**Resources:**

Medical libraries, the Internet, medical periodicals, public health departments, healthcare organizations, hospital and clinics, interviews with medical personnel, computer technology software, and clinical studies.

**Manuscripts**

| | |
|---|---|
| Title Page | Title, author(s), affiliations, submission date, for whom written |
| Abstract | 100–150 word summary |
| Introduction | Problem under study, background, purpose, rationale |
| Methods | How the study was conducted, procedure |
| Results | Tables and figures, statistics |
| Discussion | Evaluation and interpretation of results |
| Other experiments | Integration of results |
| References | Supportive interpretations |
| Appendix | Supplementary materials |

**Grants**

| | |
|---|---|
| Proposal Summary | A proposal abstract briefly describing the organization seeking funds, the scope of the project, and the cost. |
| Introduction | Background of the applicant organization, scope of financial support, related projects, and other support received. |
| Problem Statement | Situation or problem to be solved through the proposed grant; the cause for which the proposal was written. |
| Goals and Objectives | Goals: broad and unmeasurable statements that give a general focus to the grant program. |
| | Objectives: specific and measurable outcomes of the situation. |
| Methods | Detailed activities that will take place in order to achieve the objectives of the program. |
| Evaluation | Tools to determine how effective the program was in reaching its goals. |
| Future Funding | How the program will continue when the money runs out. |

Budget                          Itemized list of costs, based on the goals and objectives and strategies to implement them.

Appendix                        Supplementary materials requested by the grantor.

# Skills Review

*Circle the prepositions in the following paragraph:*

John Doe is a 23-year old male suffering from back pain and memory loss as a result of injuries sustained in a car accident three months ago. At that time, the patient was the driver of an automobile traveling across Main to State Street. Another vehicle hit Mr. Doe's car on the front passenger's side before coming to a halt. Complaining of pain with any movement of his neck, John was transported by ambulance to the emergency department of Wells Medical Center. X-rays of the cervical spine revealed an injury affecting his neck and back. He was placed on a high dose of anti-inflammatory medication and muscle relaxants and provided with a cervical collar. Because of the accident, John Doe has been unable to work since the motor vehicle accident in question.

*Write the correct preposition in the blanks:*

1. The study _____ diseases _____ the elderly is called geriatrics.

2. Proximal is _____ the point of attachment.

3. An oncologist is concerned _____ cancer.

4. Ventral and anterior pertain _____ the front of the body.

5. The patient lost much blood _____ the delivery of her child.

*Supply a coordinating or correlative conjunction:*

1. The responsibility belongs _____ to you _____ your assistant.

2. Make sure the patient is conscious enough to eat _____ swallow.

3. Explain the procedure _____ follow-up treatment.

4. _____ we obtain the blood test _____ we give glucose in the form of orange juice.

5. Each person may experience diabetes in his or her own unique way _____ pattern.

*Write the corresponding part of speech from the list below above each italicized word in the sentences.*

noun          adverb          article          adjective

pronoun          preposition          conjunction          verb

1. Patients facing death *pass* through many emotional and psychological stages.

2. Glucose tolerance testing is contraindicated for patients with recent surgery *or* myocardial infarctions.

3. *The* Patient's Bill of Rights is a set of laws that helps protect patients.

4. OSHA suggests safety *measures* that must be taken to prevent or limit the spread of germs.

5. Limiting the use of antibiotics is crucial for the prevention of bacterial growth *and* resistance.

*Answer the following questions.*

1. Arrange these components as they would appear in a manuscript:

   References

   Appendix

   Abstract

   Results

   Title page

   Introduction

2. List four types of resources used in medical research:

   _____          _____

   _____          _____

3. List four types of medical writings:

   _____          _____

   _____          _____

*Select the word that describes the type of medical writing.*

abstract          report          writing style

document          manuscript          research

appendix          journal          grant

1. A request for funds for a special project. _____

2. Work submitted for publication. _____

3. Investigation into a topic to obtain facts or theories. _____

4. Short writing summarizing a larger work. _____

5. Item usually appearing in a newspaper or magazine. _____

6. Original writing that provides evidence or information. _____

*Circle the correctly spelled word in each line:*

| | | | |
|---|---|---|---|
| 1. Trendelanburg | Trendilenburg | Trendelenburg | Trendelonburg |
| 2. hypirtension | hipertension | hypertision | hypertension |
| 3. virus' | viruss | viruses | virusas |
| 4. technikue | tehneque | tecknique | technique |
| 5. urticaria | urtkaria | urtecaria | urtocaria |
| 6. defencency | deficiency | dificiency | deficeincy |
| 7. metaztazis | metatsasis | matastasis | metastasis |
| 8. facia | fascia | faccsia | fassia |
| 9. cianotic | cyantoic | cyanotic | ciaanotyc |
| 10. diaphigm | diafragm | diaphragm | diephragm |

*Translate medical abbreviations using a medical dictionary or appendix.*

1. OOB _____
2. O.S. _____
3. OR _____
4. o.u. _____
5. ORIF _____
6. p.c. _____
7. PERRLA _____
8. p.o. _____
9. p.r.n. _____
10. PTT _____

# Comprehensive Review

*Underline the Prepositional word(s) or phrase(s) that connect to other words in the sentence.*

1. Before performing the procedure, wash your hands.
2. Goals give focus to the grant program.
3. An evaluation measures the results of the proposal.
4. Investigation is a topic of facts and theories.
5. An appendix contains material requested by the grantor.
6. Funding source requirements differ in length and format.
7. Common types of medical writings are documents and research papers.
8. Knowledge is listed among the qualities of a good doctor.
9. I'm calling because I cannot attend.
10. The doctor and lawyer came to a reasonable agreement.

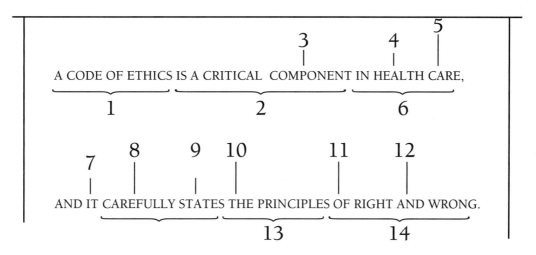

Match the numbered words in the diagram with the words listed below.

article _____

noun _____

preposition _____

verb _____

adjective _____

predicate noun _____

conjunction _____

pronoun _____

adverb _____

prepositional phrase _____

direct object _____

complete subject _____

complete predicate _____

# CHAPTER 10

# Phrases and Clauses

---

## PRACTICAL WRITING COMPONENT: PROMOTIONAL WRITING

*Upon completion of this chapter, the learner should be able to:*

❖ understand how phrases function within the structure of a sentence

❖ recognize various types of phrases

❖ understand how clauses function within the structure of a sentence

❖ recognize various types of dependent and independent clauses

❖ spell various medical terms

❖ translate various medical abbreviations

❖ understand Promotional Writing used in the medical profession

Six previous chapters explained how words are used as single parts of speech. This chapter shows how groups of words function as parts of a sentence.

## Phrases

A phrase is a group of words without a subject or a predicate.

### Examples

|  |  |
|---|---|
| *toward the patient's face* | *on the operating table* |
| *in the left kidney* | *about the curable disease* |

Consider these phrases within the context of a sentence:

| **Subject and Predicate** | **Phrase (No Subject or Predicate)** |
|---|---|
| Urticaria is spreading | *toward the patient's face.* |
| Calculi were found | *in the left kidney.* |

The patient died          *on the operating table.*

Oncologists talked          *about the curable disease.*

Note that the subjects and predicates in these sentences can function independently as complete sentences because they have a subject and a predicate:

*Urticaria is spreading.*

*Calculi were found.*

*The patient died.*

*Oncologists talked.*

The phrases—*toward the patient's face, in the left kidney, on the operating table,* and *about the curable disease*—however, cannot exist independently because they have no subject or predicate.

## PREPOSITIONAL PHRASE

Most phrases in the English language are prepositional phrases. As stated in Chapter 9, a prepositional phrase is a group of words that begins with a preposition and ends with a noun or pronoun that is its object. The phrases *toward the patient's face, in the left kidney, on the operating table,* and *to cure the disease* all contain prepositions, with nouns and their modifiers.

| Preposition | Modifier | Object (Noun or Pronoun) |
| --- | --- | --- |
| toward | the patient's | face |
| in | the left | kidney |
| on | the operating | table |
| about | the curable | disease |

# Practice 10-1

*Identify the prepositional phrases in the following sentences:*

1. Tenderness was noted over the right bicipital tendon.

2. The patient went through lithotripsy.

3. The glomerulus is the filtration unit of the kidney.

4. Nephrectomy is excision of a kidney.

5. Cirrhosis is the degeneration of the parenchyma of the liver.

## Prepositional Phrase Used As a Noun

Prepositional phrases may function in the same manner as nouns.

## Prepositional Phrase Used As an Adjective

Prepositional phrases can modify words in the same manner as do adjectives or adverbs. An adjective phrase is a prepositional phrase that describes a noun or pronoun. Adjective phrases, like adjectives, answer the questions *which one? what kind?* or *how many?* and occupy different positions in a sentence.

## *Examples*

A patient *in room 210* is scheduled for a cholecystogram. [The prepositional phrase *in room 210* describes the noun *patient* by answering *which one?* Therefore, it is an adjective phrase.]

The procedure *with few side effects* is the best alternative. [*With few side effects* describes the noun *procedure.*]

The pathology report *with tissue results* is due tomorrow. [*With tissue results* describes the noun *report.*]

## Prepositional Phrase Used As an Adverb

An adverb phrase is a prepositional phrase that describes a verb, adjective, or another adverb and answers the questions *how? what? when? why? where?* and *to what extent?* Adverb phrases occupy different positions in a sentence.

## *Examples*

Fortunately *for the students,* no additional courses were required. [The phrase *for the students* modifies the adverb *fortunately* and answers the question *why?*]

Nurses worked *without a break.* [The phrase *without a break* modifies the verb *worked* and answers the question *how?*]

The operating room is located conveniently *near the recovery room.* [The phrase *near the recovery room* modifies the adverb *conveniently* and answers the question *where?*]

 *Practice 10-2*

*Identify the prepositional phrase in each sentence as adjective or adverb:*

1. Unfortunately for the patient, the symptoms indicate glomerulonephritis.

2. The patient went to physical therapy daily.

3. Polyuria is an indication of diabetes mellitus.

4. Urology is the study of the urinary tract.

5. A nephrectomy was performed reluctantly because of kidney failure.

## VERBAL PHRASES

A verbal is a nonfinite verb—a verb form that does not make a complete sentence—used as a noun, adjective, or adverb. A verbal phrase is a group of words including a verbal and its subject, object, complement, or modifiers that functions as a noun, adjective, or adverb. There are three types of verbal phrases: participial, gerund, and infinitive.

### Participial Phrase

A participle is a verb form ending in *ing* (the present participle) or *t, d, ed, en,* or other form of the past participle that functions as part of a verbal phrase called a *participial phrase.* A participial phrase usually functions as an adjective.

## *Examples*

The patient, *feeling ill,* took the prescribed medicine. [The participial phrase, *feeling ill,* modifies the noun *patient. Feeling* is the present participle of the verb *feel.*]

The culture *taken from the wound* tested positive for streptococci. [The participial phrase, *taken from the wound,* modifies the noun *culture.*]

## *Practice 10-3*

*Identify the participial phrase in each sentence:*

1. The sterilized instruments wrapped with tape were removed from the autoclave.

2. The patient's voice, weakened from laryngitis, was barely heard.

3. Physicians experiencing the pressure of the HMO need to take control.

4. Immunizations given throughout childhood are recommended by the Public Health Department.

5. Volunteers, retired from careers, perform valuable services in hospitals.

### Gerund Phrase

A gerund is a verb form ending in *ing* that is used in any way that a noun may be used: as a subject, object, object of a preposition, or predicate noun.

## *Examples*

*Walking* is a healthy exercise. [*Walking* is a gerund formed from the verb *walk,* and it is used as the subject of the sentence.]

The patient does appreciate my *caring*. [*Caring* is a gerund formed from the verb care. It is used as a direct object of the verb *does appreciate*.]

You can pass this course by *studying*. [The gerund *studying* is used as an object of the preposition *by*.]

The medical assistant's greatest reward is *learning*. [The gerund *learning* is used as a predicate noun. It follows the linking verb *is*.]

A *gerund phrase* is a group of words consisting of a gerund and any other modifiers it may have. The gerund phrase, like a single gerund, functions as a noun and cannot be removed from the sentence.

## Examples

*Walking a mile* is healthy exercise. [*Walking a mile* is a gerund phrase used as the subject of the sentence.]

The patient does appreciate *my caring*. [*My caring* is a gerund phrase used as a direct object of the verb *does appreciate*.]

You can pass this course by *studying daily*. [The gerund phrase *studying daily* is used as the object of the preposition *by*.]

The nurse's reward is *learning compassion*. [The gerund phrase *learning compassion* is used as a predicate noun following the linking verb *is*.]

Note that both participles and gerunds end in *ing*. The difference is that a participle functions as an *adjective* and a *gerund* functions as a noun. One is essential; the other is not.

## Practice 10-4

*Identify the gerund phrase*:

1. Selecting the correct antibiotic is crucial to this infection.

2. Calculating blood gases is an easy process.

3. Analyzing medical information helps to form a diagnosis.

4. Sterilizing instruments under pressurized steam is the most common method of sterilization.

5. Monitoring blood pressure can also be done in a home environment.

### Infinitive Phrase

An infinitive is a verbal consisting of the present form of a verb usually preceded by the word *to*. It is generally used as a noun, and sometimes as an adjective or adverb.

## Examples

| | |
|---|---|
| Used as a subject | *To operate* would *ease* the *pain*. |
| Used as a direct object | The doctor wants *to operate*. |
| Used as a predicate noun | The decision was *to operate*. |
| Used as an adjective | The decision *to operate* was made by the patient. |

A clarification may be helpful in distinguishing between an infinitive and a prepositional phrase because both constructions include the word *to*. An infinitive is a *verb* plus the word *to*. A prepositional phrase, begins with the word *to* but is followed by a noun or pronoun as the object of the preposition.

## Examples

| | |
|---|---|
| Infinitive | *To smoke* causes lung damage. |
| Prepositional Phrase | Smoking causes damage *to the lungs*. |

An *infinitive phrase* includes the infinitive and any subjects, objects, or modifiers. Like the infinitive itself, it generally functions as a noun, and sometimes as an adjective or adverb.

## Examples

| | |
|---|---|
| Used as a noun | *To cure disease* became the goal of the scientist. [*To cure disease* is an infinitive phrase that functions as a subject.] |
| Used as a predicate noun | His plan is *to operate*. [*To operate* modifies *plan*. It comes after the linking verb *is*.] |
| Used as an adjective | Medical researchers found a way *to solve the problem*. [*To solve the problem* describes the noun *way*.] |
| Used as an adverb | The medical assistant was encouraged *to help nurses*. [*To help nurses* modifies the verb *was encouraged*.] |

# Practice 10-5

*Identify the infinitive phrase in each sentence:*

1. The nurse practitioner needs to analyze the test results.

2. A low fat diet given in small amounts helps to prevent cholecystitis.

3. Leukocytes help to protect the body from infection and tissue damage.

4. To excise the vermiform appendix is called an appendectomy.

5. X-rays are taken to validate any fractures.

## APPOSITIVE PHRASE

An appositive phrase contains an appositive noun along with any modifying words. The phrase is placed next to the noun or pronoun it describes or renames. Commas are used to separate an appositive phrase.

Mike, *the class president,* called the meeting to order. [*The class president* renames Mike; *president* is the appositive noun modified by *the* and *class.*]

## Practice 10-6

*Identify the appositive phrase in each sentence:*

1. Morphine, a drug used to control pain, is often given to cancer patients.

2. Infection, an invasion of a pathogen, is the cause of many diseases.

3. Some protein foods, milk and fish, help repair tissues damaged by disease.

4. The Patient's Bill of Rights, a code of ethical standards, ensures that quality care be given to patients.

5. The report contains a summary of the patient's ADL, activities of daily living.

# Clauses

A clause is a group of words that contains a subject and a verb within the structure of a sentence. Clauses are either independent or dependent.

## INDEPENDENT CLAUSES

An independent clause (also called a main clause) contains a subject and a verb and expresses a complete thought. An independent clause can stand alone as a sentence.

## Examples

*The team wrote the patient's care plan.*

*The lecturer is an HMO representative.*

## DEPENDENT CLAUSES

A dependent clause (also called a subordinate clause) contains a subject and verb but does not express a complete thought and cannot stand alone as a sentence. A dependent clause has a sense of incompleteness about it. It sounds like something more should be said or written:

## Examples

*If you order your prescription today* . . . [What about it? What happens if you order today? More information is needed to make this dependent clause complete the thought.]

*that she didn't know* [Know what?]

*while she was in the hospital* [What about it?]

To make a complete sentence, a dependent clause must be combined with an independent clause.

## Examples

*If you order your prescription today*, you will get a discount.

There were many people at the medical conference *that she didn't know.*

The patient was too sick to read *while she was in the hospital.*

Dependent clauses are usually introduced by subordinating conjunctions or relative pronouns. Examples of subordinating conjunctions are *after, although, as, as if, as long as, as though, because, before, even though, how, if, in order that, provided that, rather than, since, so, so that, though, unless, until, when, whenever, where, whereas, wherever, whether,* and *while.* The relative pronouns are *what, which, that, who, whom,* or *whose.*

## Examples

*Although diabetes can be controlled*, it presents a costly burden in the U.S.

Patients are subject to complications of diabetes *even though they follow the ADA recommendations.*

## Practice 10-7

*Identify the dependent clause in these sentences:*

1. Medical assistants must use judgment when scheduling appointments that require more evaluation time.

2. The CPT code is assigned for services rendered after a patient has a procedure.

3. While the patient was in the hospital, she developed Pseudomonas.

4. Autoimmune diseases are the cause of many chronic illnesses when a person's self-antigens are damaged.

5. Sjögren's syndrome, because it is characterized by dryness of the eyes and mouth, is an autoimmune disorder.

Different conjunctions introduce different types of dependent clauses, of which there are three: the noun clause, adjective clause, and adverb clause.

# NOUN CLAUSE

The noun clause is a dependent clause that functions as a noun. It may be used as a subject, predicate noun, or direct object. Noun clauses are easy to detect because they are introduced by such words as *how, when, where, which, who (whoever), whom (whomever), whose, that, why, what,* or *whether.*

## EXAMPLES

The problem is *that I am too dedicated to my profession.* [predicate noun after the verb *is*]

Do you know *what the emergency is?* [direct object]

The doctor didn't know *what to say.* [direct object]

*Whoever locked the office door* must open it. [subject]

*What the manager planned* was a new hospital wing. [subject]

## Adjective Clause

An adjective clause is a dependent clause that tells about or describes a noun or pronoun. It is usually joined to a main clause by a relative pronoun: *what, which, that, who whose,* or *whom.*

## EXAMPLES

The patient *whom the physician diagnosed with cancer* left suddenly. [The adjective clause, *whom the physician diagnosed with cancer,* modifies the noun *patient.*]

A medical assistant *whose name I can't remember* did a great job. [The adjective clause, *whose name I can't remember,* describes the noun *assistant.*]

## Adverb Clause

An adverb clause functions as an adverb. It tells more about a verb, adjective, or another adverb. Adverb clauses are introduced by subordinating conjunctions such as *also, beside, for example, however, in addition to, instead, meanwhile, then,* and *therefore.* They answer the questions *how, when, why, where, how often, to what extent,* and *under what condition* about the verb.

## EXAMPLES

List currency and coins *when you complete a deposit slip.* [The adverb clause, *when you complete a deposit slip,* modifies the verb *list.*]

Surgeons operate on weekends *if there is an emergency.* [The adverb clause, *if there is an emergency,* modifies the verb *operate.*]

## Practice 10-8

*Identify the dependent clauses in each sentence:*

1. Aspirin should not be used as an antipyretic with children because it may cause viral problems.

2. Phenylketonuria is a disease in which a hereditary enzyme is absent.

3. The staff was told when the patient arrived.

4. The electrocardiogram provides diagnostic information that the cardiologist needs.

5. When you finish, dispose of the syringes into the proper container.

# Phrases Summary

**Phrase:** A group of words without a subject or predicate, which functions as a noun, adjective, or adverb in a sentence.

| | Composition | Function | Example |
|---|---|---|---|
| **Prepositional phrase** | Begins with a preposition, plus nouns or pronouns and any modifiers | Group of words that acts like a single modifier. | . . . valve *in the heart* . . .<br>. . . parking lot *behind the hospital* . . .<br>. . . time *at your earliest convenience.* . . . |
| Used as an adjective | Begins with a preposition, plus nouns or pronouns and any modifiers | Modifies a noun or pronoun. Answers *which one? what kind? how many?* | . . . the blood *in the heart* . . .<br>. . . medicines *to cure infections* . . . |
| Used as an adverb | Begins with a preposition, plus nouns or pronouns and any modifiers. | Modifies a verb, adjective, or other adverb. Answers *how? what? where? when? why? to what extent?* | The blood flowed *through the aorta*<br>The doctor operated on *weekends.*<br>Nurses worked *around the clock.* |

**Verbal Phrase:** A group of words including a verbal and its subject, object, complement, or modifiers that function as a noun, adjective, or adverb.

| | Composition | Function | Example |
|---|---|---|---|
| Participial | Begins with verb ending in *ing* (present participle) or in *t, d, ed, en* (past participle). | Adjective | Nurses *dedicated to patient care* are unsung heroes.<br>The report *containing the patient's history* was sent to another hospital. |

| Gerund | Begins with an *ing* verb and includes any modifiers. | Noun | *Eating healthy food* is an excellent habit. An excellent habit is *eating healthy food.* |
| Infinitive | Begins with *to,* plus present form of a verb and any modifiers. | Noun, predicate noun, adjective, or adverb | *To question* is a sign of intelligence. The doctor asked *to see the file.* |
| Appositive Phrase: | An appositive noun and any modifiers that describe or rename a noun: "The Ethics Committee, *ten members strong,* met yesterday." "Terminology, *a study of words,* is essential in health professions." | | |

# Clauses Summary

**Clause:** A group of words containing a subject and verb. Independent clauses contain a subject and a verb, express a complete thought, and can exist alone as a sentence. Dependent clauses contain a subject and a verb but do not express a complete thought and cannot exist alone in a sentence.

Dependent clauses are introduced by subordinating conjunctions and relative pronouns:

**Subordinating Conjunctions**

*after, although, as, as if, as long as, as though, because, before, even though, how, if, in order that, provided that, rather than, since, so, so that, that, though, unless, until, when, whenever, where, wherever, whereas, whether, while*

**Relative Pronouns**

*which, that, who, whom, whose, what*

| Function | Identifier | Example |
|---|---|---|
| Noun used as a subject, predicate noun, or direct object. | Introduced by *how, when, where, which, who, whoever, whom, whomever, whose, that, why, what, whether.* | The wheelchair is *what I ordered.* I know *how you are feeling.* |
| Adjective used to tell *which one* or *what kind.* | Often introduced by a relative pronoun: *which, that, who, whom, whose, what.* | That was the house *where Dr. Brown lived.* Supplies, *which were ordered in May,* have not arrived yet. |
| Adverb used to tell about a verb, adjective, or another adverb. | Introduced by *also, because, beside, for example, however, if, in addition to, instead, meanwhile, then, therefore.* | She practices *because she wants to be a better pianist.* *If you discover a fire,* ring the alarm immediately. |

# Medical Spelling

*Become familiar with the spelling of the following words:*

| | |
|---|---|
| appendectomy | asymptomatic |
| artifacts | audiogram |
| ascites | autoclave |

| | |
|---|---|
| autoimmunity | mucous membrane |
| bronchiectasis | mucus |
| compatible | nephrectomy |
| confidentiality | oncology |
| cystoscopy | palatine |
| demographics | Papanicolaou test |
| diabetes insipidus | parenchyma |
| diabetes mellitus | pathology |
| dilemma | polyuria |
| glomerulonephritis | prescription |
| glomerulus, glomeruli | Pseudomonas |
| glycosuria | Sjögren's syndrome |
| guaiac | symptomatic |
| hematemesis | tinnitus |
| laryngitis | urology |
| leukocytes | varicella |
| lithotripsy | vermiform appendix |

The previous chapter discussed how prepositions and conjunctions connect words to form larger ideas. Here we expand that concept to include the use of phrases and clauses. Phrases and clauses can contribute greater clarity and variety in writing by expanding on the information provided in a sentence. For example, if given the sentence "Our offices are located off Exit 9," adding the phrase "to the left of Mercy Hospital" gives more exact information. Phrases and clauses may be useful in various types of medical writing, including the kind of promotional writing that may be encountered in medical professions.

# Promotional Writing

In addition to the more structured types of writing contained in reports, research papers, grant proposals, and manuscripts, medical-related writing includes promotional types such as advertisements, press releases, announcements, brochures, and informational materials.

These items are a public or formal notice to announce a product, attend an event, give information to the public, call attention to something special, or offer goods or services. There are no limits to advertising, providing the information is true and not misleading.

Medical facilities publish promotional items in brochures, newspapers, medical journals, and publications. Data included in those items may cover any of the following:

❖ Philosophy

❖ Description of office practice

VILLES MEDICAL CENTER
*One Morey Place*
*Anywhere, MA 01102*

Internal Medicine
Nutrition Counseling
School and Employment Exams
Health Education
Laboratory and X-Ray Services
Risk Factor Assessment
Smoking Cessation

**Mary Louise Norman, M.D.,**
Medical Director
**Ralph H. Masterson, M.D.**
**Mary Lane, LICSW,**
Certified Nutritionist
**Norman Giess, P.A.C.**
**William Pyne, R.N., B.S.**

**By Appointment Only**
**(555) 555-4727**

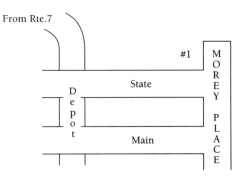

**FIGURE 10-1** *Sample Advertisement*

❖ Laboratory services

❖ Policy on appointments and cancellations

❖ Medical associations

❖ Policy of prescription renewal

❖ Map of how to get to the facility

❖ Parking facilities

❖ Financial policies

❖ Photo or logo of the facility

❖ Names of key medical and administrative staff

❖ Information for patients prior to their first visit

❖ Emergency room procedures

❖ Answering service

❖ Areas of specialization

Figure 10-1 is a sample advertisement and Figure 10-2 is a sample brochure. A brochure is a small pamphlet. The brochure shown as Figure 10-2 is the one used by the Villes Medical Center and Barry High School to announce the Teen Smoke-Out Seminars, *May I Introduce Myself? I Am A Cigarette.* And the following is an example of a news or press release:

The Davis Foundation announced an $8,000 grant award to Villes Medical Center and Barry High School to run a series of four Teen Smoke-Out Seminars. According to a

## MAY I INTRODUCE MYSELF?

TEEN SMOKE-OUT SEMINARS
October 4, 20XX
January 18, 20XX
March 11, 20XX
May 13, 20XX

A COLLABORATION
*between*
VILLES MEDICAL CENTER
*and*
BARRY HIGH SCHOOL

SPONSORED BY A GRANT
*from the*
DAVIS FOUNDATION

## I AM A CIGARETTE!!

I come in many sizes and shapes, wrapped in shiny, colorful packages that are hard to resist. Advertising agencies show the public how beautiful I am, how "real cool" it is to smoke me, and how wonderful it is to be my friend. Their words flatter me:

Fashionable!

Your basic truth!

You got what it takes!

Enjoy the best of life!

You've come a long way, Baby!

Be the one with STYLE!

You can do it!

Easygoing!

Sleek!

I'm very popular. People in every walk of life respect and hold me in high esteem:

✳ I go to the best of parties.

✳ I'm the first thing people reach for in the morning and the last thing before going to bed.

✳ My friends even leave their homes in the middle of the night to find and smoke me. Spouses and children don't get that much attention.

Others look for me in trash cans or on the street so they can have just one more puff. So what if they get a little dirty. I'm worth it!

I'm also good. The large tobacco corporations that make me provide jobs for thousands of people. From the money you spend, I contribute millions and millions of tax dollars to the world economy. You don't feel that cost when you buy me one pack or one carton at a time. So what if over a 25-year friendship, I cost you the price of a few cars or a college degree. Friends don't let money come between them.

Like everybody else, I'm not perfect. I occasionally burn holes in clothes, rugs, and furniture, causing small fires and injuries.

What really excites me, however, are the homes I burn. The flames make such a pretty sight! Some of these fires claim the lives of my friends, but I don't worry. I'm an arsonist who can't be arrested.

I also cause bad breath, yellow teeth, hacking cough, shortness of breath, heart disease, high medical bills, and even cancer. You could die by associating with me. But don't worry, these things only happen to other people. If you should die, however, your children will give me the pleasure of their friendship by following in your footsteps.

**FIGURE 10-2** *Sample Brochure*

recent health survey given at Barry, three in ten teens smoke. The goal of the program during the coming year is to reduce smoking by 20%, according to Dr. Mary Louise Norman, Director of Villes Medical Center, and Emily Prior, Ph.D., school principal.

Information sheets are a convenient way to distribute data relating to health issues. A simple format includes these parts:

Introduction

Broad Topic/Narrow Topic

Points Developed/Subtopics

Body

Paragraph 1

    Topic

    Support

    Conclusion

    Transitional Sentence

    (The same format is used for additional paragraphs.)

Conclusion

Summary

Ending Sentence

Figure 10-3 is a sample information sheet used as a handout at the Teen Smoke-Out seminars previously referred to. Its format components have been broken down and labeled for instructive purposes.

# Practice 10-9

*Using the format presented in the chapter, write an information sheet on any topic suggested by the instructor.*

*List five examples of promotional writing.*

1. _____

2. _____

3. _____

4. _____

5. _____

| Introduction | Smoking is one of the most overpracticed addictions in the world. Most people who smoke admit that it severely injures their health, but they cannot always explain how. This information sheet briefly relates some reasons why smoking is harmful and why it should be stopped at all costs. |
|---|---|
| Broad topic: | Smoking |
| Narrow topic: | Dangers of not smoking; benefits of not smoking |
| Points developed: | Contents of a cigarette; how a cigarette works in the body; rewards of not smoking |

### Body, Paragraph 1

| Topic Support | Tobacco wrapped in paper for the purpose of smoking is a lethal weapon. A cigarette is made up of thousands of different chemicals including ammonia (cleaning fluid), nicotine (insecticide), formaldehyde (embalming fluid), arsenic (poison), carbon monoxide (car exhaust), and methanol (wood alcohol). Why do people smoke when they know these chemicals are harmful? |
|---|---|
| Transition | Consider how nicotine works in the body. |

### Paragraph 2

| Topic Support | Nicotine hits the brain and makes the smoker feel relaxed and pleasant. The inhaled smoke carries nicotine into the lungs. The blood in the lungs carries the nicotine into the heart and brain—all within seven seconds! Nicotine passes quickly and easily through the entire body in three days. It leaves the bloodstream through the kidneys. If nicotine from ten cigarettes could get trapped in the bloodstream, it would be strong enough to kill a person. |
|---|---|
| Conclusion | Each year, smoking kills more people than AIDS, alcohol, drug abuse, car crashes, murder, suicide, and fire combined. |
| Transition | Consequently, people have much to gain by not smoking. |

### Paragraph 3

| | When people quit smoking, their energy improves, they breathe better, the heart works easier, pulse rate and blood pressure become lower, and body circulation improves. The risk of heart attacks and cancer lessens by 90%. More oxygen goes to the brain and the rest of the body, and the sense of taste and smell improves. |
|---|---|
| Conclusion | In other words, the person gets a second chance at a quality life. |
| Summary | Cigarettes contain chemicals harmful to the body, even though those chemicals make a person feel "high." More people die from smoke-related illnesses than alcohol, drugs, murder, and suicide combined. After quitting, the risk of a heart attack and cancer is reduced by 90%, thus providing former smokers with a new lease on life. |

**FIGURE 10-3**  *Information Sheet Example*

## Promotional Writing Summary

**Promotional Writing**

Formal notice to announce a product or event, provides information, call attention to, or offer goods or services.

**Promotional items:**

Brochures, newspapers, medical journals, and publications, advertisements, news releases, and information sheets.

# Skills Review

*Identify the italicized words as a phrase or a clause:*

1. Studying is essential *while attending college courses.* _____

2. A pregnant woman can give diseases *to her unborn child.* _____

3. Medical information is kept confidential *unless a release form is signed.* _____

4. Weight varies *according to one's exercise patterns.* _____

5. *After she completed the form,* she proofread it for errors. _____

6. The journal printed last month had an article *about cancer research.* _____

7. *Although vital signs were stable,* the patient remained *in surgical recovery.* _____

8. A physician, *with years of experience,* performed the operation. _____

9. *When you know the test results,* give me a call. _____

10. Chris's goal is to do research *in the medical profession.* _____

*Underline any phrases within the paragraph:*

Education is a vital service to both patients and physicians. Patients often experience anxiety over health concerns. Health-care providers must foster patient confidence and trust. The medical assistant tries to establish a rapport between the patient and physician. Medical assistants often suggest to patients that they prepare questions for the doctor. The assistant may also alert the physician of a patient's health concerns. Information about fees, office hours, insurance, office policies, and Medicare should also be readily available. In this manner, the medical assistant performs a vital service to both patients and physicians. The services of medical assistants are a great value to the medical profession.

*Underline any clauses within the paragraph:*

Health-care providers must educate patients who need specific health information. Patient education is an important function of the allied health professional. When a professional deals with patients, state medical information in clear, concise language that patients can understand. Gathering additional information such as pictures, pamphlets, films, and community resources is also helpful. After completing patient education, evaluate the session's effectiveness. Health-care providers who educate patients about health issues provide valuable information that could help the patient throughout life.

*Answer true or false to the statements included in promotional writing.*

1. Name of medical associations. _____

2. Patient's health condition. _____

3. Parking facilities. _____

4. Information from Source-Oriented Medical Record (SOMR). _____

5. Financial policies. _____

6. Events that occurred during a patient's stay in the hospital. _____

7. Name of key medical and administrative staff. _____

8. Medical research date. _____

9. Emergency room procedures. _____

10. Correspondence between physicians. _____

*Circle the correctly spelled word in each line:*

| | | | |
|---|---|---|---|
| 1. delemma | dilemma | dilema | dilimma |
| 2. compitible | compatable | compatibel | compatible |
| 3. appendectomy | apendectomy | appendactomy | appindectomy |
| 4. confidintiality | confidentiality | confedentiality | confidenteality |
| 5. mucos | mukus | mucus | mucuus |
| 6. patology | pothology | pathology | patholgy |
| 7. simptomatic | symtomatic | sympamatic | symptomatic |
| 8. prescriptions | priscriptions | prescreptions | perscriptions |
| 9. tinitus | tinnitus | tinnetus | tinnitis |
| 10. laringitis | larygetis | laryngites | laryngitis |

*Translate medical abbreviations using a medical dictionary or appendix.*

1. q. _____
2. q.i.d. _____
3. PVC _____
4. q.3h. _____
5. q.n.s. _____
6. RBC _____
7. R/O _____
8. Rx _____
9. RLQ _____
10. rehab _____

# Comprehensive Review

*Using the map below (and the* Writing Process Worksheet*), write the directions from 76 Elliot Street in Springfield to the Medical Doctor's Professional Building, located at 1130 Liberty Street. Use one phrase and one clause in the directions. Underline and label the phrase and clause.*

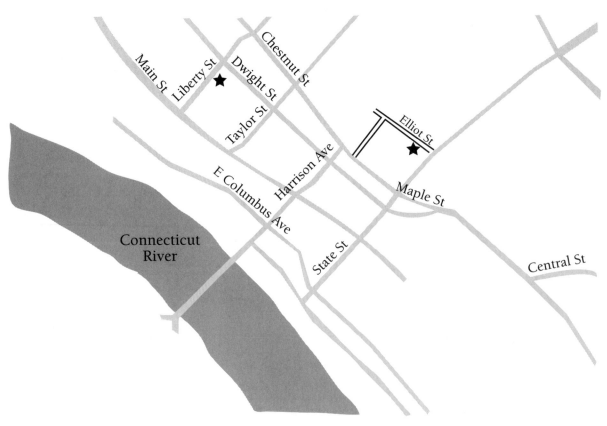

**FIGURE 10-4**

# CHAPTER 11

# The Paragraph

## OBJECTIVES

*Upon completion of this chapter, the learner should be able to:*

❖ recognize and write different types of paragraphs

❖ understand the structure and development of a paragraph

❖ organize and compose paragraphs according to various approaches to sentence progression

❖ use various techniques to attain paragraph unity

❖ spell various medical terms

❖ translate various medical abbreviations and symbols

Previous chapters show how individual parts of speech are arranged to form a coherent sentence. This chapter explains how sentences are joined together to form a coherent paragraph. A paragraph is a group of sentences that go together because they explain a common point of view called a *main idea*. A main idea is the central message that the writer wishes to convey to the reader. That message is what drives the entire passage. Every sentence in an effective paragraph must be related to the main idea.

A paragraph is easy to detect because the start of its first sentence is indented about five spaces from the left-hand margin. The length of a paragraph varies, depending on the complexity of the main idea. The average length of an effective paragraph ranges from four to eight sentences. Readers lose their focus when a paragraph is too long or too short. In medical documentation, paragraphs differ in length, depending on the amount of medical facts included in them.

## Practice 11-1

*All three of the following paragraphs give the same message. Which one is easiest to read and understand?*

1. The doctor's office is more than a professional health-care service. It is also a business. Because of this reality, an efficient system of record management is needed to maintain a well-directed medical office practice. The first component of medical records deals with a patient's health information. Data include such items as a medical history, examination results, record of treatments, laboratory reports, prescriptions, and diagnoses. Invoices, insurance forms and policies, payroll records, canceled checks, financial records, and other correspondence pertain to the business component of the operation. More than likely, business information is filed separately from a patient's health record. Medical professionals may draw on four or five different filing methods to maintain order: alphabetic, numeric, geographic, subject, and color-coding. Efficient record management is essential for the smooth operation of both components of a medical office practice.

2. The doctor's office is more than a professional health-care service. It is also a business. Because of this reality, an efficient system of record management is needed to maintain a well-directed medical office practice.

   The first component of medical records deals with a patient's health information. Data include such items as a medical history, examination results, record of treatments, laboratory reports, prescriptions, and diagnoses. Invoices, insurance forms and policies, payroll records, canceled checks, financial records, and other general correspondence pertain to the business component of the operation.

   More than likely, business information is filed separately from a patient's health record. Medical professionals may draw on four or five different filing methods to maintain order: alphabetic, numeric, geographic, subject, and color-coding. Efficient record management is essential for the smooth operation of both segments of a medical office practice.

3. The doctor's office is more than a professional health-care service. It is also a business. Because of this reality, an efficient system of record management is needed to maintain a well-directed medical office practice.

   The first component of medical records deals with a patient's health information.

   Data include such items as a medical history, examination results, record of treatments, laboratory reports, prescriptions, and diagnoses.

   Invoices, insurance forms and policies, payroll records, canceled checks, financial records, and other general correspondence pertain to the business component of the operation.

   More than likely, business information is filed separately from a patient's health report.

   Medical professionals may draw on four or five different filing methods to maintain order: alphabetic, numeric, geographic, subject, and color-coding.

   Efficient record management is essential for the smooth operation of both components of a medical office practice.

## Practice 11-2

*Separate this message into three paragraphs:*

Patients often wonder why the social history (SH) component is part of medical records. On further investigation into the meaning of social history, the reason becomes evident. Habits of smoking, physical exercises, eating, sleeping, and hobbies greatly impact the health of every individual. Facts about a patient's family history provide the physician with additional health data. Hereditary factors and parent and sibling health conditions help doctors see the larger picture. Questions on the review of symptoms (ROS) concentrate on the patient's general health condition unrelated to the present illness. The ROS provides a history of systems and organs, usually in logical order from head to foot.

_____

_____

_____

_____

_____

_____

_____

_____

_____

_____

_____

_____

_____

_____

_____

_____

# Types of Paragraphs

Many different types of paragraphs exist. The four types most commonly encountered by people in the medical profession are narrative, descriptive, expository, and persuasive.

## NARRATIVE PARAGRAPH

As the word implies, a narrative paragraph tells a story or shows a series of events that usually occur in chronological order. Narrative paragraphs may be autobiographical (about oneself), biographical (about another), or about something witnessed.

## *Example*

Elizabeth Blackwell, an immigrant from England, was the first woman in the U.S. to receive a degree in medicine. She was refused entrance into medical school many times before she was finally accepted. While practicing in this country, she established a hospital staffed by women. Returning to England, she founded the London School of Medicine for Women.

## DESCRIPTIVE PARAGRAPH

A descriptive paragraph is a pictorial representation in words that appears in most types of writing. The choice of words in this type of paragraph is deliberately specific to describe concrete details about objects, ideas, actions, settings, or persons. The wording conveys a sensory impression of appearance, smell, taste, sound, and touch or reveals a mood or an emotion.

## *Example*

The professor in the anatomy lab described the heart in the following manner:

The heart is a muscular organ located between the lungs. It weighs about nine ounces and is about the size of a fist. The heart has four chambers. The two upper chambers, the atria, are the receiving chambers and the two lower chambers, the ventricles, are the pumping chambers. Valves are located between the upper and lower chambers that open and close to let the flow of blood pass in one direction.

## EXPOSITORY PARAGRAPH

An expository paragraph is the most common type of paragraph. Its purpose is to inform, explain, or define something. The information may include facts, statistics, or specific examples. Because the language is so precise, the tone of the paragraph is very factual and unemotional.

## *Example*

The patient's chief complaint is headache pain on one side of the head. If this is a migraine, it exhibits certain characteristics. Migraines have a high hereditary influence and commonly affect more women than men. The usual symptoms are severe, intense, and of long duration. It often presents when the person wakes in the morning. One side of the head is affected more than the other. The pain may be more severe over the temporal area but also may include the face and other areas of the head. Other signs and symptoms that may occur at the attack are nausea and/or vomiting, fatigue, irritability, chilliness, edema, diaphoresis, or aphasia.

## PERSUASIVE PARAGRAPH

The persuasive paragraph is written to urge the reader to follow a certain course of action, to deal with an important issue, or to state an opinion about a debatable issue. The topic sentence clearly and concisely states the writer's point of view. Subsequent sentences develop the issue with reasonable and supportive statements.

## *Example*

One critical pathway for increasing the effectiveness of medical care in hospitals is to adopt quality assurance standards. These standards encompass every facet of the hospital from medical personnel, patients, staff, and administration. Other components include medical care, patients' rights, family satisfaction, hospital policies, cost-effectiveness, and medical records. The Joint Commission on Accreditation of Health-care Organizations establishes quality assurance standards. The implementation of these standards is a necessity if growth is to take place in the health-care industry.

## *Practice 11-3*

*Identify this paragraph as descriptive, expository, or persuasive:*

Electrolytes are chemical compounds found in all body fluids. Electrolytes break into positive and negative particles that conduct electrical impulses. Acids, bases, and salts are examples of electrolytes. Some general functions of all electrolytes are (1) to promote neuromuscular irritability, (2) to maintain body fluid volume, (3) to distribute water between fluid compartments, and (4) to help regulate the acid-base balance. Electrolytes are a necessity for life.

# *Structure of a Paragraph*

The structure of the paragraph consists of three elements: the topic sentence, supporting sentences, and a concluding sentence. The topic sentence presents the main idea. Subsequent supporting sentences offer more details about the topic. The concluding sentence brings closure to the paragraph (Figure 11-1).

## TOPIC SENTENCE

The topic sentence is the most important sentence in the paragraph because it introduces the reader to the main idea. It tells the reader what the paragraph is about and helps keep ideas organized and focused. In a sense, the paragraph is a clear and direct summary of the main idea. A paragraph without a topic sentence misdirects and confuses the reader. The topic sentence should immediately capture the interest of the reader.

## SUPPORTING SENTENCES

The supporting sentences form the body of the paragraph and comprise the details, facts, examples, descriptions, definitions, explanations, questions, causes and effects,

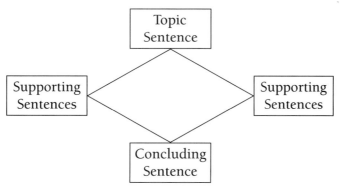

**FIGURE 11-1** *The Structure of an Effective Paragraph*

comparisons, contrasts, and proofs that support the main idea expressed in the topic sentence. The more specific the details of the supporting sentences, the better the explanation of the main idea. The content of the body usually answers any number of questions like *who? what? what kind? where? when? why?* and *how?*

## CONCLUDING SENTENCE

The final sentence brings the paragraph to a conclusion in one of several ways. It may summarize, offer a solution, predict, make a recommendation, state a conclusion, or restate the topic sentence.

## PUTTING IT ALL TOGETHER

## *Example 1*

| | |
|---|---|
| Topic Sentence | Punctuation is a crucial skill for medical assistants to possess. |
| Supporting Sentences | Many physicians do not bother to punctuate their reports, letters, notes, or correspondence. Should punctuation be included, it is often used incorrectly. The end punctuation of sentences is usually correct because the punctuation marks are obvious. The punctuation mark that causes the most problems, however, is the comma. There are more rules for the use of the comma than any other type of punctuation. |
| Concluding Sentence | Knowing where to place commas is a crucial step in acquiring punctuation skills. |
| The Complete Paragraph | Punctuation is a crucial skill for medical assistants to possess. Many physicians do not bother to punctuate their reports, letters, notes, or correspondence. Should punctuation be included, it is often used incorrectly. The end punctuation of sentences is usually correct because the punctuation marks are obvious. The punctuation mark that causes the most problems, however, is the comma. There are more rules for the use of the comma than any other type of punctuation. Knowing where to place commas is a crucial step in acquiring punctuation skills. |

## *Example 2*

| | |
|---|---|
| Topic Sentence | An operative note is one type of medical documentation. |
| Supporting Sentences | This report, dictated by the surgeon or an assistant, describes a surgical operation. The report includes pre- and postoperative diagnoses, sponge count, and blood loss. |
| Concluding Sentence | The report concludes with the patient's condition at the end of the surgical procedure. |
| The Complete Paragraph | An operative note is one type of medical documentation. The report, dictated by the surgeon or an assistant, describes a surgical operation. The report includes pre- and postoperative diagnoses, sponge count, and blood loss. The report concludes with the patient's condition at the end of the surgical procedure. |

# Practice 11-4

*Identify the topic, supporting, and concluding sentences in each paragraph:*

1.  The rate of respiration may be normal, rapid, or slow. The average rate for an adult is 12 to 20 cycles per minute. The average for infants is 30 to 60. For children age one to seven, the rate is 18 to 30 cycles per minute. The number per minute is referred to as the rate of respiration. Medical office workers should be aware of these facts.

2.  Gerontology is the study of the aging process. During this process, the chemical composition of the body changes. Among these changes are a decrease in lean body mass and an increase in vulnerability to different diseases. Stress is also an important factor in aging. Stress decreases cardiac output and brain function. As a result, the aging population is more susceptible to infections and accidents.

3.  The electrocardiogram (EKG or ECG) is a recorded picture of the electrical activity of the heart. The EKG may be normal even in the presence of heart disease. It is essential that the EKG be used in conjunction with the patient history, physical exam, and laboratory data. Arrhythmia and dysrhythmia are used interchangeably to denote an abnormal conduction. Electrocardiograms are a necessary component in assessing cardiovascular disease.

4.  Communication consists of many types. The spoken word or verbal communication is not the only one. Sometimes people communicate more with actions than with words. A smile or frown, eye contact or lack of it, gestures, postures, touch, and style of dress are expressions of nonverbal communication. In these cases, actions may speak louder than words.

5.  Fats, proteins, carbohydrates, vitamins, and minerals are all necessary nutrients for the body. A person's basal metabolic rate, growth, and physical activity determine the amount of nutrients needed. Nutrition needs change when a person is ill, is taking medications, or has a type of trauma. An imbalance occurs when nutrients are consumed in concentrated forms and reach the point that they do not help. Proper nutrition is important to everyone's health.

# Paragraph Organization

Paragraphs should be well organized in that the arrangement of their sentences should follow some order. One common way to organize a paragraph is by time. Time is a chronological approach that lists events from the earliest to the most recent, or in reverse, from the most recent to the earliest. An example of time is a paragraph describing events from 1989 to 2010; a resume is an example of reverse chronological order.

## TIME EXAMPLE

The AMA was organized in 1846 in New York City. A Code of Ethics was formulated and adopted in 1847. Its principles were revised in 1906, 1912, and 1949. In 1957, they were condensed to a preamble and ten sections.

Organizing paragraphs by time, however, is not conducive to documenting ideas. To write about ideas, you should organize the paragraphs by logic. Paragraphs organized by logic proceed from the familiar to the less familiar, simple points to more complex points, less important things to more important things and the general to the specific.

Other ways to organize paragraphs are location, deduction, induction, cause and effect, comparison, and definition or classification. The location approach involves the arrangement of content from left to right, right to left, top to bottom, edge to center, and the like.

## LOCATION EXAMPLE

Chart notes are dictated in a SOAP format. *S* refers to *subjective* or what the patient tells the doctor. The *O* for *objective* consists of what the physician finds on examination. *A* is the *assessment* the physician makes or the diagnosis. *P* stands for the *planned* course of treatment.

Organizing by deduction starts with the general and goes to the specific. The topic sentence, which is general, is followed with specific reasons, examples, facts, and details that support the topic sentence.

## DEDUCTION EXAMPLE

Follow these general rules regarding word contractions in medical transcription. Contractions may be used in informal records like chart notes. However, in formal correspondence like reports, use the words that form the contraction (do not, is not) rather than the contractions (don't, isn't).

Induction is the opposite of deduction. Specific ideas come before the general. Details, reasons, and examples follow the topic sentence.

## INDUCTION EXAMPLE

Letters to insurance companies and physicians are a few examples of correspondence dictated by specialists. To this list may be added follow-up letters concerning referred patients and letters of introduction. Medical office correspondence consists of many different types.

Cause and effect paragraphs help connect the result of something with the events or facts that precede it.

## CAUSE AND EFFECT EXAMPLE

Prilosec stops the production of stomach acid. It can turn off stomach acid production within an hour. The medication is used for conditions in which stomach acid is produced as part of a condition. Some of the drug's side effects are headache, diarrhea, nausea, fever, and vomiting.

The comparison paragraph measures one subject against another subject. The comparison is presented early. Contrasted details are given to illustrate the differences between the subjects.

## COMPARISON EXAMPLE

Legal abuses that affect health care are physical abuse and verbal abuse. Examples of physical abuse are performing the wrong treatment, hitting, holding the patient too roughly, or failing to answer the call light. Verbal abuse is using profanity or raising a voice in anger. Failure to obey laws regarding abuse results in fines or imprisonment.

Paragraphs organized by definition or classification explain words and ideas in a clear fashion.

## DEFINITION EXAMPLE

Pulse, respiration, temperature, and blood pressure are called vital signs. Pulse is the regular throbbing of the arteries echoing contractions of the heart. Respiration is the process of breathing and is measured by watching a patient breath in and out. Temperature is the degree of heat within the body. Blood pressure is the amount of force exerted by the heart pumping blood though the arteries. Vital signs are extremely important because appropriate medical care depends on these readings.

*Practice 11-5*

*Identify the following paragraphs as organized by time, location, deduction, induction, cause and effect, comparison, definition, or classification:*

1. *Advice* is a noun that means an opinion or a recommendation: My *advice* to you is to get a second opinion. *Advise* is a verb that means to inform or to recommend: I would *advise* you to get a second opinion. _____

2. When arranging flight reservations for the medical conference, obtain departure date and time, flight number, and estimated time of arrival. Make hotel reservations and arrange transportation from the airport to the hotel in time for the conference. The same information is required for the return trip: transportation to the airport, departure and arrival times, and arrangements for the traveller to be picked up at the airport and driven home. _____

3. Alzheimer's disease is caused by changes in nerve endings and brain cells that interfere with normal brain function. Symptoms of Alzheimer's progress from simple forgetfulness to severe loss of memory about how to dress, eat, or call people by name. Other signs are unpredictable moods and personality changes. _____

4. *Effect* is a noun that means the result of some action: A side *effect* of antihistamine is sleepiness. *Affect* is usually a verb that means to impress or influence, usually in the mind or feelings: The death of the patient *affected* us. _____

5. Locating a file on the computer is likened to locating a file in a file cabinet. Entering the A or C drive on the computer is similar to opening a drawer of the file cabinet. Clicking the subdirectory on the computer (A:Dr. Villes/consults) is comparable to opening a file pulled from the drawer. _____

# Paragraph Unity

In addition to structure and organization, an effective paragraph should also have unity. Unity means that sentences should flow logically from one statement to another. Ideas are arranged and connected so they will read smoothly and sensibly. Paragraph unity is achieved in a number of ways, one of which is called *transition*. A transition is a word, phrase, or structural element that appropriately links one sentence to the next by referring to previously used words or ideas:

> *Bathing* is as important to the sick as it is to persons who are well. *Besides* removing dirt and perspiration, *bathing* helps patients relax.

Examples of transitional words are *finally, consequently, also, thus, in another sense, in the same way, specifically, nevertheless, nonetheless, besides, on the other hand, above, below, meanwhile, moreover, however, as I said above, still, therefore, furthermore, in addition, similarly, in contrast, on the contrary, for example, accordingly, as a result, consequently, next, finally, yet, that is, in particular, at last, likewise, more important, then, in summary, on the whole, as a matter of fact, during, after, before,* and *the first point.*

Transitional words can be grouped by location, time, comparison, contrast, emphasis, summary, additional information, or clarity:

| | |
|---|---|
| Location | *across, around, away from, beyond, in back of, over, outside* |
| Time | *while, first, during, next, as soon as, finally, till, at, after* |
| Comparison | *in the same way, likewise, also, similarly* |
| Contrast | *although, on the other hand, yet, however* |
| Emphasis | *to repeat, in fact, for this reason, again* |
| Summary | *as a result, therefore, in conclusion, to sum up, all in all* |
| More information | *additionally, besides, for instance, likewise, along with* |
| Clarity | *in other words, for instance, that is, put another way* |

Other ways to unify a paragraph include these strategies:

❖ Repeating words from one sentence to the next:

> The patient was *examined* in the emergency room. On *examination*, the patient's chest and lungs sounded relatively clear.

> The medical history contained many *errors*. An incorrect spelling of the patient's surname was one of the major *errors*.

❖ Using pronouns that refer to a noun in a previous sentence:

> *The nurse instructor* insisted that her students use *medical abbreviations* correctly. *She* gave the class a test on *them* daily.

❖ Repeating a sentence structure:

> *A diagnostic report describes* the pathological findings of a sample of tissue. The *MRI uses* electromagnetic energy to produce images of body tissue.

❖ Substituting another word in place of a previous one:

> The *Hb, Hct, WBC,* and *RBC* are normal. The *complete blood count (CBC)* is normal.

❖ Stating at the beginning of a sentence that there are a particular number of points to be mentioned:

> According to Dr. Elizabeth Kubler-Ross, patients facing death pass through *five* stages. *The first* stage is denial and *the second* is anger.

# Paragraph Summary

### Types of Paragraphs

| | |
|---|---|
| Narrative | Relates a story or series of events, usually in chronological order. |
| Descriptive | Describes details, ideas, actions, settings, or persons. |
| Expository | Informs, explains, or defines something. |
| Persuasive | Urges the reader to follow a certain course of action, deal with an issue, or state an opinion about a debatable issue. |

### Paragraph Structure

| | |
|---|---|
| Topic sentence | Introduces the reader to the main idea. |
| Supporting sentences | Comprise the details, facts, examples, and questions that support the topic sentence. |
| Concluding sentence | Brings the paragraph to conclusion. |
| **Paragraph Organization** | The orderly arrangement of sentences. |
| Time | Organizes by time. |
| Location | Arranges from left to right, top to bottom, and edge to center. |
| Deduction | Starts with the general and goes to the specific. |
| Induction | Starts with specific and goes to the general. |
| Cause and effect | Connects results of something to an event or fact. |
| Comparison | Measures one subject against another subject. |
| Definition | Explains words or ideas in clear fashion. |

### Paragraph unity

| | |
|---|---|
| The manner in which sentences are formed smoothly, sensibly, and logically. | Methods:<br>—Repeat words from one sentence to another.<br>—Use pronouns that refer back to another noun.<br>—Repeat sentence structure.<br>—Substitute new words in place of previous ones.<br>—Use transition words. |

# Medical Spelling

*Become familiar with the spelling of the following words:*

| | |
|---|---|
| affect | complement |
| Alzheimer's disease | compliment |
| arrhythmia | course |
| aural | cytology |
| cite | defuse |
| coarse | diffuse |

| | |
|---|---|
| effect | osteopenia |
| elicit | ostalgia |
| explicit | pedal |
| facial | perfusion |
| fascial | petal |
| illicit | profusion |
| implicit | reflex |
| infarction | reflux |
| infraction | sight |
| keratosis | somatic |
| ketosis | vesical |
| moral | vesicle |
| morale | waive |
| oral | wave |

# Skills Review

*Match these words to the statements listed below.*

| persuasive | deduction | topic sentence |
|---|---|---|
| induction | expository | comparison |
| supportive sentence | cause and effect | |

_____1. Introduces reader to the main idea.

_____2. Informs, explains, or defines something.

_____3. Starts with the specific and goes to the general.

_____4. Starts with the general and goes to the specific.

_____5. Connects results of something to an event or fact.

_____6. Measures one subject against another subject.

_____7. States an opinion about a debatable issue.

_____8. Details, facts, and examples that build on the topic sentence.

*Divide this passage into appropriate paragraphs.*

Many patterns of nursing care are being used today. In the functional method of organizing care, each nursing employee is assigned specific duties to be carried out on all patients in a given unit. For example, a nurse's aide might be assigned to take all the patients' temperatures and the practical nurse to take all the patients' blood pressures. In primary nursing, the nurse is responsible for planning and caring for patients until they leave the hospital. One of the advantages of this pattern is that the nurse is able to give more individualized care. Progressive patient care groups the patients according to degrees of illness, including the patients on the following units: intensive care, intermediate care, self care, long-term care and home care. When the specialized care pattern is used, the patients are grouped according to age or diagnoses. Examples include orthopedics, pediatrics, obstetrics, or geriatrics.

*Identify the correct word:*

1. Pertaining to the ears _____ (oral, aural)

2. Having to do with the face _____ (facial, fascial)

3. Pertaining to the foot _____ (petal, pedal)

4. To voluntarily postpone, to relinquish _____ (wave, waive)

5. Not allowed by law _____ (illicit, elicit)

*Circle the correctly spelled word in each line:*

| | | | |
|---|---|---|---|
| 1. complament | complument | compliment | complment |
| 2. Alxhiemers | Alzheimer's | Alzhimers | Alzhimmers |
| 3. ostealgia | ostalgia | ostialgia | osstalgia |
| 4. arrhythmia | arrithmya | arthythmia | arrythmia |
| 5. karatosis | keratosis | ceratosis | kerotitis |
| 6. rephix | reflux | rephulx | refulx |
| 7. infraxtion | infracshun | infarction | inpharction |
| 8. corse | coarse | korse | coussre |
| 9. fascial | fasial | facsial | fassial |
| 10. purfusion | pirfusion | perfushun | perfusion |

*Translate medical abbreviations using a medical dictionary or appendix.*

1. VD _____
2. VDRL _____
3. v/o _____
4. w/c _____
5. WNL _____
6. p̄ _____
7. STAT _____
8. PWB _____
9. POMR _____
10. postop _____

# Comprehensive Review

*Use the* Writing Process Worksheet *to write a three to five paragraph essay on* **one** *of the following topics:*

Why are you studying in the medical profession at this time?

What hospital experience do you remember most?

What was your most memorable experience at the doctor's office?

# Writing Process Worksheet

1. PREWRITING – write down facts, organize ideas

_____     _____
_____     _____
_____     _____
_____     _____

2. WRITING – write without concern for grammar or punctuation

_____
_____
_____
_____
_____
_____
_____

3. REWRITING – correct grammar, make changes using proofreaders' marks

_____
_____
_____
_____
_____
_____
_____
_____
_____

4. FINALIZING – type or write final copy

_____
_____
_____
_____
_____
_____

5. PROOFREAD – read the final copy aloud for a final check

_____
_____

# APPENDIX A · Spelling Rules

Spelling correctly is a real challenge. Many medical terms are long, uncommon, and somewhat tricky: *tourniquet, pneumonia, scirrhous, diarrhea, ecchymosis,* and *herniorrhaphy*. The allied health professional must be careful about spelling, especially since medical reports are legal documents. Sometimes the incorrect use of simple words like *their* and *there* or *its* and *it's* are easily overlooked by the careful eye of the most conscientious proofreader. (In the word *conscientious*, does the *i* come before the *e* or the *e* before the *i?*)

When uncertain about how to spell a word, it should become a habit to look it up in the dictionary. A good idea for allied health workers is to keep an on-going list of spelling words that are most often misspelled in a small pocket notebook. Such lists of misspelled words are different from person to person, but the effort is rewarding.

Another helpful hint in building spelling efficiency is to divide words and spell them syllable by syllable. However, words are often misspelled because they are not pronounced correctly. In many words, letters are silent. One example is the word *often*. According to the dictionary, the first pronunciation of the word *often* sounds like *offen*. Spelling the word as it sounds is often incorrect.

Knowledge of a few basic spelling rules is helpful when documenting medical reports. Following are rules applicable in four basic areas that make spelling easier.

1. Using *ei* or *ie*
    - ❖ In most words, the letter *i* goes before *e: chief, view, piece, quiet, brief, hygiene, achieve, relief, grief, believe, review, friend, orient, belief,* and *died.*
    - ❖ The letter *i* goes before *e* after the *sh* sound: *shield, patient, proficient,* and *species.*
    - ❖ When the letters *i* and *e* are sounded separately, the spelling is easier: *sci-ence, a-li-en,* and *ex-pe-ri-ence.*
    - ❖ The letter *i* goes before *e* except after the letter *c: receipt, receive, conceive, ceiling, perceive, deceive,* and *conceit.* Exceptions include *leisure, height, weird, seize, foreign, Alzheimers, neither,* and *either.*
    - ❖ The letter *e* goes before *i* when *ei* sounds like the letter *a: weigh, weight, neighbor, their, heir, reign, veil,* and *eight.*
    - ❖ Change *ie* to *y* before adding *ing: die = dying, lie = lying.*

2. Doubling the Final Consonant

A student wrote about an experience that she had when trying to secure gainful employment as a medical assistant:

I recently graduated from a medical assistant course and hopped to secure a position in a medical office. During one interview, I was given many pre-programed tests to determine if I possesed the potential to handle the job. I was quized on the many tasks required of a medical assistant Initially I reactted calmly to the test. It never occured to me that I would find anything difficult. One of the exercises was to proof-read a document written by a doctor who transfered a patient from one hospital to another. Because the physician refered the patient to another specialist, there was a lot of information. I regreted only that the test took so long to complete. After two weeks, I was notiffied that someone else received the position. I wondered why.

The most predominant spelling error in this paragraph involves whether to double or not double the final consonant. The final consonant is doubled when the following criteria are met:

1. The word is one syllable: *fit*.
2. The word ends in a single consonant: *fit*.
3. The final consonant is preceded by a vowel or the letter y: fit.
4. What is added (the suffix) begins with a vowel: *ed* or *ing*.

Under these conditions, the final consonant is doubled: *fitted*. Here are other examples:

ship + ed = shipped            run + ing = running

hot + est = hottest            ship + ing = shipping

Exceptions to this rule involve word ending in the letter *w* (*showing*) or *x* (*boxed*), and the word *bus*.

What happens to words of more than one syllable? Double the final consonant in words of more than one syllable under these conditions:

1. The accent must be on the last syllable: re*gret*.
2. The ending must be a single consonant: regre*t*.
3. The last letter is preceded by one vowel: regr*e*t.
4. What is added begins with a vowel: *ed* or *ing*.

When all these conditions are present, double the final consonant: *regretted*. Here are other examples:

transfer + ed = transferred        transfer + ing = transferring

occur + ed = occurred              occur + ence = occurrence

acquit + ed = acquitted            acquit + ing = acquitting

A critical point to remember about this rule is that a dictionary is necessary to be sure that the accent is on the last syllable of the word.

Another way to look at this rule is to identify when NOT to double the final consonant:

❖ When the accent is *not* on the last syllable: *offer, offering*.

❖ The word does *not* end in a single consonant: *cold, colder*.

❖ The last letter is *not* preceded by a *single* vowel: obtain, *obtained*.

❖ What is added does *not* begin with a vowel: *ness*, goodness.

## *Examples*

differ + ent = *different,* the accent is not on the last syllable.

cancel + ed = *canceled,* the accent is on the first syllable.

leap + ed = *leaped,* there are two vowels before the final consonant.

film + ed = *filmed,* the word ends in two consonants instead of one.

There are, of course, exceptions. Many words in the dictionary have two acceptable spellings.

## *Examples*

travel + ers = *travelers* or *travellers*

counsel + or = *counselor* or *counsellor*

label + ed = *labeled* or *labelled*

program + ing = *programming* or *programing*

3. Adding Suffixes to a Final Silent *e*
   What happens to the letter *e* at the end of a word when a suffix is added, particularly when the *e* is silent? Several rules help to answer that question.

1. Drop the final *e* before adding a suffix that begins with a vowel:

   state + ing = *stating*

   like + ing = *liking*

   use + ing = *using*

   Exceptions:     eye + ing = *eyeing*

   dye + ing = *dyeing*

   shoe + ing = *shoeing*

2. Do not drop the final *e* if the suffix begins with a consonant:

   state + ment = *statement*

   like + ness = *likeness*

   use + ful = *useful*

   awe + some = *awesome*

   Exceptions:     judge + ment = judgment

   acknowledge + ment = acknowledgment

3. Do not drop the *e* from words ending in *ce* or *ge* when adding *able* or *ous:*

   notice + able = *noticeable*

   outrage + ous = *outrageous*

4. Drop the *e* before adding the suffix *y:*

   edge + y = *edgy*

   ice + y = *icy*

5. When the word ends in *ie* and the suffix begins with *i,* change the *i* to *y* and add the suffix:

   vie + ing = *vying*

   untie + ing = *untying*

4. Adding Suffixes to Words Ending in *y* and *c*

❖ For words ending in *y* preceded by a consonant, change the *y* to *i* before adding a suffix:

fancy + ful = fanci*ful*

glory + ous = glor*ious*

accompany + ment = accompan*iment*

happy + ness = happ*iness*

Exception: shy + ness = *shyness*

❖ For words ending in *y* preceded by a vowel, keep the *y* before adding the suffix:

annoy + ance = annoyance

obey + ed = obeyed

Although these four basic rules seem lengthy, common sense dictates their usage. They concretize and reinforce spelling habits writers already practice.

# Capitalization Rules

Capitalize the following except as noted:

| | |
|---|---|
| The pronoun *I* | After *I* read the book, you can have it. |
| The first word in a sentence | *Poems* are made by fools like me. |
| People's names | Roberta, *F. Scott Fitzgerald* |
| Titles as part of a person's name | Senator Kennedy, *Prime Minister Abouti* |
| Do *not* capitalize a title used without a person's name. | secretary of state, the senator from Ohio |
| Words like mother, father, aunt, uncle used alone. | I asked Mother to go. |
| Do *not* capitalize family members when accompanied by a possessive pronoun. | I asked my *mother* to go. |
| Title after a name | Jonathan Harlan, *M.D.*, Randy Kane, *Jr.* |
| Geographic names, streets, towns, and regions of a country. | *China, Dade County, West Side, the Southeast, Rodeo Drive, France, Atlantic Ocean* |
| Do *not* capitalize directions. | Drive *west.* Face *south.* |
| Languages, races. | *Spanish, French* accent, *Black* history |
| Do *not* capitalize *the* before these names. | *the* Nile River, *the* French people |
| Important buildings or structures | Vietnam Memorial, *Trump Tower* |
| Historical ages, events | Romantic Era, *Senior Prom* |
| Do *not* capitalize *the* before these names. | *the* Senior Prom |
| Names of products | Avon, *Bayer* |

| | |
|---|---|
| Names of companies, stores, banks | Delta Airlines, Mercy Medical Center, Pathology Department, Ford truck . |
| Names of specific courses | English Grammar 101 |
| Do *not* capitalize subject matter. | English grammar. |
| Organizations | American Medical Association, Special Olympics |
| Political parties | Democrat, Republican |
| Religions, deity, worshipped figures | Baptist, Judaism, Catholicism, Buddha, Christ, Allah, God, Bible, Promised Land |
| Important words in the title of a book, movie, etc. | Bill of Rights, Gray's Anatomy |
| Unless they are the first word in a title, articles and prepositions are not capitalized. | The Grapes of Wrath, The Return of the Native |
| Holidays, days of the week, months | Christmas, Sunday, July, Hanukkah |
| Do *not* capitalize seasons. | spring, summer, winter, fall |
| Do *not* capitalize academic years. | freshman, sophomore, junior, senior |
| First word in a direct quote | "The pain is here," said Mary. Mary said, "The pain is here." |
| Do *not* capitalize the first word of the continuation of an interrupted quote. | "The pain," said Mary, "is in the stomach." |
| Eponyms | Parkinson's disease, Babinski's reflex, Apgar score, Fowler's position, Bell's palsy, Epstein-Barr virus |
| Certain abbreviations | B.C.   Ph.D.   A.D.   M.D. |

# APPENDIX C — *Number Use*

- ❖ In general spell out numbers ten and under: one, four, six, nine.
- ❖ Use figures for numbers over ten: 16, 26, 785, 591.
- ❖ Spell out numbers used as the first word in a sentence: Sixteen x-rays were taken.
- ❖ Spell out indefinite numbers and amounts: a few hundred dollars, a bunch of fifties.
- ❖ Be consistent with numbers in a sentence: five computers and twelve scanners; 5 computers, 16 scanners, and 24 lap tops.
- ❖ When two numbers modify the same noun, spell out one (the shorter number) and use numerals for the other: We mailed over 200 five-page reports.
- ❖ Separate unrelated numbers with a comma: On July 1, 28 people were laid off from work.
- ❖ A fraction alone is written in words with a hyphen: Three-fourths of the population go to bed hungry.
- ❖ Use numerals for mixed fractions: Give her $1\frac{1}{2}$ ounces of medicine.
- ❖ Use figures with a.m., p.m: 11:30 a.m., 6:15 p.m.
    - *Note:* Omit :00 on the hour time: 7 a.m.
        - Do not use a.m. and p.m. with the word *o'clock*: The meeting is at 4 o'clock.
- ❖ Always use figures with symbols and abbreviations: pH 7.5, 33%, # 21 gauge, 2 cc. t.i.d., 3+, pulses 2+.
- ❖ Use figures with drugs: Give 75 mg of meperidine IM STAT.
- ❖ When the day precedes the month, use ordinal endings (th, rd, nd, st): The 2nd of February is my anniversary.
- ❖ Spell out an ordinal with no month: It is my twenty-eighth wedding anniversary.
- ❖ Spell out street names under 10: Fifth Avenue
- ❖ Use numerals for all house numbers but one: She lives at One 24th Street.
- ❖ Use numerals for money: 45 cents, $3.45, $15 for membership.
    - *Notes:* Use the word *cents* for amounts under a dollar. Use a dollar sign for money over one dollar. Omit .00 with even dollars.
- ❖ Use numerals for ages: The patient is 46 yrs. old. John is 16 years and 2 months old.

❖ Use numerals with numbers that have decimal fractions: An incision was made 4.5 cm below. . . .

>    *Note:* Always put a zero before a decimal that is not a whole number: Two capsules of Marcaine 0.2% were used.

❖ Dimensions, sizes, and temperature readings are expressed in figures: 43° below zero; My shoe size is $6\frac{1}{2}$, and I weigh 120 lbs.

## Arabic and Roman Numerals

| | | | |
|---|---|---|---|
| 1 | I | 20 | XX |
| 2 | II | 30 | XXX |
| 3 | III | 40 | XL |
| 4 | IV | 50 | L |
| 5 | V | 60 | LX |
| 6 | VI | 70 | LXX |
| 7 | VII | 80 | LXXX |
| 8 | VIII | 90 | XC |
| 9 | IX | 100 | C |
| 10 | X | 200 | CC |
| 11 | XI | 300 | CCC |
| 12 | XII | 400 | CD |
| 13 | XIII | 500 | D |
| 14 | XIV | 600 | DC |
| 15 | XV | 700 | DCC |
| 16 | XVI | 800 | DCCC |
| 17 | XVII | 900 | CM |
| 18 | XVIII | 1000 | M |
| 19 | XIX | | |

# APPENDIX D    Clichés

A cliché is a word or phrase that has lost its effectiveness through overuse. There are thousands of clichés in the English language. Following are some examples:

| | |
|---|---|
| after all is said and done | food for thought |
| as luck would have it | fresh as a daisy |
| as old as the hills | golden opportunity |
| at a later date | good as my word |
| better late than never | grin and bear it |
| busy as a bee | in a nutshell |
| by leaps and bounds | in one ear and out the other |
| calm before the storm | in the final analysis |
| cart before the horse | in the nick of time |
| cool as a cucumber | it goes without saying |
| crystal clear, clear as a bell | knowing the ropes |
| days are numbered | lap of luxury |
| dead as a doornail | last but not least |
| don't rock the boat | lesser of two evils |
| easier said than done | light as a feather |
| few and far between | miss the boat |
| finger in every pie | more than meets the eye |
| fish out of water | no time like the present |
| flat as a pancake | playing with fire |
| fly off the handle | put your foot in your mouth |

| | |
|---|---|
| quick as a wink | sink or swim |
| raining cats and dogs | skating on thin ice |
| red as a beet | snug as a bug in a rug |
| regular as clockwork | so far so good |
| safe and sound | straight as an arrow |
| see eye to eye | tough as nails |
| short and sweet | without rhyme or reason |
| shot in the arm | |

Because clarity and conciseness are so essential in medical documentation, clichés should not be used. Notice how clichés in this memo distort its meaning:

**Re:** Stress Management Workshop

Believe it or not, Williams Hospital is offering a workshop on Stress Management. The cost of the workshop is a drop in the bucket compared to the benefits received. Applicants will come through with flying colors and learn how to be good to themselves. First and foremost, they will learn how to relate to difficult people, save time, and handle stress. This is just the icing on the cake. If you should feel that you are not satisfied, your costs will be returned. Leave no stone unturned. Openings are few and far between. Put your best foot forward and apply today.

# APPENDIX E

# Titles and Salutations

Effective letters require that the appropriate titles and salutations be used.

| Position or Title | Styling for Address | Styling for Salutation |
|---|---|---|
| *Executive branch of the federal government* | | |
| the president | The Honorable (full name)<br>President of the United States<br>The White House | Dear Mr. President: |
| wife of president | Mrs. (full name)<br>The White House | Dear Mrs. (surname): |
| vice president | The Honorable (full name)<br>Vice President of the United States | Dear Mr. Vice President: |
| cabinet member | The Honorable (full name)<br>Secretary of _____<br>The Secretary of _____ | Dear Mr. Secretary: |
| attorney general | The Honorable (full name)<br>The Attorney General | Dear Mr. Attorney General: |
| postmaster general | The Honorable (full name)<br>The Postmaster General | Dear Mr. Postmaster General: |
| commissioner | The Honorable (full name)<br>Commissioner of _____ | Dear Mr. Commissioner:<br>Dear Madam Commissioner:<br>Dear Mr. (full name):<br>Dear Ms. (full name): |
| chief justice | The Honorable (full name)<br>The Chief Justice of the United States | Dear Mr. (Madam) Chief Justice: |
| federal judge | The Honorable (full name)<br>Judge of _____ | Dear Judge (surname): |
| director or head of<br>an agency | The Honorable (full name)<br>(title, name of agency) | Dear Mr./Mrs./Ms. (surname): |

| Position or Title | Styling for Address | Styling for Salutation |
|---|---|---|
| *congress* | | |
| senator | The Honorable (full name) United States Senate | Dear Senator (surname): |
| representative | The Honorable (full name) House of Representatives | Dear Representative (surname): |
| Speaker of the House | The Honorable (full name) Speaker of the House of Representatives | Dear Mr. Speaker: Dear Madam Speaker: |
| Chairman of a Committee | The Honorable (full name) Chairman of _____ | Dear Mr. Chairman: Dear Madam Chairman: |
| Librarian of Congress | The Honorable (full name) Librarian of Congress | Dear Mr./Mrs./Ms.(surname): |
| *American diplomatic officials* | | |
| Ambassador | The Honorable (full name) American Ambassador | Dear Mr./Madam Ambassador: |
| Minister | The Honorable (full name) American Minister | Dear Mr./Madam Minister: |
| Chargé d'Affaires | (full name), Esq. American Chargé d'Affaires | Dear Mr./Madam Chargé d'Affaires: |
| Consul | (full name), Esq. American Consul | Dear Mr./Mrs./Ms.(surname): |
| Representative to the United Nations | The Honorable (full name) United States Representative to the United Nations | Dear Mr./Mrs./Ms.(surname): |
| *Foreign diplomatic officials* | | |
| Foreign Ambassador | His/Her Excellency (full name) | Dear Mr./Madam Ambassador: |
| British Ambassador | His/Her Excellency The Right Honorable (full name) | Dear Mr./Madam Ambassador: |
| Chargé d'Affaires | Mr./Mrs./Ms. (full name) Chargé d'Affaires of _____ | Dear Mr./Madam Chargé d'Affaires: |
| Consul | The Honorable (full name) Consul of _____ | Dear Sir/Madam: |
| Minister | The Honorable (full name) Minister of _____ | Dear Mr./Madam Minister: |
| Prime Minister | His/Her Excellency (full name) | Excellency Dear Mr./Madam Prime Minister: |
| Premier | His/Her Excellency (full name), Premier of _____ | Excellency Dear Mr./Madam Premier: |
| President of a Republic | His/Her Excellency (full name) | Excellency Dear Mr./Madame President: |
| Secretary General of the United Nations | His/Her Excellency (full name) Secretary General of the United Nations | Dear Mr./Madam Secretary General: |

| Position or Title | Styling for Address | Styling for Salutation |
|---|---|---|
| *State and local officials* | | |
| Governor | The Honorable (full name)<br>Governor of _____ | Dear Governor (surname): |
| Lieutenant Governor | The Honorable (full name)<br>Lieutenant Governor of _____ | Dear Mr./Mrs./Ms.(surname): |
| Secretary of State | The Honorable (full name)<br>Secretary of State of _____ | Dear Mr./Madam Secretary: |
| Chief Justice of the<br>State Supreme Court | The Honorable (full name)<br>Chief Justice, Supreme Court of<br>the State of _____ | Dear Mr./Madam Chief<br>Justice: |
| State Senator | The Honorable (full name)<br>The Senate of _____ | Dear Senator (surname): |
| State Representative | The Honorable (full name)<br>House of Representatives | Dear Mr./Mrs./Ms. (surname): |
| State Treasurer | The Honorable (full name)<br>Treasurer of (state) | Dear Mr./Mrs./Ms. (surname): |
| Local Judge | The Honorable (full name)<br>Judge of the Court of _____ | Dear Judge (surname): |
| Mayor | The Honorable (full name)<br>Mayor of _____ | Dear Mayor (surname): |
| City Attorney | The Honorable (full name)<br>(title) for the City of _____ | Dear Mr./Mrs./Ms. (surname): |
| Commissioner | The Honorable (full name)<br>Commissioner of _____ | Dear Commissioner (surname): |
| Councilperson | The Honorable (full name)<br>Councilman/Councilwoman | Dear Mr./Mrs./Ms.(surname): |
| *Academic officials and professionals* | | |
| President of a university<br>or college | President (full name) | Dear Dr. (surname): |
| President who is a priest | The Very Reverend (full name) | Dear Father (surname): |
| Chancellor of a university | Dr./Mr./Mrs./Ms. (full name) | Dear Dr./Mr./Mrs./Ms. (surname): |
| Dean of a school, university,<br>or college | Dean (full name) | Dear Dean (surname): |
| Professor (with doctorate) | Dr. (full name)<br>Professor of _____ | Dear Dr. (surname): |
| Professor or instructor<br>with no doctorate | Mr./Mrs./Ms. (full name) | Dear Mr./Mrs./Ms.(surname): |
| Attorney | Mr./Mrs./Ms. (full name)<br>Attorney at Law | Dear Mr./Mrs./Ms.(surname): |
| Physician or surgeon | (full name), M.D.<br>or Dr. (full name) | Dear Dr. (surname): |

| Position or Title | Styling for Address | Styling for Salutation |
|---|---|---|
| Dentist | (full name), D.D.S.<br>or Dr. (full name) | Dear Dr. (surname): |
| Veterinarian | (full name), D.V.M.<br>or Dr. (full name) | Dear Dr. (surname): |
| Certified public accountant | (full name), C.P.A. | Dear Mr./Mrs./Ms.(surname): |
| Engineer or scientist<br>  with doctorate | Dr. (full name), (title) | Dear Dr. (surname): |
| *Members of the clergy* | | |
| Pope | His Holiness the Pope | Your Holiness: |
| Archbishop | The Most Reverence (full name)<br>Archbishop of _____ | Dear Archbishop (surname):<br>My Dear Archdeacon: |
| Archdeacon | The Venerable (full name)<br>Archdeacon of _____ | |
| Cardinal | His Eminence Cardinal (full name) | Your Eminence: |
| Bishop, Roman Catholic | The Most Reverend (full name) | Dear Bishop (surname): |
| Bishop, Episcopal | The Right Reverend (full name) | Dear Bishop (surname): |
| Bishop, other denominations | The Reverend (full name)<br>Bishop of _____ | Dear Bishop (surname): |
| Dean of a cathedral | The Very Reverend (full name)<br>Dean of _____ | Dear Dean (surname): |
| Priest | The Reverend (full name) | Dear Father (surname): |
| Minister or pastor | The Reverend (full name) | Dear Reverend (surname): |
| Rabbi | Rabbi (full name) | Dear Rabbi (surname): |
| Mother Superior | The Reverend Mother Superior<br>Convent of _____ | Reverend Mother: |
| Sister, Roman Catholic | Sister (full name), (order) | Dear Sister (full name): |
| Military chaplain | Chaplain (full name)<br>(rank and service) | Dear Chaplain (surname): |
| *Military ranks* | | |
| General* | General (full name)<br>(branch of service) | Dear General (surname): . |
| Admiral* | Admiral (full name)<br>(branch of service) | Dear Admiral (surname): |
| Colonel | Colonel (full name)<br>(branch of service) | Dear Colonel (surname): |
| Major | Major (full name)<br>(branch of service) | Dear Major (surname): |

*It is common practice to show the specific rank, such as Major General; Lieutenant General; Rear Admiral; Vice Admiral; First Lieutenant; Lieutenant, j.g., if that rank is known to the sender. This distinction, however, is not made in the salutation.

| Position or Title | Styling for Address | Styling for Salutation |
|---|---|---|
| Captain | Captain (full name)<br>(branch of service) | Dear Captain (surname): |
| Commander | Commander (full name)<br>(branch of service) | Dear Commander (surname): |
| Lieutenant* | Lieutenant (full name)<br>(branch of service) | Dear Lieutenant (surname): |
| Chief Warrant Officer | Chief Warrant Officer (full name)<br>(branch of service) | Dear Mr./Ms. (surname): |
| Petty Officer | Petty Officer (full name)<br>(branch of service) | Dear Mr./Ms. (surname): |
| Ensign | Ensign (full name)<br>(branch of service) | Dear Ensign (surname): |
| Master Sergeant | Master Sergeant (full name)<br>(branch of service) | Dear Sergeant (surname): |
| Cadet | Cadet (full name)<br>(branch of service) | Dear Cadet (surname): |
| Midshipman | Midshipman (full name)<br>(branch of service) | Dear Midshipman (surname): |

*It is common practice to show the specific rank, such as Major General; Lieutenant General; Rear Admiral; Vice Admiral; First Lieutenant; Lieutenant, j.g., if that rank is known to the sender. This distinction, however, is not made in the salutation.

# APPENDIX F Instructor's Symbols for Correction

| | |
|---|---|
| Agreement problem | agr. |
| Awkward expression | awk. |
| Common fault | cf. |
| Double negative | d. neg. |
| Sentence fragment | frag. |
| Be more specific | gen. |
| Grammatical error | gram. |
| Incomplete | inc. |
| Not clear | n.c. |
| Begin paragraph | ¶ |
| Not parallel | // |
| Punctuation | P |
| Redundant | red. |
| Run-on sentence | RO |
| Sentence structure | s. s. |
| Spelling | sp. |
| Word choice | w.c. |
| Word order | w.o. |
| Be concise | wordy |

# APPENDIX G

# General Rules for Abbreviations

Abbreviations and acronyms are used often in the medical field. They are the shorthand of the medical profession. Abbreviations may contain both upper- and lowercase letters and may or may not take periods. Here are some general rules:

❖ Educational degrees are abbreviated and punctuated: M.D., Ph.D., D.D.S., M. Ed., B.A.

❖ Certification and registrations do not have to be punctuated with periods: RN, CAGS, CMA, CMT.

❖ Acronyms are capitalized and follow their formal name:

Acquired Immunodeficiency Syndrome, AIDS

Problem-oriented medical record, POMR

pupils, equal, regular, react to light and accommodation, PERRLA

❖ Abbreviations are used in chart notes but not in formal correspondence:

Chart note: *Pt* is to have an *FBS* in the *a.m.*

Formal correspondence: The patient is to have a fasting blood sugar test in the morning.

❖ Chemical abbreviations use upper- and lowercase letters: KCI, K, Na.

❖ Do not use the same courtesy title at the beginning and end of a name:

Incorrect      Dr. Chris Villmare, M.D.

Correct        Chris Villmare, M.D., or Dr. Chris Villmare

❖ Do not abbreviate the days of the week or the months of the year:

Incorrect      Feb. 18, 1999        2-18-2006        2-18-2020

Correct        February 18, 2006

❖ Latin abbreviations are usually in lowercase letters: i.e., a.c., p.m., a.m., o.d., a.u.

❖ Measurements are abbreviated without using a period: cm, 500 mg, 30 ml, 30 cc.

❖ A comma is not necessary when II or III follows a surname: John Archie III.

❖ Abbreviations are acceptable in formal reports, as long as the word has been spelled out previously.

❖ Spell out diagnoses and procedures to prevent misinterpretations: Marshall-Marchetti operation, tonsillectomy and adenoidectomy.

❖ Symbols are acceptable as a shortened form of communication: 4-0 silk suture, 56% bone loss, 2+.

❖ All abbreviations and symbols must be accepted and approved by the medical staff for use at a particular facility.

❖ In medical correspondence, use the two letter abbreviations (without periods) for the states:

| | |
|---|---|
| Alabama, AL | Montana, MT |
| Alaska, AK | Nebraska, NE |
| Arizona, AZ | Nevada, NV |
| Arkansas, AR | New Hampshire, NH |
| California, CA | New Jersey, NJ |
| Colorado, CO | New Mexico, NM |
| Connecticut, CT | New York, NY |
| Delaware, DE | North Carolina, NC |
| District of Columbia, DC | North Dakota, ND |
| Florida, FL | Ohio, OH |
| Georgia, GA | Oklahoma, OK |
| Hawaii, HI | Oregon, OR |
| Idaho, ID | Pennsylvania, PA |
| Illinois, IL | Rhode Island, RI |
| Indiana, IN | South Carolina, SC |
| Iowa, IA | South Dakota, SD |
| Kansas, KS | Tennessee, TN |
| Kentucky, KY | Texas, TX |
| Louisiana, LA | Utah, UT |
| Maine, ME | Vermont, VT |
| Maryland, MD | Virginia, VA |
| Massachusetts, MA | Washington, WA |
| Michigan, MI | West Virginia, WV |
| Minnesota, MN | Wisconsin, WI |
| Mississippi, MS | Wyoming, WY |
| Missouri, MO | |

# APPENDIX H — Medical Abbreviations and Symbols

A thorough understanding of the meaning and proper usage of medical abbreviations and symbols is extremely important. Refer to a medical dictionary for details. Abbreviations may appear with or without periods or capital letters, depending on the facility that adopts them.

| | |
|---|---|
| A&P | auscultation and percussion |
| a.c. | before meals (ante cibum) |
| A.D., a.d. | right ear (auris dextra) |
| A.S., a.s. | left ear (auris sinistra) |
| A.U., a.u. | both ears (aures unitas) |
| A | assessment |
| aa | of each |
| AAMA | American Association of Medical Assistants |
| AAROM | active assistive range of motion |
| ABD | abdomen |
| abd. | abduction; abdomen |
| ABG | arterial blood gas |
| ACS | American Cancer Society |
| ACTH | adrenocorticotropic hormone |
| ad lib | as desired |
| AD | Alzheimer's disease |
| ADA | American Diabetic Association |
| ADH | antidiuretic hormone |
| ADHD | attention-deficit hyperactivity disorder |
| ADL | activities of daily living |
| Adm | admission |
| AF | atrial fibrillation |
| AHIMA | American Health Information Management Association |
| AIDS | Acquired Immunodeficiency Syndrome |
| AIHA | autoimmune hemolytic anemia |
| AJ | ankle jerk |
| AK | above the knee |
| ALL | acute lymphocytic leukemia |

| | |
|---|---|
| ALS | amyotrophic lateral sclerosis (Lou Gehrig's disease) |
| alt. dieb. | every other day |
| alt. hor. | every other hour |
| alt. noc. | every other night |
| ALT | alanine amniotransferase (formerly SGPT) |
| AMA | American Medical Association; against medical advice |
| amb | ambulatory |
| AML | acute myelocytic leukemia |
| amp. | ampule |
| ANA | American Nurses Association, antinuclear antibody |
| Ant. | anterior |
| ap | before dinner |
| A-P | anterior-posterior |
| AQ, aq | water |
| aq. dest. | distilled water |
| aq. frig. | cold water |
| AR | apical rate |
| ARD | atrial septal defect |
| AROM | active range of motion |
| AS | aortic stenosis; ankylosing spondylitis |
| ASA | aspirin |
| ASAP | as soon as possible |
| ASCVD | arteriosclerotic cardiovascular disease |
| ASD | atrial septal defect |
| ASH, ASHD | arteriosclerotic heart disease |
| ASIS | anterior superior iliac spine |
| AST | serum aspartate amniotransferase (formerly SGOT) |
| A-V, AV | atrioventricular, arteriovenous |
| ax | axillary |
| B cells | lymphocytes produced in the bone marrow |
| b.i.d., bid | twice a day (bis in die) |
| b.i.n. | twice a night |
| B/S; BS | bedside; blood sugar; breath sounds |
| Ba | barium |
| bands | banded neutrophils |
| baso | basophils |
| BBB | bundle branch block |
| BE | barium enema; below the elbow |
| bib. | drink |
| bilat. | bilaterally |
| BK | below the knee |
| BM | bowel movement |
| BMR | basal metabolic rate |
| BMT | bone marrow transplant |
| bol. | pill |
| BP | blood pressure |
| BPH | benign prostatic hypertrophy |
| bpm | beats per minute |
| Bronch. | bronchoscopy |
| BRP | bathroom privileges |
| BT | bleeding time |
| BUN | blood, urea, nitrogen |
| Bx | biopsy |

| | |
|---|---|
| C&S | culture and sensitivity |
| C/O, co | complains of |
| c/w | compare with |
| C | centigrade; calorie; Celsius |
| C1–C7 | cervical vertebrae |
| Ca | calcium |
| CA | cancer; chronological age; cardiac arrest |
| CABG | coronary artery bypass graft |
| CAD | coronary artery disease |
| cap. | capsule |
| CAT scan | computed axial tomography |
| Cath | catheter |
| CBC, c.b.c. | complete blood count |
| CBS | chronic brain syndrome |
| cc | cubic centimeter |
| CC, C/C | chief complaint |
| CCU | coronary care unit |
| CDC | Centers for Disease Control and Prevention |
| CF | cystic fibrosis |
| cf. | compare |
| CHD | coronary heart disease |
| Chem. | chemotherapy |
| CHF | congestive heart failure |
| chol | cholesterol |
| chr | chronic |
| CIS | carcinoma in situ |
| CLD | chronic liver disease |
| CLL | chronic lymphocytic leukemia |
| cm | centimeter |
| CMA | Certified Medical Assistant |
| CMF | cytoxan, methotrexate, 5-fluorouracil |
| CNS | central nervous system |
| $CO_2$ | carbon dioxide |
| COLD | chronic obstructive lung disease |
| COPD | chronic obstructive pulmonary disease |
| COTA | Certified Occupational Therapy Assistant |
| CP | cerebral palsy |
| CPK | creatine phosphokinase |
| CPR | cardiopulmonary resuscitation |
| CRF | chronic renal failure |
| C-section | cesarean section |
| CSF | cerebrospinal fluid |
| CT scan | computed tomography |
| CTA | clear to auscultation |
| CTS | carpal tunnel syndrome |
| CV | cardiovascular |
| CVA | cerebrovascular accident |
| CVP | central venous pressure |
| Cx | cervix |
| CX, CXR | chest x-ray |
| cysto | cystoscopy |
| D&C | dilation and curettage |
| D/C | discontinue |

| | |
|---|---|
| d. | day |
| dc | discharge |
| DD | discharge; diagnosis |
| DDS | Doctor of Dental Surgery |
| Decub | decubitus ulcer |
| Derm. | dermatology |
| DES | diethylstilbestrol |
| DI | diabetes insipidus |
| diff | differential (white blood count) |
| DIG | digoxin; digitalis |
| DM | diabetes mellitus |
| DMD | Doctor of Dental Medicine |
| DNA | deoxyribonucleic acid |
| DNR | do not resuscitate |
| DO, D.O. | Doctor of Osteopathy |
| DOA | dead on arrival |
| DOB | date of birth |
| DOE | dyspnea on exertion |
| DPT | diptheria-pertussis-tetanus vaccine |
| DRE | digital rectal exam |
| drg | drainage |
| DRGs | diagnostic related groups |
| DTR | deep tendon reflex |
| DTs | delirium tremens |
| DUB | dysfunctional uterine bleeding |
| DVT | deep venous thrombosis |
| Dx | diagnosis |
| EBV | Epstein-Barr virus |
| ECC | endocervical curettage |
| ECF | extended care facility |
| ECG, EKG | electrocardiogram |
| ECHO | echocardiography |
| ECT | electroconvulsive therapy |
| EEG | electroencephalogram |
| EENT | eye, ear, nose, and throat |
| EGD | esophagogastroduodenoscopy |
| ELISA | enzyme-linked immunosorbant assay (AIDS test) |
| EM | electron microscope |
| EMB | endometrial biopsy |
| EMG | electromyogram |
| EMS | emergency medical service |
| ENT | ear, nose, throat |
| EOM | extraocular movement |
| eos., eosin | eosinophils |
| ER | Emergency Room |
| ERT | estrogen replacement therapy |
| ESR | erythrocyte sedimentation rate; sed rate |
| ESRD | end-stage renal disease |
| ESWL | extracorporeal shock-wave lithotripsy |
| ETT | exercise tolerance test |
| eval. | evaluation |
| ext. | extension |
| 5-FU | 5-fluorouracil |

| | |
|---|---|
| f | female |
| F | Fahrenheit |
| FACP | Fellow, American College of Physicians |
| FACS | Fellow, American College of Surgeons |
| FB | foreign body |
| FBS | fasting blood sugar |
| FDA | Food and Drug Administration |
| FEF | forced expiratory flow |
| FEV | forced expiratory volume |
| FHT | fetal heart tones |
| FHx, FH | family history |
| flex | flexion |
| FP | Family Practice |
| FROM | full range of motion |
| FSH | follicle-stimulating hormone |
| FU, F/U | follow-up |
| FUO | fever of unknown origin |
| FWB | full weight bearing |
| Fx, fx | fracture |
| g, gm | gram |
| G | gravida (number pregnancies) |
| GB | gallbladder |
| GBS | gallbladder series |
| GERD | gastroesophageal reflux disease |
| GGT | gamma-glutamyl transpeptidase |
| GI | gastrointestinal |
| gm | gram |
| gr | grain |
| Grav.1 | first pregnancy |
| gt, gtt | drop, drops |
| GTT | glucose tolerance test |
| GU | genitourinary |
| guttat. | drop by drop |
| GYN | gynecology |
| H&H | hematocrit and hemoglobin |
| H&P | history and physical |
| h, hr | hour |
| H | hydrogen |
| h.s., hor. som. | hours of sleep, bedtime |
| H/A, HA | headache |
| $H_2O$ | water |
| HCG | human chorionic gonadotropin |
| HCl | hydrochloric acid |
| HCT, Hct, hct | hematocrit |
| HCVD | hypertensive cardiovascular disease |
| HD | hemodialysis |
| HDL | high-density lipoprotein |
| HEENT | head, ears, eyes, nose, and throat |
| Hct and Hgb | hematocrit and hemoglobin |
| Hg | mercury |
| HGH; GH | human growth hormone; growth hormone (somatotropin) |
| HIV | human immunodeficiency virus |
| HOB | head of bed |

| | |
|---|---|
| hor. decub. | bedtime |
| HPI | history of present illness |
| HR | heart rate |
| HSV | herpes simplex virus |
| ht. | height |
| Htn., Htn | hypertension |
| Hx | history |
| I | iodine |
| I&D | incision and drainage |
| I&O | intake and output |
| I.U. | international unit |
| IBD | inflammatory bowel disease |
| ICSH | interstitial cell-stimulating hormone |
| ICU | intensive care unit |
| IDDM | insulin-dependent diabetes mellitus (Type I) |
| IHD | ischemic heart disease |
| IM | intramuscular |
| imp. | impression |
| inf. | infusion; inferior |
| INF. | interferon |
| INH | isoniazid |
| inj. | injection |
| instill. | instillation |
| IOP | intraocular pressure |
| IPPB | intermittent positive-pressure breathing |
| IQ | intelligence quotient |
| IT | inhalation therapy |
| ITP | ideopathic thrombocytopenic purpura |
| IUD; IUCD | intrauterine device; intrauterine contraceptive device |
| IV | intravenous |
| IVP | intravenous pyelogram |
| J | joule |
| JCAHO | Joint Commission on Accreditation of Healthcare Organization |
| K | potassium |
| kg | kilogram |
| KS | Kaposi's sarcoma |
| KUB | kidney, ureter, bladder |
| l | liter |
| L | left |
| L1–L5 | lumbar vertebra |
| Lab. | laboratory |
| lap. | laparotomy |
| lb. | pound |
| LBP | low back pain |
| LDL | low-density lipoprotein |
| LE | lower extremity; lupus erythematosus |
| LFTs | liver function tests |
| LH | luteinizing hormone |
| liq. | liquid |
| LLL | left lower lobe |
| LLQ | left lower quadrant |
| LMP, lmp | last menstrual period |
| LOA | leave of absence |

| | |
|---|---|
| LOC | loss of consciousness; level of consciousness |
| LOM | limitation of motion |
| LP | lumbar puncture |
| LPN | Licensed Practical Nurse |
| LS | lumbosacral |
| LT | left |
| LTH | luteotropic hormone (prolactin) |
| LUL | left upper lobe |
| LUQ | left upper quadrant |
| lymphs | lymphocytes |
| lytes | electrolytes |
| m | male; meter |
| MA | mental age |
| MAO | monoamine oxidase |
| max. | maximal |
| mcg | microgram |
| M.D., MD | Medical Doctor |
| MED | minimum effective dose |
| meds., med. | medications |
| mEq | milliequivalents |
| mets | metastases |
| MFT | muscle function test |
| mg | milligrams |
| MG | myasthenia gravis |
| MI | myocardial infarction |
| min. | minimal; minute |
| ml | milliliter |
| mm | millimeter |
| MMR | measles, mumps, rubella |
| mol. wt. | molecular weight |
| mono | monocyte; mononucleosis |
| MR | medical record; mitral regurgitation |
| MRI | magnetic resonance imaging |
| MS | multiple sclerosis; mitral stenosis |
| MTX | methotrexate |
| multip | multiparous |
| MVR | mitral valve replacement |
| N | normal; nitrogen |
| N/V | nausea and vomiting |
| Na | sodium |
| NB | newborn |
| NBS | normal bowel sounds; normal breath sounds |
| neg | negative |
| neuro | neurological |
| nitro | nitroglycerin |
| NKA | no known allergies |
| NMR | nuclear magnetic resonance |
| noc | night |
| noct. maneq. | night and morning |
| non rep, n.r. | do not repeat |
| NPO, n.p.o. | nothing by mouth |
| NS | no show; normal saline |
| NSAID | nonsteroidal anti-inflammatory drug |
| NSR | normal sinus rhythm |

| | |
|---|---|
| NWB | non-weight-bearing |
| O&P | ova and parasites |
| O.D., o.d. | right eye; once daily |
| O.S., o.s. | left eye |
| O.U., o.u. | both eyes |
| O | objective |
| $O_2$ | oxygen |
| OB | obstetrics |
| OBS | organic brain syndrome |
| OOB | out of bed |
| OP, O.P. | outpatient |
| OR, O.R. | operating room |
| ORIF | open reduction and internal fixation |
| Orth, Ortho | orthopedics |
| OT | occupational therapy; |
| OTC | over the counter |
| OTR | official signature for registered occupational therapist |
| oz. | ounce |
| P&A | percussion and auscultation |
| P.A., P/A | Physician's Assistant; posterioanterior |
| p.c. | after meals |
| P.O., po, per os | by mouth |
| p.r. | through the rectum |
| p.r.n. | whenever necessary |
| P | plan; pulse; para (number of births); phosphorus |
| PA view | x-ray of the posteroanterior view |
| PACU | postanesthesia care unit |
| Palp. | palpable |
| Para 1,2,3 | unipara, bipara, tripara |
| PAT | paraoxysmal atrial tachycardia |
| Path | Pathology |
| PBI | protein-bound iodine |
| PCP | *Pneumocystic carinii* pneumonia |
| PD | peritoneal dialysis |
| PDR | *Physicians' Desk Reference* |
| PE, P.E. | physical examination |
| peds | pediatrics |
| per | by; through |
| PERRLA | pupils equal, round, reactive to light and accommodation |
| PFTs | pulmonary function tests |
| pH | hydrogen ion concentration |
| PHx | past history |
| PI | present illness; previous illness |
| PID | pelvic inflammatory disease |
| PKU | phenylketonuria |
| plts. | platelets |
| PM | post mortem; afternoon; petit mal seizures |
| PMN, poly | polymorphonuclear leukocytes |
| PND | paroxsymal nocturnal dyspnea |
| PNF | proprioceptive neuromuscular facilitation |
| PNI | peripheral nerve injury |
| POMR | problem-oriented medical record |
| pos. | positive |
| post. | posterior |

| | |
|---|---|
| postop. | postoperative |
| PPD | purified protein derivative (test T.B.) |
| Preop. | preoperative |
| primip | primipara |
| pro time | prothrombin time |
| PROM | passive range of motion |
| PSA | prostate-specific antigen |
| PSIS | posterior superior iliac spine |
| pt. | patient |
| PT | physical therapy; pro time; prothrombin time |
| PTH | parathyroid hormone |
| PTT | prothrombin time |
| PVC | premature ventricular contractions |
| PVD | peripheral vascular disease |
| PWB | partial weight bearing |
| q., q | every |
| q.d., qd | every day |
| q.h., qh | every hour |
| q.i.d., qid | four times a day |
| q.l., ql | as much as wanted |
| q.n., qn | every night |
| q.n.s., qns | quantity not sufficient |
| q.o.d., qod | every other day |
| q.p., qp | as much as desired |
| q.s., qs | quantity sufficient; as much as needed |
| q2h, q.2h. | every two hours |
| q3h, q.3h. | every three hours |
| q4h, q.4h. | every four hours |
| QA | quality assurance |
| qam. | every morning |
| qt | quart |
| quotid. | daily |
| R, rt., r. | right |
| R.A. | rheumatoid arthritis |
| R.N., RN | Registered Nurse |
| R/O, r/o | rule out |
| Ra | radium |
| RBC | red blood cell count |
| RD | Registered Dietician |
| RDS | respiratory distress syndrome |
| rehab | rehabilitation |
| REM | rapid eye movement |
| reps | repetitions |
| resp. | respiratory; respiration |
| Rh | Rhesus factor (blood) |
| RHD | rheumatic heart disease |
| RLL | right lower lobe |
| RLQ | right lower quadrant |
| RML | right middle lobe |
| RNA | ribonucleic acid |
| ROM | range of motion |
| ROS | review of systems |
| RQ | respiratory quotient |
| RROM | resistive range of motion |

| | |
|---|---|
| RT | respiratory therapist |
| RUL | right upper lobe |
| RUQ | right upper quadrant |
| Rx | treatment or therapy |
| s.o.s. | if necessary |
| s.q. | subcutaneous |
| S/P | status post, no change after |
| S | subjective |
| S-1, S-2 | sacral vertebra |
| SA | sinoatrial |
| SBE | subacute bacterial endocarditis |
| SC, sc, s.c. | subcutaneous |
| sed. rt. | erythrocyte sedimentation rate |
| segs | segmented neutrophils |
| SGOT | serum glutamic oxaloacetic transaminase (See AST) |
| SGPT | serum glutamic pyruvic transaminase (See ALT) |
| SIDS | sudden infant death syndrome |
| sig | label the prescription |
| SLE | systemic lupus erythematosus |
| SOB | shortness of breath |
| sol, soln | solution |
| sp. gr. | specific gravity |
| spec. | specimen |
| stat, STAT | immediately |
| STD | sexually transmitted disease |
| Sx | symptoms |
| syr. | syrup |
| T&A | tonsillectomy and adenoidectomy |
| t.i.d. | three times a day |
| t.i.n. | three times a night |
| T/O, t.o., TO | telephone order |
| T1–T12 | thoracic vertebra |
| T | temperature |
| tab. | tablet |
| TB | tuberculosis |
| temp. | temperature |
| TFT | thyroid function test |
| THR | total hip replacement |
| TIA | transient ischemic attack |
| tinct, tr. | tincture |
| TKR | total knee replacement |
| tlc | total lung capacity |
| TLC | tender loving care |
| TM | tympanic membrane |
| TMJ | temporomandibular joint syndrome |
| top. | topically |
| TPR | temperature, pulse, respiration |
| TSH | thyroid-stimulating hormone |
| TURP | transurethral resection of the prostate |
| Tx | treatment or therapy |
| UA, U/A | urinalysis |
| UE | upper extremity |
| UGI | upper gastrointestinal tract series |
| ung. | ointment |

| | |
|---|---|
| URI | upper respiratory infection |
| US, U/S | ultrasound |
| USP | United States Pharmacopeia |
| UTI | urinary tract infection |
| UV | ultraviolet |
| V/O, VO, v.o. | verbal order |
| v | vein |
| VD | venereal disease |
| VDRL | Venereal Disease Research Laboratory (tests) |
| vol. | volume |
| VS, V/S, v.s. | vital signs |
| vv | veins |
| w/d | well-developed |
| w/n | well-nourished |
| w/v | weight in volume |
| WBC | white blood cell count |
| WC, w/c | wheelchair |
| WDWN | well-developed, well-nourished |
| WF/BF | white female/black female |
| WM/BM | white male/black male |
| WNL | within normal limits |
| wt. | weight |
| × | times; multiplied by |
| x-match | crossmatch |
| YO, y/o | years old |
| Z | atomic number |

## Medical Symbols

| | | | |
|---|---|---|---|
| degree | ° | with | c̄ |
| negative; deficiency | − | without | s̄ |
| positive; excess | + | approximately | ≈ |
| equal to | = | change (or heat) | Δ |
| not equal to | ≠ | assistance (of one or | +1 |
| greater than | > | of two people) | +2 |
| less than | < | ratio | : |
| number; gauge; weight | # | grain | gr. |
| forward | → | tablet | tab. |
| backward | ← | one half | s̄s̄ |
| increased; elevated | ↑ | inch; second | " |
| decreased; depressed | ↓ | feet; minute | ' |
| of each | āa | reversible; back and forth | ⇌ |
| degree centigrade (Celsius) | °C | | ↔ |
| degree Fahrenheit | °F | male | ♂ |
| infinity | ∞ | female | ♀ |
| take; prescription; recipe | ℞ | primary | 1° |
| plus or minus; positive | | secondary | 2° |
| or negative | ± | tertiary | 3° |
| therefore | ∴ | divided by; per | / |
| after | P̄ | parallel bars | // |
| left | Ⓛ | right | Ⓡ |
| before | ā | | |

# APPENDIX I  *Use of a Thesaurus*

A thesaurus is a reference book containing synonyms—words having the same or nearly the same meaning as another word—and antonyms—words meaning the opposite of another word. Words are listed alphabetically like a dictionary. The purpose of a thesaurus is to vary the expressions of the entry word in order to provide more interesting writing. The best-known thesaurus is *Roget's*.

As an example, consider the entry for *medicine/medication:*

(N) Substance that helps cure, alleviate or prevent illness.

anesthetic, antibiotic, antidote, antiseptic, antitoxin, balm, biologic, capsule, cure, dose, drug, elixir, injection, inoculation, liniment, lotion, medicament, ointment, pharmaceutical, physic, pill, potion, prescription, remedy, salve, sedative, serum, tablet, tincture, tonic, vaccination, vaccine

# APPENDIX J

# Use of the English Dictionary

A dictionary is a reference or resource book that contains a great deal of information, depending on its size and organization. The most common purposes of a dictionary are to provide the definitions and correct pronunciation of words and to identify parts of speech. But a dictionary, medical or English, may contain much more information:

- capitalization and punctuation rules (English)
- meaning of frequently used foreign terms
- history of words (etymology)
- comparisons of adjectives and adverbs (English)
- proofreaders' marks
- cross-references
- various tables and charts

- signs and symbols
- measurements
- bibliographies
- illustrations
- footnotes
- diseases (medical)
- units of measurement (medical)
- guide for writers (English)

Each word listed in the dictionary is referred to as an *entry* word, which is broken into syllables. The phonetic spelling of the word indicating its pronunciation is found in parenthesis after the entry. The part of speech is usually identified in italic print.

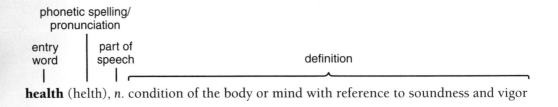

**health** (helth), *n.* condition of the body or mind with reference to soundness and vigor

To save time and facilitate the location of words in the dictionary, *guide words* are placed at the top of each page. The first guide word is the first word on the page. The second guide word is the last word on the page. All entries that fall *alphabetically* between the guide words are located on that page.

*guide words:* masthead _____ maw

Unfortunately, many words are spelled incorrectly because they are spoken incorrectly. That is why the respelling of words is so important. The respelling of the word *health* shows that the letter *a* is silent. On the other hand, the respelling of the word *khaki* shows that the phonetic respelling is quite different from the entry word.

**health** (helth)     **khaki** (kak'ē)

Note that the phonetic respelling uses symbols to assist in the pronunciation of words. To decipher the symbol, consult the pronunciation key found in every dictionary, whether at the bottom or side of each page, or in the front or back of the book. The accent mark after the first syllable (kak') shows which syllable to stress.

The most common phonetic symbols are the long and short vowels and the *schwa* that looks like an upside down letter *e* (ə). The schwa sounds like *uh* as in the word *about* (ə bout). The vowels are *a, e, i, o, u,* and sometimes *y.* Long vowels have the sound of their own letter name. The symbol above a long vowel is a short horizontal line (¯) called a *macron.*

# Examples

ā, as in *late*     ī, as in *ripe*     ū, as in *blue*

ē, as in *be*     ō, as in *note*

Short vowels have a small u-like symbol (˘) above the vowel called a *breve.*

# Examples

ă, as in *bat*     ĭ, as in *it*     ŭ, as in *cut*

ĕ, as in *pet*     ŏ, as in *pot*

The symbols in the pronunciation key mean that the letters have the same sound as in vowels in these words:

| | |
|---|---|
| ă, *pat* | oi, *boy* |
| ā, *pay* | ou, *cow* |
| âr, *car* | o͝o, *took* |
| ä, *father* | o͞o, *boot* |
| ĕ, *pet* | ŭ, *cut* |
| ē, *be* | ûr, *urge* |
| ĭ, *pit* | th, *thin, ether* |
| ī, *pie* | t, *attack, lateral* |
| îr, *pier* | hw, *which* |
| ō, *toe* | zh, *vision* \vi-ᶾhen\ |
| ô, *paw* | ə, *about* \ə-bout\ |

# APPENDIX K
# *Use of the Medical Dictionary*

A medical dictionary has most of the same features as an English dictionary—abbreviations, illustrations, tables, and symbols—but it focuses exclusively on medical terms and topics. Many medical entries have information beyond these features. For example, after the word *ostomy* is defined, further information is provided under subheadings titled ostomy care, stoma care, irrigation of colostomy, and miscellaneous considerations.

Other subheadings might include nursing implications, caution, nursing diagnoses, etiology, first aid, poisoning, prognosis, systems, and treatment. An appendix further augments medical information under the titles of anatomy, phobias, nutritional value of foods, minerals and vitamins, universal precautions, physical content of elements, dietary allowances, major diagnostic category (MDC), nursing diagnosis, medical emergencies, and diagnostic-related groups.

Entry words in the medical dictionary are not divided into syllables, nor do they provide the part of speech as found in the English dictionary. However, they do have phonetic spellings. Because medical words are long and difficult to pronounce, the respelling is especially helpful.

## Examples

influenza (ĭn"floo-ĕn'-ză)

physiology (fĭz"ē-ŏl' ō-jē)

APPENDIX

L

# Answers to Practice Exercises

## CHAPTER 1: GUIDELINES FOR EFFECTIVE WRITING SKILLS

**Practice 1-1:** Answers will vary.

**Practice 1-2:** Answers will vary.

## CHAPTER 2: NOUNS

**Practice 2-1**
1. artery, common; aorta, common
3. veins, common; DNA, proper
5. cholesterol, common; fats, common

**Practice 2-2**
1. faculty, school
3. faculty
5. union

**Practice 2-3**
1. satisfaction, abstract; care, abstract
3. group, collective
5. evidence, abstract

**Practice 2-4**
1. doctor, neuter; aware, neuter
3. winner, neuter; prize, neuter
5. hospital, neuter; nurses, neuter; signs, neuter; line, neuter

**Practice 2-5**

1. children, outlets
3. diagnoses
5. vertebrae

| **Singular of Nouns** | **Plural of Nouns** |
|---|---|
| 1. nucleus | 1. septa |
| 3. stratum | 3. thoraces |
| 5. ovum | 5. aponeuroses |

**Practice 2-6**

1. approach
3. symptoms
5. otologist

**Practice 2-7**

1. message
3. term
5. Mrs. Leclair

**Practice 2-8**

1. medication
3. right
5. structures

**Practice 2-9**

1. residents
3. doctor
5. patient

**Practice 2-10**

1. intestines
3. families
5. communication, team

**Practice 2-11**

1. doctor's
3. children's
5. pharmacy's

**Practice 2-12**

1. direct address
3. appositive
5. direct address

**Practice 2-13**

1. subject noun
3. collective noun
5. number
7. direct object
9. appositive

1. report is subject, physician is object of preposition by
3. nurse is direct address, medication is direct object
5. Susan is subject, nurse is predicate noun, floor is object of preposition on

**Practice 2-14**
1. G
3. I
5. H
7. B
9. C

# CHAPTER 3: PRONOUNS

**Practice 3-1**
1. third person singular
3. second person singular or plural
5. third person plural

**Practice 3-2**
1. you
3. It
5. it

**Practice 3-3**
1. I
3. she
5. they

**Practice 3-4**
1. he, subject
3. They, subject; him, object of the preposition
5. she, subject

**Practice 3-5**
1. themselves
3. herself
5. himself

**Practice 3-6**
1. who
3. that
5. that

**Practice 3-7**
1. Either, S
3. Many, P
5. Few, P

**Practice 3-8**

1. demonstrative

3. interrogative

5. interrogative

**Practice 3-9**

1. me, personal

3. We, personal; ourselves, reflexive

5. I, personal

**Practice 3-10**

1. doctor

3. Val and I

5. personnel

1. she, their

3. they

5. their

**Practice 3-11**

Writing Assignment: Answers will vary.

# CHAPTER 4: VERBS (AQ A.6)

**Practice 4-1**

1. are

3. prevent

5. is

**Practice 4-2**

1. have read

3. Has been stabilized

5. stimulates

**Practice 4-3**

1. transitive

3. transitive

5. transitive

**Practice 4-4**

1. is

3. need

5. disclose

**Practice 4-5**

1. decides, present

3. circulate, present

5. will be published, future

**Practice 4-6**

| | | | |
|---|---|---|---|
| 1. accumulate | accumulating | accumulated | had accumulated |
| 3. reveal | revealing | revealed | had revealed |
| 5. palpate | palpating | palpated | had palpated |

**Practice 4-7**

1. elicited
3. occurred
5. shook

**Practice 4-8**

1. lain, to recline
3. laid, to place
5. laying, to place

**Practice 4-9**

1. raise
3. raise
5. raised

**Practice 4-10**

1. can
3. may
5. can, can

**Practice 4-11**

1. saw to sees
3. we had cleaned to cleaned
5. wanted to want

**Practice 4-12**

1. Passive
3. Passive
5. Active

**Practice 4-13**

1. subjunctive
3. imperative
5. imperative, subjunctive

**Practice 4-14**

1. a history of a patient's health, medical treatment, research purposes, legal purposes, and answers that the instructor may require.
3. Joint Commission on Accreditation of Health Care Organizations.
5. C

1. F
3. T

Practice 4-15

1. F

3. F

5. T

# CHAPTER 5: SENTENCES

### Practice 5-1

1. operation

3. physician

5. breach

### Practice 5-2

1. compound

3. simple

5. simple

### Practice 5-3

1. interrogative

3. imperative

5. declarative

### Practice 5-4

1. fragmented

3. complete

5. complete

### Practice 5-5

1. T

3. F

5. T

### Practice 5-6

1. parallel

3. parallel

5. nonparallel

### Practice 5-7

1. Your age makes you eligible for Medicare.

3. The group accepts the physician's plan.

5. A $100 check is enclosed.

### Practice 5-8 Answers will vary.

1. Doctors' chart notes are hard to read.

3. The patient held his right arm during the exam.

5. Credit must be given to original materials used in the report.

Practice 5-9

1. B

3. B

5. B

Practice 5-10

1. Some people can change.

3. The doctor's office is open between 9 a.m. and 5 p.m.

5. Call the doctor right away.

Practice 5-11

1. patient complains of shortness of breath

3. diagnosis: upper respiratory infection

5. urinalysis for red blood count

1. immediately

3. c) POMR

# CHAPTER 6: PUNCTUATION

Practice 6-1

1. period

3. question mark

5. period

Practice 6-2

1. The division of the vertebrae are cervical, thoracic, lumbar, sacral, and coccygeal.

3. Prior to antibiotics, her sinusitis caused headaches.

5. The patient with the CABG needs blood work.

7. I don't believe it!

9. Is there a history of myocardial infarctions in the family?

Practice 6-3

1. I wanted a response from Dr. Ville, a forensic pathologist from Boston, but as of today, I received none.

3. Val visited the medical library on Tuesday; she also did further research on Saturday.

5. Some redness, pain, and swelling appeared in the right ankle; consequently, ice packs were applied.

Practice 6-4

1. SOCIAL HISTORY: The patient neither smokes nor drinks.

3. Many medical assistants were at the Cancer Conference: Chris, Luke, John, Valerie, and Sarah.

5. Discharge diagnoses:  A Excision of benign cyst on left lung

    B Emphysema

    C Klebsiella pneumoniae infection

7. To Whom It May Concern:

9. The cases were arterial insufficiency, diabetes, gangrene, glomerulonephritis, and anemia.

## Practice 6-5

1. The chapter entitled "Punctuation" is the most important chapter in the book.

3. We got the article out of *The New England Journal of Medicine.*

5. Yogurt is a form of curdled milk caused by *Lactobacillus bulgaricus.*

7. The side effects of the medication are (1) headaches, (2) possible vomiting, and (3) diarrhea.

9. *Yellow fever is caused by the bite of the female mosquito Aedes aegypti.*

# CHAPTER 7: ADJECTIVES

## Practice 7-1

1. A

3. Two

5. Each

1. state-of-the-art

3. up to date

5. well-known

## Practice 7-2

1. likeable, friendly

3. Allied health, responsible

5. Triangular

## Practice 7-3

1. The computer, which doesn't work, is in Dr. Ville's office.

3. The hospital with central air conditioning provides comfort for people.

5. A psychotherapist described him as someone with multiple problems.

## Practice 7-4

| | | |
|---|---|---|
| 1. weak | weaker | weakest |
| 3. painful | more painful | most painful |
| 5. hearty | heartier | heartiest |

## Practice 7-5

1. most colorful

3. more difficult

5. competent, more competent

## Practice 7-6

1. Fallot

3. Epstein-Barr

5. Bell's

## CHAPTER 8: ADVERBS

**Practice 8-1**

1. extremely, to what extent
3. surgically, how
5. today, when

**Practice 8-2**

1. only, adjective
3. grossly, adjective
5. probably, verb; later, verb

**Practice 8-3**

1. more
3. fastest
5. better

**Practice 8-4**

1. safely
3. orally
5. painfully

**Practice 8-5**

1. The insurance company can't pay its bills. The insurance company can't pay any of its bills.
3. The DRGs used by Medicare had no effect on the building. The DRGs used by Medicare didn't have any effect on the building.
5. She wants none of my help. She doesn't want any of my help. She doesn't want any help.

**Practice 8-6**

1. Sue always has a yearly physical.
3. The office seldom opens earlier than 9 a.m.
5. For this reason, nurses probably need help.
7. Get her immediately to the operating room.
9. The patient courageously signed a health care proxy.

**Practice 8-7**

1. F
3. T
5. F

## CHAPTER 9: PREPOSITIONS AND CONJUNCTIONS

**Practice 9-1**

1. Throughout the exam, without pain
3. in the clotting, of blood, for the production, of prothrombin
5. for toddlers, to 100 pulsations per minute

**Practice 9-2**

1. according to the <u>physician</u>, in spite of his <u>injury</u>

3. in support of the <u>consultation</u>

5. With respect to the involved <u>personnel</u>

**Practice 9-3**

1. for its coverage, noun is premium

3. in the treatment room, noun is autoclave

5. to heart attacks, noun is contributor

**Practice 9-4**

1. during normal aging, remains

3. in surgery, removed; to pathology, are sent

5. within other cells, live; by electron microscopes, can be seen

**Practice 9-5**

1. Besides

3. beside

5. between

**Practice 9-6**

1. into

3. into

5. in, into (either is correct)

**Practice 9-7 Answers will vary.**

1. I never heard of these symptoms.

3. After physical therapy, I changed the dressing.

5. The patient was put under by the anesthesiologist. The patient had anesthesia.

**Practice 9-8**

1. or, coordinating

3. and, coordinating

5. either, or, correlative

**Practice 9-9**

1. T

3. F

5. T

# CHAPTER 10: PHRASES AND CLAUSES

**Practice 10-1**

1. over the right bicipital tendon

3. of the kidney

5. of the parenchyma, of the liver

**Practice 10-2**

1. for the patient, adverb

3. of diabetes mellitus, adjective

5. because of kidney failure, adverb

**Practice 10-3**

1. wrapped with tape

3. experiencing the pressure of the HMO

5. retired from careers

**Practice 10-4**

1. Selecting the correct antibiotic

3. Analyzing medical information

5. Monitoring blood pressure

**Practice 10-5**

1. to analyze the test results

3. to protect the body

5. to validate any fractures

**Practice 10-6**

1. a drug used to control pain

3. milk and fish

5. activities of daily living

**Practice 10-7**

1. when scheduling appointments that require more evaluation time

3. While the patient was in the hospital

5. because it is characterized by dryness of the eyes and mouth

**Practice 10-8**

1. because it may cause viral problems

3. when the patient arrived

5. When you finish

**Practice 10-9 Answers will vary.**

## CHAPTER 11: THE PARAGRAPH

**Practice 11-1**

Paragraph 2 is the easiest to read and understand.

**Practice 11-2**

Patients often wonder why the social history (SH) component is part of medical records. On further investigation into the meaning of social history, the reason becomes evident. Habits of smoking, physical exercise, eating, sleeping, and hobbies greatly impact the health of every individual.

Facts about a patient's family history provide the physician with additional health data. Hereditary factors and parent and sibling health conditions help doctors see the larger picture.

Questions on the review of symptoms (ROS) concentrate on the patient's general health conditions unrelated to the present illness. The ROS provides a history of systems and organs, usually in logical order from head to foot.

**Practice 11-3 expository**

**Practice 11-4**

1. Topic sentence—The rate of respiration may be normal, rapid, or slow.

   Concluding sentence—Medical office workers should be aware of these facts.

3. Topic sentence—The electrocardiogram (EKG or ECG) is a recorded picture of the electrical activity of the heart.

   Concluding sentence—Electrocardiograms are a necessary component in assessing cardiovascular disease.

5. Topic sentence—Fats, protein, carbohydrates, vitamins, and minerals are all necessary nutrients for the body.

   Concluding sentence—Proper nutrition is important to everyone's health.

**Practice 11-5**

1. definition

3. cause and effect

5. comparison

# Index